# Fighting Slavery in the Caribbean

# Latin American Realities

Robert M. Levine, Series Editor

# Fighting Slavery
## in the Caribbean

## The Life and Times of a British Family in Nineteenth-Century Havana

### Luis Martínez-Fernández

### M.E. Sharpe
Armonk, New York
London, England

**Library of Congress Cataloging-in-Publication Data**

Martínez-Fernández, Luis, 1960–
Fighting slavery in the Caribbean : the life and times of a British family
in nineteenth-century Havana / Luis Martínez-Fernández.
p. cm. — (Latin American realities)
Includes bibliographical references (p.  ) and index.
ISBN 0–7656–0247–4 (alk. paper). — ISBN 0–7656–0248–2 (pbk. :alk. paper)
1. Cuba—History—1810–1899.  2. Havana (Cuba)—Social conditions.
3. Havana (Cuba)—Description and travel.  4. British and Spanish Mixed
Commission for the Suppression of the Slave Trade.  5. Slave-trade—Cuba—
History—19th century.  6. British—Cuba—Havana—Attitudes.
7. Visitors, Foreign—Cuba—Havana—Attitudes.  8. Backhouse, George Canning.
9. Cuba—Race relations.  I. Title.  II. Series
F1783.M386 1998
972.91'05—dc21
97–32665
CIP

Printed in the United States of America

The paper used in this publication meets the minimum requirements of
American National Standard for Information Sciences—
Permanence of Paper for Printed Library Materials,
ANSI Z 39.48-1984.

BM (c)  10   9   8   7   6   5   4   3   2   1
BM (p)  10   9   8   7   6   5   4   3   2   1

A mis abuelos maternos, Luis Fernández, de Pinar del Río,
y Lourdes Cisneros, de Camagüey.
Y a la memoria de mis abuelos paternos,
Celestino Martínez, de Asturias,
y María de la Concepción Lindín, de Galicia.
Por los cuentos que me hicieron y los
otros tantos que me hubieran querido hacer.

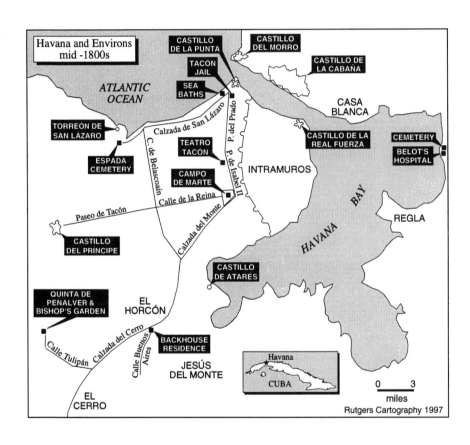

Havana and Environs
mid -1800s

ATLANTIC
OCEAN

CASTILLO
DE LA PUNTA

CASTILLO
DEL MORRO

CASTILLO DE
LA CABAÑA

TACÓN
JAIL

SEA
BATHS

CASA
BLANCA

TORREÓN DE
SAN LÁZARO

Calzada de San Lázaro

C. de Belascoaín

P. del Prado

CASTILLO DE LA
REAL FUERZA

CEMETERY

TEATRO
TACÓN

P. de Isabel II

BELOT'S
HOSPITAL

ESPADA
CEMETERY

CAMPO
DE MARTE

INTRAMUROS

Calle de la Reina

BAY

Paseo de Tacón

Calzada del Monte

HAVANA

REGLA

CASTILLO
DEL PRÍNCIPE

CASTILLO
DE ATARÉS

QUINTA DE
PENALVER &
BISHOP'S GARDEN

EL
HORCÓN

Calle Tulipán

Calzada del Cerro

Calle Buenos Aires

BACKHOUSE
RESIDENCE

JESÚS
DEL MONTE

Havana

CUBA

0       3
miles

EL
CERRO

Rutgers Cartography 1997

# Contents

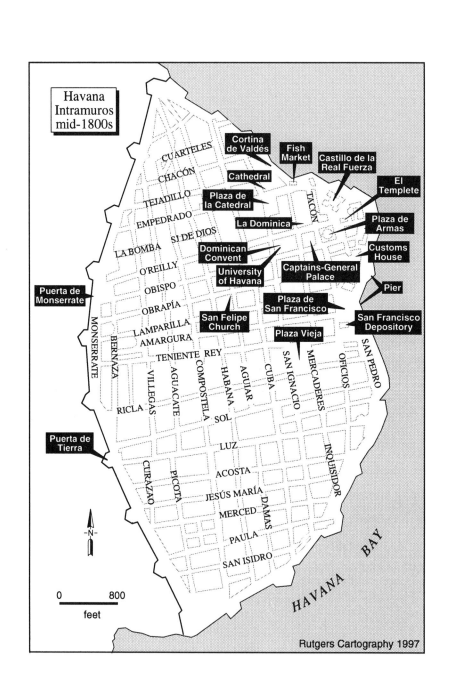

Havana
Intramuros
mid-1800s

Cortina de Valdés
Fish Market
Castillo de la Real Fuerza
Cathedral
El Templete
CUARTELES
CHACÓN
TEJADILLO
Plaza de la Catedral
TACÓN
EMPEDRADO
La Dominica
Plaza de Armas
SJ DE DIOS
LA BOMBA
Dominican Convent
Customs House
O'REILLY
University of Havana
Captains-General Palace
Puerta de Monserrate
OBISPO
Pier
OBRAPÍA
Plaza de San Francisco
LAMPARILLA
San Felipe Church
San Francisco Depository
AMARGURA
Plaza Vieja
MONSERRATE
BERNAZA
TENIENTE REY
SAN IGNACIO
MERCADERES
OFICIOS
SAN PEDRO
VILLEGAS
AGUACATE
COMPOSTELA
HABANA
AGUIAR
CUBA
RICLA
SOL
LUZ
INQUISIDOR
Puerta de Tierra
CURAZAO
PICOTA
ACOSTA
JESÚS MARÍA
DAMAS
MERCED
PAULA
SAN ISIDRO
HAVANA BAY

-N-

0        800
feet

Rutgers Cartography 1997

# List of Illustrations

# Foreword

The Latin American Realities series presents aspects of life not usually covered in standard histories that tell the stories of governments, economic development, and institutions. Books in this series dwell on different facets of life, equally important, but not often analyzed or described. How have underground economies worked? What strategies have poor people employed to cope with hardship and to improve their lives? How have government policies impacted everyday life? What has been the importance of popular culture? How have members of minority or disadvantaged peoples in Latin America—blacks, recent immigrants, indigenous peoples, men and women of intermediate racial status—fared? How have social and economic changes affected them?

George Backhouse's story not only offers a fascinating traveler's account of nineteenth-century Cuba, but it offers invaluable insight into the history of the Cuban sugar industry, its reliance on slave labor, the island's race relations, and the movement to abolish slavery, of which Backhouse played a leading role as a member of the Mixed Commission for the Suppression of the Slave Trade. Luis Martínez-Fernández's book is invaluable on several levels. Not only does it focus on the lives of real people, setting traditional historical events into an accessible context, but it offers rare insights into Cuba's economic life, its social organization, and its racial conundrum. Extensive research went into this book: private papers, diaries, correspondence, newspapers, and dozens of contemporary studies, travel accounts, and political tracts. Readers will be grateful for the author's sensitive analysis of the nuances of human relations against a background of tense historical change.

Robert M. Levine

# Acknowledgments

I worked on this book, on and off, from the time I first laid eyes on the Backhouse family documents over ten years ago. In the process I have accumulated debts of gratitude with many individuals and institutions who in some way made possible the research, writing, and publication of this book.

I remain grateful to my wife, Margie Fernández, and my sons Luis Alberto and Andrés, for all they have taught me and for their love, patience, and understanding. My parents, Celestino Martínez and Luisa Fernández, were the first to read an early version of the manuscript. Their encouraging assessment may have been biased but I took it. I thank them for their love and support. My grandparents, Luis Fernández and Lourdes Cisneros, and my aunt and cousin, Mercedes Fernández and Mercedes Almuíña, opened their home and hearts during my research visits to Havana, that wonderful city I call home. I am grateful for all their help.

Over the past decade I have enjoyed the friendship and have benefited from the guidance of former professors, now colleagues, and other fellow historians. John J. TePaske, my mentor at Duke University, has guided and encouraged my work over the years. I also carry a debt of gratitude toward Louis A. Pérez, Jr., who more than anybody else outside of Cuba has promoted and led the field of Cuban historical studies. I also wish to acknowledge other colleagues and friends, who in some way have been a part of the making of this book: Luis E.

Agrait, Jorge Alonso, Carlos Alvarado, Silvia Álvarez Curbelo, Carlos Bartolomé, Herman L. Bennett, Sagrario Berti, Nigel and Ellie Bolland, Stephen E. Bronner, Keith de Lellis, Georgette Dorn, Joseph Dorsey, Faye Dudden, William R. Erwin, Jr., Ramiro Fernández, Richard Foley, Araceli García Carranza, Humberto García Muñiz, Blanca Gómez, Betty González, Filiberto González, Lydia Milagros González, Jane Grimshaw, Manuel Hernández González, Gad Heuman, H.L. Hoffenberg, Franklin W. Knight, Robert M. Levine, Valentín Llanes, Linda McCurdy, Tomás Eloy Martínez, James Masschaele, Mary Moran, Robert L. Paquette, Lizabeth Paravisini-Gebert, Hernán Pérez, Ángel Quintero Rivera, Richard Ramos, Lynn Roundtree, Francisco Scarano, Michael Siegel, Roslyn Turborg-Penn, Diane Wachtell, James Walvin, Oscar Zanetti, and Nancy Zingrone.

Various institutions have made possible the research and writing of this book. I should first thank the staff of the Special Collections Library of Duke University for acquiring, cataloguing, and making available the Backhouse Papers; I consider myself very fortunate to have found these documents and to now have the privilege of sharing their intimate and dramatic contents. I also wish to acknowledge the support provided by Duke University, the Johns Hopkins University, the Tinker Foundation, the Pew Evangelical Scholars Program, and Rutgers University.

Different versions of chapters 3 and 4 were published as articles in the journals *Slavery and Abolition* and *Cuban Studies*. My gratitude goes to their respective editors for granting me the permission to publish revised versions of the articles. I am also grateful to Stephen J. Dalphin, executive editor; Peter Coveney, executive editor; Susanna Sharpe, the copyeditor; and the other editors of M.E. Sharpe for believing in this rather unconventional project and for their role in making it a reality.

Last, but certainly not least, I thank God for giving me the strength to go on.

# Fighting Slavery in the Caribbean

# Introduction

The way we write and teach history has changed dramatically over the past four decades. Through contact with related disciplines, influenced by contemporary political preoccupations, and armed with new approaches and methodologies, history has become more interpretative and analytical and has expanded to include subjects it had previously ignored. There is no doubt that the historian's craft has been redefined and revitalized.

Yet many still become historians because they like to read and tell stories. I wrote this book, in part, to remind my colleagues and myself that our origins are in storytelling, that good stories carry forward the wisdom of the ages, and that the society that supports our toil still expects at least a bit of that. This book tells the story of the Backhouses, a British family living in mid-nineteenth-century Havana. If some of what follows seems closer to the realm of fiction, it is not so. It is solely the reflection of the dramatic times and fascinating surroundings in which they lived.

In the spring of 1987, I stumbled upon a unique collection of sources that became the documentary core of this book. The Special Collections Library of Duke University had a few years earlier acquired the John Backhouse Papers, which contained the diaries of George Canning Backhouse, judge at the Havana Mixed Commission for the Suppression of the Slave Trade (1853–55); the diaries of his wife, Grace Margaret Backhouse; dozens of letters which they wrote to relatives in England; and other items such as newspaper clippings, property inventories, and other documents.[1] George Backhouse's official correspondence and other contemporary documents housed at the Public Record Office in Kew, England, and at the Archivo Histórico Nacional, in Madrid, later provided vital information from the official perspective. At later stages in the preparation of this book, the fall of 1994 and the summers of 1996 and 1997, I was able to visit Havana and conduct further research at the Archivo Nacional de Cuba, at the Biblioteca Nacional José Martí, and at various local archives in El Cerro.

The very broad and rich travelers' literature of Europeans and North Americans in nineteenth-century Cuba provides richly textured descriptions and insights about the life of foreigners and natives on the island and complements very nicely the Backhouse materials. In spite of their distortions, shortcomings, oftentimes ethnocentric views, and condescending air, the travelers' accounts are excellent raw materials for our understanding of life in nineteenth-century Cuba. Foreigners, as uninformed as some may have been, recorded information that native Cubans took for granted and therefore failed to write about. The travel accounts' authors, furthermore, shared many of the biases that the Backhouses had and thus help recreate the context as the Backhouses perceived it.[2]

The chronological context of the Backhouses' arrival in Havana, the middle years of the 1850s, is of particular importance for several reasons. It was an explosive and pivotal juncture, at which coincided the maturation of myriad interrelated contradictions within Cuba's economy and society, and its political sphere. During these years, the island's sugar industry entered its apogee, spurred by two seemingly contradictory, frantically paced processes: the industry's mechanization and the massive importation of African slaves. With feudal lords who lived in fortified palaces acquiring the most sophisticated sugar-making technology the industrial age had to offer, and with hordes of slaves enduring the factory-like regimentation and exploitation of the sugar plantations, Cuba's economy and society combined the worst of slavery and agro-industrial capitalism.[3]

Sugar and slavery were at the heart of other mid-century contradictions that seemed on the verge of exploding when the Backhouses arrived in Havana. The wealth accumulated by Cuba's Creole planters and the growing distance between their interests and those of the Spanish colonial state pointed toward an impending rupture of the colonial bond between Cuba and its decaying metropolis. The sugar industry's labor demands, however, created the potentially explosive circumstance of a black and slave majority, a demographic reality that forced Cuba's whites to depend on Spain's military might to advert or suffocate a massive slave revolt. Cuba's whites, particularly the master class, had thus been traumatized into colonial submission by the bloody example of Haiti's turn-of-the-century abolitionist war of independence. The sharp divisions within Cuba's racial castes and social classes remained, furthermore, a major obstacle to the formation of a nationalist front that could successfully bring about the island's separation from an increasingly oppressive Spain.[4]

Yet another contradiction peaking at mid-century consisted of the fact that while Spain tightened the reigns of colonial despotism and fiscal exploitation, the crown jewel of its once vast imperial domains gravitated closer and closer to the United States, the market for the bulk of Cuba's sugar and an increasingly important supplier of the island's foodstuffs and manufactured imports. Precisely in the late 1840s and early 1850s, some within Cuba's propertied classes began conspiring to sever their ties with Spain and to annex the island to the United States, where slavery flourished in the South. More important than commercial considerations were the Cuban elites' fears that British abolitionist pressures could lead to a sudden abolition, to the island's "Africanization," and potentially to the extermination of all whites. It was precisely within this cresting wave of Anglophobia that George Backhouse arrived in Havana to serve on the Mixed Commission for the Suppression of the Slave Trade.

Thus far George Backhouse is barely a footnote in the historiography of nineteenth-century Cuba and Britain's crusade against the slave trade.[5] His heretofore untold story is not only alluring and valuable in and of itself, it is also important because of the role Backhouse played as a judge in the British and Spanish Mixed Commission for the Suppression of the Slave Trade. Sugar was the Cuban economy's backbone, and without slavery there was no sugar, or so believed the planters and many others. Slavery and the threat of a bloody racial war was also the bugbear that Spanish colonial authorities used to keep the island's white Creoles in line. Backhouse thus found himself in a very difficult position, entrusted by the British government to prosecute slave-trading vessels in a foreign and hostile society that seemingly could not operate without them.

The richly documented day-to-day experiences of the Backhouses also provide an excellent window into the lives of thousands of other foreigners from Britain, Germany, and the United States, who for one reason or another lived in or passed through Havana during the nineteenth century. At mid-century, more than 2,500 non-Spanish foreigners lived in Havana and an approximately equal number visited the city each year.[6] The Backhouse story provides insights into important aspects of the foreign population's daily life: for example, what was it like to be an unacclimated traveler in a city deemed a "hot-bed of pestilence," where yellow fever was endemic and often fatal; what was it like for a foreign woman, used to finding her way freely around London, to be forced into seclusion because in Havana "ladies" were not allowed to walk on the streets; what was it like to be a Protestant and to seek the basic sacraments in a country where non-Catholics were not allowed to reside let alone worship freely according to their faith; or what was it like to deal with Havana's frustratingly slow colonial bureaucracy concerning any matter ranging from applying for a temporary exit visa to securing licenses to have the mortal remains of a loved one shipped abroad.

Researching and writing this book gave me the opportunity to know the Backhouses at their happiest and saddest moments, to learn about their hopes, fears, and frustrations, and about their loved ones halfway across the world. I cannot help but wonder what they would have thought and done had they known that their story would some day be told. I find comfort in the thought that they would have still kept their diaries and that they would have liked what I have written in the pages that follow.

# I

## Havana Bound

The morning of Friday, December 17, 1852, was rainy and cold, a typical London late fall morning as far as the weather went. It was quite a significant day, however, in another respect, for the ten-month-old cabinet of Prime Minister Lord Derby had all but collapsed the previous night, beaten in Parliament in a failed attempt to pass a national budget and fiscal plan.[1] As the day unfolded, Britain's conservative ministers and their assistants found themselves busy with plenty of exit business to attend to before making official their impending resignations. With one of his last breaths of political life, the Earl of Malmesbury, Secretary of State for Foreign Affairs, through his Under Secretary H.U. Addington, extended an offer that would forever change the lives of thirty-four-year-old George Canning Backhouse, a clerk at the Foreign Office; his twenty-nine-year-old wife, Grace Margaret Backhouse; Alice Grace Catherine, their baby of six months; and their other children yet to be born.

That morning Addington summoned George to his office and offered him an appointment to serve in Cuba as Her Majesty's Judge in the Havana Mixed Commission for the Suppression of the Slave Trade, a position to judge over cases relating to captured slave ships. Thomas Staveley, George's friend and superior at the Foreign Office, was also present and explained the terms of the appointment. The duties were described as "being very plain," with the yearly salary to be £1,600, more than triple George's current salary as second-class clerk, and the liberty to retire after twelve years of service, at the age of forty-six, with a generous £600 yearly pension. The government would also pay for the passage costs and allot £400 toward Backhouse's relocation expenses. George was taken aback.[2]

The offer of appointment coincided with a brewing renewed offensive by the British government in response to a dramatic upsurge in the slave trade in Cuba, a trade that had been banned bilaterally by Britain and Spain in a treaty dating to 1817. In Cuba, however, sugar was king and its insatiable demand for more and more slaves remained a formidable obstacle to any attempt at abolishing the trade or slavery itself. An estimated total of 12,500 slaves were to arrive clandestinely in Cuban waters in 1853, the largest number since 1840 and more than two and a half times the yearly average for the previous decade.[3]

The political circumstances under which George received the offer demanded an immediate response; he had to accept or reject it before the end of the day. That morning George left the old Foreign Office building at 16 Downing Street, took a cab and rushed home to 28 Hans Place, his family residence, in the plush section of Belgrave Square in London's West End. George explained to Grace what little he knew about the appointment to the Havana court and sought her opinion on the matter. Her good Victorian wife's response was that she "was ready to go with him wherever he liked & hoped he would act exactly as he thought best." George returned to the office that afternoon and accepted the appointment.[4]

A clerk in the Foreign Office since his graduation from Christ Church College of Oxford University in 1838, George lived in the shadow of his deceased father, John Backhouse, who had had a distinguished public service career that began with six years of service as personal secretary to English statesman George Canning and culminated with fifteen years of service as Permanent Under Secretary of State for Foreign Affairs until his retirement in 1842. While John Backhouse served at the Foreign Office, he also held the well-remunerated post of Receiver General of the Excise, a sinecure arranged by Canning that required minimal attendance. The senior Backhouse died in November 1845 at age sixty-two, following a long and debilitating illness.[5] Surprisingly for career Foreign Office officials, George, like his father before him, had minimal actual experience outside of Britain.[6] The Backhouses were by no means members of London's stale aristocracy but they enjoyed the security and comfort of an upper-middleclass family.

Dissatisfied and unchallenged by his bureaucratic duties at the Foreign Office and hoping for better remuneration, for some time George had unsuccessfully sought an overseas appointment within the British consular corps. His appetite for the exotic and remote most probably had been stimulated by the splendid collections of the Great Exhibition of 1851, held at the Crystal Palace that was temporarily erected at Hyde Park, a few blocks from the Backhouse residence. A few months into their marriage, George and Grace discussed the possibilities of a consulship abroad. She liked the idea and George applied directly to then Foreign Secretary Lord Palmerston for an appointment in Tripoli. Discouraged by a negative response, George rationalized the rejection as probably the best thing, given that the Tripoli appointment would have represented a salary reduction. Following the birth of their first child, Alice, in June 1852, the Backhouses renewed their interest in service abroad and George applied for consular positions in Elsinore, Venice, and Lima. Just three days before learning about the opportunity at Havana, George had received his latest rejection.[7] It seemed that his family's long-time relations with the Cannings—George had been named after the late George Canning (1770–1827)—had been of little help in these pursuits. Regarding the promotion aspirations of George's younger brother, Johnny Backhouse, Charles John Canning, son of George Canning, candidly told their mother that his "six or seven years of severance from the F.O. incapacitated" him from writing letters of recommendation based on his own knowledge. He added, however, that he had written to Lord Malmesbury that Johnny's "father's long and valuable service give him to a favorable consideration."[8]

At the time, Johnny Backhouse was serving Her Majesty's Government halfway around the world in China, where he held a viceconsulship at Amoy, one of a handful of Chinese ports opened to European trade after the Opium War of 1839–42.[9] Coincidentally, with George's deployment to Havana, the two Backhouse brothers would now be serving at the two poles of the infamous China–Cuba trade of contract workers that began in earnest precisely in 1853 as a supplement to the illegal slave trade. The Liverpool-based company Tait and

Co., with a base in the port city of Amoy, recruited and organized some of the first shipments of Chinese contract workers to reach Havana. In 1853, according to the records of the Empresa de Colonización, 4,307 Chinese laborers began their eight-year contracts in Cuba. Over the next two decades, an estimated 150,000 unfortunate Chinese contract workers would arrive in the island to endure exploitation and abuse, comparable to that of the slaves. A small portion of them survived the duration of their terms, and an even smaller portion managed to return home. Many among those who remained succumbed to the numbing fumes of opium, the evasive promise of games of chance, and the ultimate escape offered by suicide.[10]

The invitation to join the Havana court came at a point when, following numerous failed applications for service abroad, George had all but lost hope of getting any such appointment. Like many other pivotal events in the Backhouses' lives this offer came about suddenly, as a complete surprise. It terminated a long and emotionally draining journey of applications and rejections that took the Backhouses's hopes all around the globe, to Lima and Tripoli, to Venice and Elsinore, and finally and quite unexpectedly to Cuba's tropical shores.

Grace had all along proven supportive of her husband's aspirations but seemed less eager to leave behind her familiar surroundings and those she loved. She also found it easier to rationalize George's earlier disappointments. On November 7, 1852, she jotted in her diary: "We are both I think *somewhat* disappointed, as we had entertained serious thoughts of the change [to Tripoli]. However one good thing is we need not now look forward to wishing our friends goodby, that is pleasant." Grace's doubts and ambivalence continued even after George received the Havana offer, as confided in a letter to her aunt: "he has been so happy ever since, and likes the prospects of it so much that I trust we may really have no cause to repent. It is very melancholy indeed to think of leaving all we love in England; this is the *great* drawback to our happiness. We must pray to be re-united in joy & safety once more."[11]

George's appointment, on his superiors' instructions, had to be kept secret at first, but within a day or two it was official and the Backhouses were free to share the news with their family and friends. It all became public on December 21, when the London *Gazette* published the following notice: "The Queen has also been graciously pleased to appoint George Canning Backhouse, Esq., to be Her Majesty's Judge in the Mixed Court established at the Havannah [*sic*], under the treaty of 28th of June, 1835, between Great Britain and Spain, for the abolition of the slave trade, in the room of James Kennedy, Esq., retired." Letters of congratulations from relatives, friends, and acquaintances began to pour into 28 Hans Place. Everyone seemed to agree that this was a very special opportunity.[12]

Realizing the intense material, educational, and emotional preparation that moving an entire household halfway around the world required, George requested a two-month postponement for his departure. On New Year's Day 1853 he wrote to Addington on this subject, asking him to seek the new Foreign Secretary, former Prime Minister Lord Russell's, permission to delay his trip to Havana until March 2, to leave on board the Royal West India Mail Steamer. Three days later Addington replied that Lord Russell had granted George's petition.[13]

Shopping for necessities that George and Grace would not—or believed they would not—find in Havana became an almost daily activity for the Backhouses that winter, a winter that to them seemed grayer and colder than previous ones had. During their last few weeks in London, Grace and George frequented the seemingly endless succession of shops that lined Piccadilly and Coventry Streets; they bought books, articles of clothing, and of course, their favorite teas.[14] Seeking to leave images of their likeness behind for the consolation of their loved ones, they hired an artist, a Mr. Blakely, to paint their portraits. The first sitting took place on January 22. By February 3, the portraits were either finished or close enough for George to pass judgment: "Grace's & Baby's very good—very pretty picture. Mine good likeness."[15]

Relocation to the strange context of Cuba required that George familiarize himself with the environment and situations that he would encounter in a matter of a few weeks. On the day following the offer, he met with James Kennedy, the man he was replacing, an old-time protégé of Lord Palmerston. Kennedy, whom George most probably had already met, had served as the Havana British Commissary Judge for fifteen years, beginning in 1837. He left Havana in August 1851 without intending to return. Kennedy finally resigned in December 1852 after negotiating the maximum pension of £600 per year and securing for his son the Foreign Office post that George left vacant.[16]

During his tenure in the Mixed Commission, Kennedy witnessed dramatic changes in Cuban society and several ups and downs in the controversial slave trade. In response to the exponential growth of

Cuba's sugar industry and its concomitant increased demand for servile labor, a total of around 560,000 slaves were introduced to the island during the first half of the century; most of them ended up in the island's sugar plantations, where a brutalizing system of exploitation prevailed. Some 315,500 of this total were clandestinely imported after the slave trade was prohibited in 1821. Ironically, this slave trading orgy, which Britain now sought to suppress, had its origins during the ten-month-long British occupation of Havana (1762–63), during which period the British opened the port city to free trade—including the slave trade—with the outside world. In that short span of time an estimated 10,000 slaves arrived in Havana, an import rate twelve times the rate for the previous decade. After the British returned Havana to Spain in exchange for the Florida Peninsula at the end of the Seven Years' War, the flow of slaves dropped to about 2,000 a year, still twice the rate preceding the British capture of Havana.[17]

Kennedy arrived in Havana in 1837 in the middle of an upsurge in the slave trade. During his fifteen-year tenure at the Mixed Commission an estimated 131,500 African slaves arrived in Cuba, an annual average of 8,766. The slave trade particularly shot up in 1852–53 following Kennedy's departure. In an 1853 report, a seemingly scandalized British official stationed in Havana reported to the Foreign Office: "The Spanish Officers are bribed; the Slave Traders interested commit their offences and repeat them with the most complete impunity; Commissions sent by the Chief Authority of the Island to investigate such offences are baffled, or corrupted; the Masters and Crews are not punished, the Vessels are allowed to escape."[18]

Perhaps no one, save the slave traders themselves, knew more about the business than Kennedy did. He met with George several times, wrote letters of introduction for him, and gave him tips on housing and other matters.[19] Addington also wrote to the British consul-general at Havana, Joseph T. Crawford, instructing him to seek Backhouse upon his arrival and to render him all the official assistance in his power. George followed up Addington's letter, directly writing to Crawford asking for help in finding a place to live in Havana.[20] Overall, Kennedy painted a very positive picture of life in Havana. He presented the city as quite beautiful and healthy and attested that during his entire tenure "he never had a day's illness!!"[21]

Other testimonies and written accounts seemed to confirm

Kennedy's portrayal. "[T]he climate I am told," George wrote his mother, "is very good for the West Indies,—cooler and better than that of Jamaica." Gustave D'Hespel D'Harponville's *La reine des Antilles,* with its generally positive depiction of Cuba, became George's main reference on the island. George also bought a copy of a Spanish history text and read numerous books and reports on the slave trade.[22] Among his preparatory readings were most probably included three books by fellow Britons who earlier in the century had served the British government in various posts at Havana. The first British arbitrator appointed to the Havana Mixed Commission, Robert Francis Jameson, published his *Letters from the Havana* in 1821. David Turnbull and Richard Robert Madden, both British officials active in the struggle against the slave trade, also left published books on Cuba (1840, 1853) that were probably of use to George.[23]

George also engaged in some language preparation in anticipation of a long stay in a Spanish-speaking country. He purchased Spanish dictionaries and hired a tutor surnamed Mr. Calderón to teach him and Grace Spanish. They agreed on five or six lessons. George took them quite seriously but Grace absented herself from at least two of the sessions, which made George upset enough to remark on her absences in his diary.[24]

Late at night on February 9, 1853—it was Ash Wednesday— George received some unexpected instructions from Under Secretary of State for Foreign Affairs Lord Wodehouse; he was to leave for Havana not in three weeks as he planned but anytime within the next few days on board the HMS *Medea.*[25] No doubt this urgency obeyed to the Foreign Office's renewed abolitionist offensive beginning in 1853. The news must have greatly unsettled the Backhouse household for they had counted on more time for preparation. The unexpected appointment, the hasty response it demanded, the many necessary preparations, and the unexpectedly hurried good-byes all seemed to fall like a torrent on this young English family. Exactly two months after receiving the appointment offer the Backhouses began their journey to Havana.

George viewed the move and the opportunities that came with it as a definite watershed in their lives. The last entry in his diary for 1852, his song for that New Year's Eve, vividly reflects how he viewed the past he was leaving behind and the future he was about to embrace:

Farewell departed fifty two!
Last year of Wellington adieu.
Farewell to late alarming floods
Farewell to coming vernal buds
Farewell F.O.—farewell Protection
and fifty objects of affection
Farewell to F.O. dreary drudgery
Farewell to pipes smoked in the Nudgery
Farewell to every London manner
Farewell

Next to the poem George drew a sketchy picture of the events about to take place: three fully dressed figures, a man and a woman with a baby, leave behind an urban landscape over which reads the caption "England"; a steamship puffing a scribbling of smoke points its prow to another land over which George has written "HAVANA." Underneath stand two black figures, seemingly undressed and with open arms; one appears to be dancing, the other hanging from a tree.[26]

At 4:30 in the afternoon of February 17, 1853, George and Grace Backhouse, their eight-month-old daughter, Alice, and the family nursemaid, Harriet Wilson (Hilton), boarded the 835-ton HMS *Medea* in the port of Portsmouth. George scribbled a quick note to his Foreign Office superiors informing them of his departure. Soon after, Commander John Baile's *Medea* sailed into the sunset with its crew of 145, four civilian guests, and a cargo of provisions to last five months.[27]

The steamship struggled in rough Atlantic waters over the next few days. On the second day of the journey George jotted in his diary: "Grace, & Hilton, & Baby all sick during night." It most certainly did not help that Grace was about one-month pregnant with their second child, although apparently she did not know it at the time. The ship's log states that the rough surf continued to shake and rock the *Medea* for several days.[28] Grace had already begun to complain about the monotony of life on board a navy ship when their vessel anchored in the port of Funchal in Madeira, where the Backhouse party momentarily disembarked. They toured the harbor and mailed some letters home. The natives struck George as indolent, "owing," he concluded, "perhaps to their climate," while Grace was critical of the fact that their "Romish" temple remained open throughout the day and at night.[29]

The journey to Havana brought them sights of unfamiliar sea creatures that became stranger and more exotic as the latitudes dropped and the longitudes increased. First, formations of dolphins playfully escorting Her Britannic Majesty's ship, then large blue sharks, one of which Commander Baile suspected bit off part of the ship's steering equipment; closer to the Caribbean, flying fish flew out of the water for distances of fifteen to twenty feet, the increasingly bright sun rays reflecting off their tiny scales until they sank again into the undulating, dark blue surf.[30]

On March 17, exactly one month into their sea journey, the Backhouses saw land for the first time since Madeira; it was the north coast of Hispaniola. On the following day on port bow La Punta de Maisí, the eastern tip of Cuba, emerged gently out of the horizon. During the next four days and nights the *Medea* continued to coast the jagged profile of the 800-mile-long island that would soon become the Backhouses' home. The hundreds of inlets, coves, and bays that scarred Cuba's long coastline were indeed the slave traders' and smugglers' dream come true, and a nightmare to the British squadrons patrolling Cuba's coasts in search of slave-trading vessels. At around noon on March 21, the majestic Pan de Matanzas jumped out of the coastal profile. The *Medea* continued its westward trajectory, and about three hours later the ship steamed slowly into the contrastingly calm waters of the Havana Bay.[31]

To the vessel's left as it penetrated the long stem of the treborshaped bay stood the magnificent Castillo del Morro protected by a battery of twelve high-caliber cannons, each one named after one of Christ's apostles. From within El Morro shot up a monumental lighthouse of 78 feet with its light towering at 158 feet above sea level. At night its powerful beam shone a distance of 40–45 miles winking invitingly at thirty-second intervals.[32] Opposite El Morro, at the other side of the bay's entrance, the smaller and flatter Castillo de la Punta clung tenaciously to the rocky foundations that lined the bay. A narrow channel, 350 yards wide at its narrowest point, separated the two fortifications that guarded the mouth of the bay, which many described as the safest in the world. Further into the harbor and on the same side as el Castillo de la Punta stood yet another fortification, La Real Fuerza, the oldest of the harbor's forts. Across from it, at a higher elevation, emerged el Castillo de la Cabaña, the largest and one of the newest in the defensive network.[33]

As a defensive complex, Havana's fortifications had no match else-

**Castillo del Morro and Castillo de la Punta.** (Print by Federico Mialhe from B. May, *Álbum pintoresco de la Isla de Cuba.*)

where in the Americas. This monumental legacy of stone, mortar, and brick testified to the port city's strategic location at the crossroads of shipping lanes and to the unrelenting manner in which empire builders coveted the precious isle and its capital city. As early as 1537, when Havana was but a small settlement of a few hundred souls, a fleet of French corsairs raided and occupied the town temporarily. In 1555 the legendary Jacques de Sores paid a visit to Havana, sacked it, and left behind a scorched shell of a village.[34] In response to these and other attacks, Spanish authorities began the systematic fortification of Havana. The new forts and the city's militarization succeeded in discouraging any major attack on the island's capital during the 1600s and the first two-thirds of the 1700s. In 1762, however, during the Seven Years' War, the British sieged and later occupied Havana for ten months.

Though the threat of foreign aggression abated after the sobering British capture of Havana, in part due to the defensive reforms that it helped spark, the city's forts and increased military presence began during the middle decades of the nineteenth century to serve in the defense of the island from a filibustering thrust that combined the

**View of Havana from Casa Blanca.** (Print by Federico Mialhe from B. May, *Álbum pintoresco de la Isla de Cuba.*)

agendas of land-hungry southern United States expansionists, international adventurers, and Cuba's anti-abolition conspirators seeking to defend slavery by annexing Cuba as a slave state of the United States.

A first wave of filibusterer conspiracies, under the leadership of Venezuelan-born annexationist Narciso López, came to a tragic end. López's troops departed hastily from New Orleans in the summer of 1851 in an attempt to join an ongoing insurrection in Camagüey. The Camagüey rebels suffered defeat at the hands of Spanish soldiers and their leaders were executed before López's men landed off the shores of Bahía Honda, at the western tip of the island. Finding no support among the populace, López and his troops retreated to the hinterland. One eyewitness recounted the pathetic retreat: "He marches in shirt sleeves, over which crosses a rain-soaked discolored red flag; his beard is long and white. . . . Another ten or twelve are riding with him. They appeared shocked and wordless." Within a few days, roughly 500 expeditionaries had been either killed in action or taken captive. Firing squads under the command of Captain-General José de la Concha executed fifty of the survivors on August 15, including Colonel William Crittenden, nephew of the U.S. attorney general. Two weeks later López was garroted in the yard of el Castillo de la Punta.[35]

Following two years of reduced filibusterer threat, precisely at the time of George's arrival, rumors began to circulate of an impending large-scale filibuster invasion. It was in part an expansionist-annexationist reaction to erroneous perceptions that Britain and Spain were plotting to liberate Cuba's slaves to make the island less appealing to U.S. pro-slavery expansionists. An anonymous broadside circulating in Havana in the fall of 1853 warned that as soon as the Crimean War (1853–56) ended, a formidable British naval squadron would be deployed to enforce the abolition of slavery. To prevent such outcome, an association of wealthy Havana planters recruited John A. Quitman, a former governor of Mississippi, to organize and lead a filibusterer expedition against the island.[36]

The hills surrounding the fortified port city of Havana, covered with lush tropical vegetation and dotted with quaint suburban villages, added to the splendor of the view and its sense of protection. The sight of the harbor presented a spectacular picture that elicited compliments from even the best traveled of the city's visitors. Earlier in the century, Alexander von Humboldt had described the view as "one of the most picturesque and pleasing on the northern equinoctial shores of America." George himself conceded that "[i]n certain points of view the harbour here is in its way one of the finest things I have ever seen."[37]

The harbor bustled in unending maritime activity. On a March day like the one in which the *Medea* called in Havana, an average of twenty-two ships entered the port while hundreds of boats and smaller vessels frantically crisscrossed the quadrants of the fine bay. The month of March was in fact the busiest of the entire year, with the bulk of sugar exports leaving the island around that time of year. Havana's harbor was indeed a hub of converging sea routes and one of the world's busiest ports, either the sixth or the eighth busiest, depending on the source consulted. In 1852 a total of 1,594 commercial vessels called in the port of Havana; 1,004 of the total were foreign ships.[38] U.S. vessels had for some time come to dominate Havana's mercantile trade, particularly its exports of sugar and its by-products. Navigation statistics for 1856 registered a total of 776 U.S. ships, which represented 43 percent of all vessels calling in the port of Havana.[39] One contemporary described the cosmopolitan character of the port thus: "There are the red and yellow stripes of decayed Spain; the blue, white and red—blood to the fingers' end—of La Grande Nation; the Union crosses of the Royal Commonwealth; the stars and stripes of the

Great Republic, and a few flags of Holland and Portugal, of the states of northern Italy, of Brazil, and of the republics of the Spanish Main."[40]

A wide variety of export and import products were loaded and unloaded every day in Havana's busy piers. As Cuba was well on its way to becoming a monocrop economy, the bulk of its exports (84 percent) consisted of sugar, molasses, and rum. Tobacco, cigars, coffee, and some lesser quantities of minor crops completed the balance of Havana's export flow. In the other direction arrived cargoes from the four corners of the world: rice from the Carolinas and jerked beef from Argentina and Uruguay; wheat flour barrels from Castile via the port of Santander and table wine from Portugal; along with iron and wood manufactures from England and the Northern United States, and human cargoes from China's ancient ports.[41]

Shortly before 3:00 in the afternoon, the *Medea* sailed past another British man-of-war, the *Devastation*; its tired keel cut through the last folds of murky bay water with the precision of a surgeon's scalpel until it came to a complete halt and laid anchor. The Backhouses were elated to see their month-long journey come to an end. "Hurrah!" wrote Grace in her diary, "We anchored in the fine harbour of Havana to day to our great joy."[42]

Foreigners moving into or visiting Havana usually got their first taste of the Spanish colonial state even before setting foot on the island of Cuba. Because of their official status and the military nature of the vessel in which they arrived, the Backhouses were probably spared some of the delays, expenses, and inconveniences that marked the arrival of the average Londoner or Bostonian. No one, however, could disembark the *Medea* or any other ship coming from a foreign port unless the harbor's health inspectors were satisfied first.[43] Quite a few contemporary travelogues recount long waits before health officers boarded incoming vessels. These functionaries reportedly took long breaks throughout the day for breakfast, lunch, and naps, and would not allow the arrival of any ship to interfere with such activities. Usually the health officer arrived at his convenience in a small boat flying the imperial colors of Spain. Wearing a white linen suit and panama hat, smoking a fine cigar, and displaying an attitude to match, the inspector eventually proceeded to board the incoming vessel. The entire ritual was but a formality, for scores of "invalids" from the United States with clear signs of illness arrived each day during the winter months yet apparently no one was denied entrance to the island. A contemporary Briton remarked in his travelogue that the whole procedure struck him as "somewhat amusing" given that Havana was "such a deadly place."[44]

By five o'clock, two hours after laying anchor, the Backhouses had disembarked. They were most probably transported to the pier in one of the *Medea*'s own tender boats. Passengers arriving in other sorts of vessels were taxied for a few coins by conductors of small awning-covered boats that approached the recently arrived passenger ships. Other boatmen, mostly blacks and mulattoes, peddled fruits to the incoming passengers and yet others advertised and provided transportation to some of Havana's hotels and inns. Scores of shirtless black pier workers, most of them slaves, loaded and unloaded trunks, crates, and barrels into and out of departing and incoming ships.[45] Though most certainly these were not the first blacks that the Backhouses had ever seen, this would have been George's first encounter with the slaves about whom he had read much. The multiracial scene at the pier was a stark contrast to London's relative racial homogeneity.

In Cuban society there coexisted seemingly contradictory caste and class social structures, stemming from the simultaneous realities of slavery and agrarian capitalism. A slave-based society, Cuba's complex social structure rested, above all else, on status: people were either free or slave. There was, to be sure, a close correlation between race and status: all whites (around 49 percent of the population) were free and potential or de facto members of the master class, and 83 percent of all blacks (who constituted 41 percent of the population) were slaves. A significant intermediate population of free people of color (mulattoes and blacks) constituted 16 percent of the population. More than 91 percent of all mulattoes were free.[46]

A variety of sociodemographic factors beyond status and skin color conspired to produce a social structure more akin to a bewildering maze than a symmetric pyramid. Not only was there a primary three-tier caste-like social hierarchy based on status and race, there were also class-like hierarchies within each of the three castes, responding to a multitude of factors and circumstances. Amount of wealth, place of birth, place of residence, the color and status of one's parents, and one's status at birth determined one's place within Cuba's complex social hierarchy.[47]

Havana's racial and social composition, given its economic and social roles as the island's largest city, main port, and capital, differed somewhat from that of the island as a whole. Havana was whiter than the rest of the island and proportionately had a much lower percentage of slaves. Havana also had a disproportionately high population of free people of color, who gravitated to the city in search of employment as bakers, butchers, tailors, mechanics, and the like. While the white population of Cuba's capital was more male than the white population of the rest of the island, the city's slave population was more equally balanced among the sexes but still exhibited a larger male–female ratio; among Havana's free people of color, females predominated at about the same rate as in the rest of the island.[48]

Regardless of their nationality, status, or the type of vessel in which they arrived, passengers entering the port of Havana from abroad had to pass through customs. A total of 36,871 passengers passed through the port of Havana in 1855; 2,693 of them were non-Spanish foreigners. Inside the customs building, as solemn as saints in their niches, stood the customs officials, separated from the rest of the world by iron bars through which passed back and forth passports and the required disembarkment fees that cost two Spanish pesos. The exit visa was a steeper seven pesos and fifty cents.[49] One contemporary of the Backhouses described what she encountered there in these terms: "We pass the Customs-house, where an official in a cage, with eyes of most oily sweetness, and tongue, no doubt, to match, pockets our gold, and imparts in return a governmental permission to inhabit the island of Cuba." Other customs officials inspected the arriving luggage in search of contraband and banned publications such as political pamphlets, foreign newspapers, Bibles, and Protestant tracts.[50] Not far from the main customs building stood its monumental depository, the towered former church and monastery of San Francisco. This imposing old temple had been used momentarily as a place for Anglican worship during the British occupation of Havana in 1762–63. When the British left the city, the returning Roman Catholic prelates deemed the temple desecrated and, therefore, unusable for further Catholic worship.[51]

Perceptions of the search process and other customs proceedings varied, of course, from observer to observer, and depended on the timing of the arrival, the manners and mood of the individual agents conducting the inspections, and the tolerance of those being searched. Most agreed that the searches were neither thorough nor rigid, but

**Plaza and depository of San Francisco.** (Print from B. May, *Álbum pintoresco de la Isla de Cuba.*)

more of a nuisance during which the contents of the baggages were disarranged and sometimes broken. A woman arriving from the United States at a moment of high tension stemming from the filibuster scares of the early 1850s, remarked that the authorities tormented her ship's crew and she wondered whether "it [was] a crime . . . to have a fair Saxon skin, blue eyes, and red blood?" Others, on the contrary, felt that they had been treated politely and with respect.[52] The Backhouses' experience, given their official status, should have been closer to the latter. Grace later remarked, however, that the customs people had been "nasty [and] careless" and that they had broken the glass of George's official portrait of Queen Victoria.[53] Anglo–Spanish relations had at the time reached a peak of tension and animosity over Britain's renewed abolitionist pressures and thus the breaking of Queen Victoria's portrait by a Spanish customs officer would have certainly been a symbolically charged act.

By the time the Backhouse party had gone through customs it must have been around six in the afternoon, about the time the sun set at that time of the year.[54] George had intended to seek Consul-General Crawford, whom he addressed from London soliciting help in finding temporary lodging. Commander Baile, however, who for some reason was in a hurry to return to the *Medea,* advised George to seek rooms for the night within the city. He told George that Crawford lived quite a distance from Havana (as George later discovered, Crawford's house was only one mile away). George then decided to hire a carriage to take his family and Hilton to Miss Gilbert's boarding house, which was not far from the pier.[55]

To the average newcomer from more northerly latitudes, Havana, a sprawling city of over 150,000 souls, invariably afforded a shocking spectacle of poignant sights, sounds, and smells. For one thing, the amount of sunlight and heat pouring over Havana was far greater than in Liverpool, England, or Portland, Maine. Colors were sharper and brighter and the unrelenting glare was uncomfortably blinding to many visitors from the North. One traveler complained of not being able to read or write. Another stated that without toning down the glare "one's eyes would hardly be able to sustain the power of vision." Yet another remarked that the sun's rays pierced one's brain "well-nigh as an arrow would." The exuberant vegetation, the unfamiliar physiognomies of the multiracial population, the "Moorish" style of the architecture, all stood out sharply in the eyes of the newly arrived.[56] On her very first day in Havana, Grace recorded in her diary that everything and everyone looked new and strange to her "English eyes." George wrote in one of his first letters from Havana that "this place has a great deal about it very strange to an eye fresh from England."[57]

Havana was also by foreign standards a noisy place. Habaneros, described by a visitor as a "motley crowd of negroes, Chinese and whites" whose voices were "comparable only to the confusion of tongues at the Tower of Babel," spoke and laughed louder and more often than the average Briton or North American. The cries of the street vendor assailed the ears of the newly arrived foreigner as did the chant of the ubiquitous lottery vendor: "*Loteria! Loteria!*" A raggedy legion of strategically located street beggars added to the palate of sounds with their more contained but equally insistent pleas. A United States official stationed in Havana complained about the "cries from hoarse and screeching throats," which produced the impression "that someone is being murdered." A compatriot of the Backhouses reminisced in his travelogue that two weeks into his stay in Havana the noise drove him "utterly frantic as it did on the first day." After enduring the sounds of Havana for several months George wrote a letter home in which he complained of the noise and its effects: "I should think this Country must be unfavorable to voice & ear, judging by the monotonous unmusical howling one hears from the brutal natives who make a noise for nothing but to keep ghosts off I believe." "I have very good authority," George continued, "for saying this is not a musical place."[58]

**Havana urban scene.** (Print by Federico Mialhe from B. May, *Álbum pintoresco de la Isla de Cuba*.)

The sensitive Victorian noses of Europeans and Anglo-Americans also fell prey to the sensorial onslaught that shocked most visitors from the North. One former member of the Mixed Commission had written that the stench of dried fish and salted meat combined with "the swarm of *black population*" produced "a very fair *olfactory* catalogue." Later in the century visitors and foreign residents continued to complain about Havana's "offensive" odors. One woman from the United States described the city's smell as "smoke of tobacco, four parts; steam of garlic, three parts; aroma of negro, two parts; miscellaneous garbage, one part." Another traveler stated quite dramatically that "[t]he smells and noises ... nearly killed" him. Yet another foreign nose dubbed Havana "a hot-bed of pestilence." "The dryness of the atmosphere," explained the Bostonian Maturin Murray Ballou, "transforms most of the street offal into fine powder, which salutes nose, eyes, ears, and mouth under the influence of the slightest breeze."[59]

Piercing through this sensorial gauntlet for the first time, the Backhouse party soon arrived at Miss Gilbert's Inn. Their arrangement with the black cab driver who taxied them to the hotel turned out to be the first of many disputes over money that they would have during their

**Mosquitoes in a Havana hotel room.** (Sketch by George W. Carleton from his book *Our Artist in Cuba.*)

sojourn in Havana. Cab drivers were in the habit of demanding excessive fares from unsuspecting foreigners, sometimes twenty times the legally established fares. Fortunately for the Backhouses, Miss Gilbert intervened in the dispute on their behalf and the "troublesome" driver received much less than he hoped to get.[60]

That was the only area, it turned out, in which Miss Gilbert was of help. We "[h]ad great trouble," remarked George "to get anything we wanted." According to most accounts Havana's hotels and boarding houses were incredibly expensive and lacking in basic comforts such as mattresses, clean towels, and mosquito nets. Most of the city's public lodgings were dirty and roach and flea infested. George W. Carleton, one traveler who fell prey to the city's pests, left a series of humorous sketches of Havana's hotels with torn-down appearance, their walls covered with insects of all kinds. George scorned their hotel as "a beastly hole—a low American Boarding House." Grace described it as "very dilapidated," a "horrid house" from which they could not wait to get out.[61] It was at Miss Gilbert's establishment where the Backhouses, not having been provided with mosquito nets, had their first encounter with the potentially deadly mosquito (*Aëdes aegyptis*); little Alice came out badly bitten by the blood-thirsty mosquitoes, moving her worried mother to jot in her diary "Poor dear Baby's face . . . such a disfigurement."[62]

Thus went the Backhouses' first afternoon and night in Havana, the city to which they had been so anxious to arrive. Delayed by bureaucratic procedures, assailed by strange sights, sounds, and smells, cheated by a dishonest postilion, and quartered in a filthy boarding house, they came face to face with some of the uglier aspects of Havana. On his very first day in the city, a rather shocked and disappointed George wrote in his diary "We could not have done worse."[63] Perhaps in his mind, at a great emotional cost, he had already realized that Havana was much less than what they had come to expect. George had committed himself to twelve years' service at the post; as stipulated in the appointment, it would be eleven years and ten months before he could retire and return home.

# II

## Settling in the Tropics

If the Backhouses' first night's experience in Havana was anything like that of most foreign visitors, they must have had a very poor night's sleep, turning and turning on thin, insect-infested mattresses, awakened at perfect thirty-minute intervals by the loud cries of patrolling *serenos* who circulated the streets announcing what time it was and that all was tranquil outside. The barking of street dogs and the passing of horse-drawn carriages pounding their way through the cobble stone–paved streets added to the noisy experience of a first night's sleep—or lack of it—in Cuba's capital.[1]

The next morning George set out to meet Joseph T. Crawford, Her Britannic Majesty's consul-general at Havana for the past eleven years. A veteran consular official, Crawford had previously served twenty years in Lisbon, Portugal, and Tampico, Mexico, before arriving in Havana in 1842 to clean up the mess left by his controversial predecessor, David Turnbull.[2] He was married to Sally Crawford, the daughter of Charles D. Tolmé, an English merchant who had served as British consul prior to Turnbull. Tolmé had been notoriously accommodating to the slave interests, and his own wife owned a plantation worked by slaves. The Tolmés were also associated with the infamous slave trader–fishmonger–theater producer Francisco Marty y Torréns in schemes to import Yucatecans as an alternative source of servile labor.[3] Much to his disappointment, George soon discovered that Crawford had failed to make arrangements for their temporary housing, something he had agreed to do in a letter. He also soon learned that there were tensions between the office of the consul-general and the Mixed Commission. According to George, Crawford, who had been serving as acting judge for the two previous years, spoke sneeringly of Kennedy, the former judge. George, nonetheless, described Crawford as "very civil" and appreciated the fact that he invited him to his house and his son offered to provide temporary storage for their baggage.[4]

Later in the day, George went off to find a more acceptable hotel, which he found in la Calle Obrapía; it was probably the one run by Mrs. Chambers, one highly recommended by John George F. Wurdemann, a frequent visitor to the city, physician, and author of a Cuba travel guide for invalids.[5] While George was out, a man whom Grace described as not looking "very prepossessing" and having a "very doubtful appearance" came to Miss Gilbert's boarding house looking for George. The suspicious character turned out to be James Pilgrim Dalrymple, son of the late British arbitrator of the Mixed Commission, himself a clerk in the court since 1842. Dalrymple would remain in his post as George's assistant, the only other Briton serving at the time in the Anglo–Spanish court.[6]

One of the most pressing matters for the Backhouse household was finding a permanent place to call home. Dalrymple, who knew the city well and spoke perfect Spanish, proved helpful in this quest. For about a week and a half George and Dalrymple combed the streets of suburban Havana chasing leads of adequate vacant houses. After one such expedition George recorded in his diary that they were "very much knocked up & very hungry, thirsty & exhausted altogether." The search for a spacious house, in a healthy part of town, with a large garden—where George could pursue his gardening hobby—lead them to focus their house-hunting efforts in and around the suburban village of El Cerro.[7]

To reach El Cerro from the Intramuros (walled) section of Havana one had to cross, at one of several gates, the five-foot-thick wall that guarded the older part of the city. The city's population had spilled over the walls to the point that, by 1846, 65 percent of the capital city's residents lived outside its walls. According to census statistics, by 1841 there were twice as many houses outside the walls as there were

**La Calzada del Monte**. (Drawing by Samuel Hazard from his book *Cuba with Pen and Pencil*.)

inside. The demolition of this monumental relic would begin only in 1863. Once in the Extramuros section of the city, streets became wider, residences grew bigger, the noise level dropped, and the air became fresher.[8] Directly in front of la Puerta de Tierra, in a southwesterly direction, la Calzada del Monte pushed into the surrounding hills; once it reached the village of El Horcón, in an area known today as La Esquina de Tejas, la Calzada del Monte turned into la Calzada del Cerro. Most contemporary observers described the *calzada* as "handsome" and one of Havana's finest thoroughfares. It was, no doubt, by the city's standards, a majestic suburban vein, flanked by houses that increased in size and opulence as it penetrated deeper into the suburban hills.[9] One traveler described a drive to El Cerro as a delicious experience. Another, however, warned his readers that during the rainy season the calzada developed holes as big as two feet deep, and that during the dry season one had better "put on a linen duster; otherwise [one] will be likely to come back looking like a miller's apprentice."[10]

Beginning at the dawn of the eighteenth century, El Cerro gradually evolved from one of the forests that provided the timber for the port city's shipyards to become one of Havana's most expensive and fashionable suburbs. Sugar money poured ostentatiously into El Cerro throughout the nineteenth century. One hundred fifty years later, the once palatial homes stubbornly remained standing, their dilapidated facades echoing the glory days of Havana's sugar barons. The center of El Cerro sat on a high place next to a granite mound, which gave it its name, and commanded a privileged view of the city and its fortified harbor. By mid-nineteenth century, El Cerro had a population of a little over 2,000 people, half of them whites, two-thirds of the remaining half, black slaves. The village included some of the finest residences in all of Havana. Five of them qualified as *quintas,* palatial estates, and two dozen others as resort homes. According to the 1846 census there were also 273 masonry homes, a dozen or so commercial establishments, and four inns, among them the popular Miss Woolcot's Inn, at la Calzada del Cerro #91. The average residence of El Cerro, according to most accounts, was quaint yet quite comfortable and "modernized." It stood elevated from the level of the street, a characteristic that along with a high ceiling and an interior patio added to its freshness and good air circulation. The dominant style of El Cerro's architecture was neoclassical with profusion of colonnades. Many if not most of the wealthier British and North American residents of Havana lived in and around El Cerro. La Calle Tulipán, in particular, included a large and visible population of North Europeans and North Americans. Their presence influenced the street's architecture, marking it with rather plain facades and English-style gardens. La Calle Tulipán included several schools run by foreign teachers as well as the laboratory of Cuba's renowned scientist Carlos J. Finlay.[11]

One of the most striking and attractive aspects of El Cerro were its gardens. The Swedish visitor and prolific writer Fredrika Bremer remarked, significantly, that the village was "composed of gardens *with their little dwellings.*" Referring to these gardens, another contemporary traveler conceded that "never before did [his] eyes behold such

***Quinta* of the Count of Fernandina, El Cerro**. (Contemporary sketch from José García de Arboleya, *Manual de la Isla de Cuba*.)

beauty, grandeur and loveliness." A network of streams, flanked by irregular bamboo palisades, crisscrossed the landscape of El Cerro, a scenery dominated by imposing royal palms and other forms of exuberant vegetation that created the impression of a wild and irregular succession of gardens. It was "[n]ature refusing to be kept down," as put by a woman traveler from the United States.[12] The tropical flora of Havana's environs presented an exotic spectacle to the eyes of most visitors from colder latitudes. Referring to the "strange palm trees," Massachusetts native and author Richard Henry Dana, Jr., remarked in his travelogue, "I cannot yet feel at home among them." Another visitor, the Englishman Henry Ashworth, commented that the vegetation looked like nothing he had seen before. George was struck by the unfamiliar vegetation too: "The cocoa nut [*sic*] trees . . . I rather like the look of," he wrote home, "though I very much prefer a fine beech or oak, or ash; but I like them better than palm trees which a novice might confound them with though the stem is very different."[13]

The village of El Cerro had an abundant, diverse, and ubiquitous fauna, most of which was also strange to foreign eyes. The solemn

**La Calzada del Cerro.** (Photograph from the Charles DeForest Fredricks Collection reprinted by permission of Dirección de Servicios Audiovisuales del Instituto Autónomo Biblioteca Nacional y de Servicios de Bibliotecas de Venezuela.)

profiles of pasturing brahmin bulls dotted the landscape while packs of loud dogs patrolled the village's streets. Bright-colored flamingoes (*Phoenicopterus ruber*), blackbirds (*Quiscallus barytus*), described by George as "nasty sort[s] of bird[s]," the even nastier turkey buzzards (*Cathares aura*), and countless other bird varieties dotted the bright blue skies of suburban Havana. The Backhouses and other foreigners noticed the absence of birds of song, however. El Cerro was also quite rich in living organisms of the lower orders. According to George there was an abundance of "varieties of lizards; Grace is quite used to them. Fireflies, mosquitoes, glow worms & frogs. . . ." One afternoon as Grace was writing a letter, a frog jumped at her face and "horrified" her. Mosquitoes, scorpions, and other pests were also regular uninvited guests at the Backhouses' suburban home.[14]

Shortly after settling in the outskirts of Havana, George and Grace witnessed an episode that struck them to the point that they were both compelled to make note of it in their respective diaries. On a May Sunday afternoon, the Backhouses were out for a stroll around the

**La Calle Tulipán, El Cerro.** (Photograph from the Charles DeForest Fredricks Collection reprinted by permission of Dirección de Servicios Audiovisuales del Instituto Autónomo Biblioteca Nacional y de Servicios de Bibliotecas de Venezuela.)

house, when they spotted a solo-flying flamingo piercing the sky above their heads; the colorful bird landed in a nearby cornfield, where suddenly out of the wilderness came several black men and children in pursuit of the fallen bird. They surrounded the unfortunate animal, screamed at it, and waved their arms until one of its tormentors got hold of the bird's long pink neck. As the flamingo fell captive, George and Grace moved closer to the scene for a better look. "Silly thing to be made a prisoner so foolishly," wrote Grace in her diary that night.[15]

Past the village of El Horcón, off la Calzada del Cerro, and not far from the center of El Cerro itself, the Backhouses found a house to rent: Calle Buenos Aires #3. The house belonged to a Mr. Igaguride, who owned a cigar factory in Havana. It rented for 7 gold ounces ($119) a month, a small fortune, but an expense that the Backhouses needed not worry about; as stipulated by the Anglo–Spanish treaties, the Spanish Government must pay the house rent of the British officials to the Havana Mixed Commission.[16] At first, George was a bit concerned about the fact that the property had a small cabin in which a slave of Igaguride's would continue to reside. Given his official position and his mission in Cuba, this posed him a serious moral dilemma. He consulted Crawford on this matter, who without hesitation calmed the younger official's concern. "[T]here is not a washerwoman in this place," Crawford assured him, "who [is] not a slave."[17]

The house in la Calle Buenos Aires commanded a formidable view of the city and the bay. From it the Backhouses could not only see the road traffic to Havana, which moved up and down la Calzada del Cerro, they could also scan the bay for incoming and departing ships, which, with the help of George's telescope, could be identified from a distance. The house had spacious living and dining rooms, which George hesitated to call such, once remarking that it was "absurd to translate the names of the airy verandah & venetian blind affairs into those of anything like such close shut up fully furnished rooms with roaring fires." Being in the heart of the tropics, it appeared, did not calm George's nostalgia for the fireplaces of his youth. Pictures of the English countryside and familiar landmarks hung on the walls to remind them of the place they called home. There were service rooms on the bottom floor and two large rooms above: a master room and a nursery. Attached to the main building was the bathroom, a metal-clad structure with a plunge bath. All around the property, a large garden, which Grace described as "a regular wilderness," satisfied George's passion for gardening; from it, he gathered flowers almost every day, as well as guavas, bananas, and other tropical fruits.[18]

The Backhouses' relations with their landlord, Mr. Igaguride, were very problematic. "[D]uring the week that elapsed between our engaging & entering the house," George wrote his sister,

> the landlord clearly gave himself not the slightest trouble to fulfil his engagement except when forced to do one thing or another that I specified to him; the day before we entered, the last order was given for removing an enormous bird-cage which filled the kitchen & which I had mentioned from the first. I at last, since we came to live here [about a month], got the landlord (for the first time I believe) to come here himself & see the state of things.

Finally, Igaguride hired a carpenter to make the necessary repairs, which must have not proceeded as George wished, given his description of the man as "the laziest, slowest, clumsiest, civillest carpenter I ever met with." Problems with Igaguride continued as attested to by Grace who, in a letter home, described him as a "disagreeable landlord" who would not make repairs.[19]

Besides problems with the landlord, the house at Buenos Aires #3 was not totally suiting, especially after the Backhouses learned that a little Habanero would soon swell their numbers. They also felt that the lack of an extra room kept them from being able to dispense their hospitality to relatives and friends in a proper way. When Mrs. Scharfenberg, their friend and next door neighbor, announced her intention to vacate her house and move to England, the Backhouses saw an opportunity to move to a bigger house with one extra bedroom. Only fourteen months into their stay at their first house they decided to cut short their two-year-lease with Igaguride and to move 150 yards up the road to Buenos Aires #1. Six men from a moving company worked all day on June 13, 1854, without carts or horses; they were done with the moving by the end of the day. Although the new landlord, Mr. Pozo, had just had the house painted and "done up," Grace deemed it necessary to hire five slaves who belonged to a neighbor to work in the new house. Grace also bought some of Mrs. Scharfenberg's furniture to add to their vast inventory of more than a dozen tables, fifty chairs of different sizes and shapes, six beds and cots, four chests, an escritoire, and dozens of other pieces of furniture. The accumulation of furniture as symbols of mobile wealth was, to be sure, one of the propensities of the Victorian English middle class.[20]

After moving into their first house, the Backhouses dedicated much time and energy to assembling their domestic service staff. This was primarily Grace's task. She devoted more time in her diaries and correspondence to domestic service issues than to any other matter except her children. The first thing that becomes evident from reading Grace's accounts is that there was a continuous turnover in the Backhouses' domestic staff. Aside from Hilton, the young nursemaid who came with them from England, their household servants proved highly transient; at least fourteen different servants are referred to by name in the Backhouse documents; countless others who passed through for just days or even hours either remain nameless or are not mentioned at all. It appears that few of their Cuban servants stayed with them for more than six months. At any given time the Backhouses had a staff of five or six native servants: an under nurse, a cook (sometimes male), a washerwoman, a housemaid, a gardener, and often a service boy. Such a large coterie of servants was one of the marks of English aristocratic life that tropical Victorians of all classes saw fit to emulate.[21]

The ethnic, status, gender, and age composition of the service proved highly diverse, which added to its instability and volatility. Above all of them was Hilton. Another British maid, Caroline Langley, joined the Backhouse household in September 1853 but did not stay long, apparently for health reasons.[22] There were other white servants, some Cuban-born, some Canary Islanders. At least two of their many housemaids, Juana and Cándida, and three of their male servants were white. There were also slaves whom the Backhouses rented from different masters and free blacks who arranged their service contracts directly with Grace.

Grace was never satisfied with those who served her. She found her servants too unreliable, too dirty, too lazy, too violent, and too immoral. Grace and Hilton insisted on imposing a Victorian work ethic on a ragtag crew of hired-out slaves and assorted free laborers in the context of a slave-based colonial society. The Backhouse domestic staff was, thus, under constant surveillance and mortification. Before hiring them, Grace inspected her workers like she would a horse on the auctioneer's block. After contracting a young slave woman named Merced, she jotted in her diary: "[She is] black a trim looking girl with good teeth and small waist." Grace's diaries and correspondence are peppered with derogatory remarks about those she brought home to work for her. She referred to Martha, an English-speaking housemaid, as an "immensely fat black woman"; George also disliked her and thought her vain. Juana, the "Canary girl" was in Grace's words "shockingly dirty to be sure." Of a boy servant named Antonio, she wrote in her diary that he had a weakness for the house wine and "he told lies besides." After being confronted with his drinking habit, Antonio decided to leave the very next day because, as he put it, "it was the Spanish fashion to go off quick." Grace also grumbled about Cándida's bad habits and immoral behavior.[23]

The Backhouses complained repeatedly about their servants' carelessness and dishonesty. In a letter home, Grace wrote, "I have often wondered whether we are particularly unfortunate in our breakages or whether (as I imagine) our servants are particularly careless." She continued by spelling out in great detail how many glasses and pieces of china had been broken since their arrival in Havana. One boy servant named Pedro was let go because, according to Grace, "he would not beg my pardon for laughing when I scolded him about a broken egg cup." When Grace lost her Geneva watch, she had Santiago, a white boy servant, searched, along with his trunk and bed. On another occasion, George paid a visit to one of their servants, who lay convalescing in a hospital bed, not to see how he was doing but to interrogate him about a missing egg spoon. Although the Backhouses probably never did such a thing, it was customary to punish and humiliate servants suspected of stealing by shaving their heads.[24]

The Backhouse documents and other contemporary sources attest that episodes of violence were common among members of domestic staffs. One contemporary recounts a fight between two domestics in which one threw a knife at another. At the Backhouses', Josefa, a black housemaid, once bit Santiago. George intended to dismiss her but Grace convinced him not to do so for this had been "her first offence of the kind." On a later occasion, another servant quarreled with Hilton and two black maids, Cecilia and Martina. A disturbed Grace described the incident as "such a blow up in our household . . . just when we were thinking we were rather comfortable with our servants." The volatile Hilton had repeated rows with black servants, whom she unabashedly despised.[25]

That so many servants had to be dismissed or simply chose to look for work elsewhere forced George and Grace to search continuously for new helping hands. Many times their servants left without prior notice, forcing the Backhouses to run off to the "very tumble down street[s]" of the city to hire new ones. One of their main suppliers of servants was Madame Fillete, a black woman whom Grace described as "excessively well off." She had lived with a Frenchman with whom she had six children until the day he decided to return to France. She remained in their spacious mansion and owned many slaves, whom she rented out as domestics. Her business allowed Fillete to support a numerous family with lots of grandchildren, who were all, according to Grace, "brought up like ladies & gentlemen." Grace, the wife of the British anti-slave trade judge, had no qualms about renting Fillete's slaves but it struck her as odd that "a black woman . . . have slaves of her own colour." Another way to come by reliable servants was to inherit those of other members of the foreign elite who because of their leaving the island or some other reason no longer had use for them.[26]

Whether rented out or hired as free laborers, domestic workers were very expensive in Havana. Consul-General Crawford once reported that in no country were servants as expensive as they were there. Another British observer calculated that wages for house servants were twice as high as they were in England. Part of the problem stemmed from a special tax on domestic slaves directed at reducing the excessive number of slaves destined to such tasks. No doubt the growth of the city's population and the island's export economy and the worsening scarcity of labor contributed to the expense and independence of service labor. Juan, who cooked for the Backhouses for some time, drew a respectable monthly salary of 20 pesos, while another of their cooks earned 13 pesos a month. Another servant, Manuel, reportedly first earned 14 pesos per month and later 19 pesos. The Backhouse records also show that at one point one of their boy servants received the significant monthly salary of 8 pesos per month. All in all, the Backhouses spent £300 a year on their service staff, a necessity that Grace felt was *"dreadfully* expensive."[27]

Servants' wages were reflective of the general exorbitant cost of life in mid-nineteenth-century Havana. Housing, clothing, food, and entertainment were also exceedingly expensive. Most travelers and foreign residents agreed that Havana was one of the most costly places they had ever been to. In one of his many letters requesting a salary increase from the Foreign Office, Consul-General Crawford referred to Havana as "outrageously expensive." On another occasion he certified that it was easier to live in London with $6,000 than in Havana with $10,000. His United States counterpart echoed these assessments, estimating that the cost of living in Havana was "greater than at any city in Christiendom [*sic*]." Antonio C.N. Gallenga, an Italian-born English journalist, referred to Havana as the "nastiest and most expensive hole in the world," and even the Spanish captain-general believed the island to be "probably the country where money is worth less."[28]

The Backhouses, who had had financial difficulties from the beginning of their marriage in 1851, were set back further by many unexpected relocation expenses. In spite of the fact that their rent was paid by the Spanish government and that they received a moving allowance from the British government, only a few weeks into their residence in Havana, George began to send signals of financial distress. On a letter dated May 1, 1853, he confided in his sister Mary that their relocation expenses had "drained" them through their "unsettled mode of living a part of the time & having so much to pay on starting housekeeping, & the expensiveness of everything except cigars, many things costing . . . fully four times as much as in England."[29]

The expense of goods and services aside, George confronted many problems conducting business in Havana, not only with Cubans and Spaniards but with all those creolized in their business habits. The first transaction in which George was involved upon arriving in Havana ended in a tense discussion with the postilion who taxied them to Miss Gilbert's inn. Not understanding—or not wishing to understand—the negotiated or bargaining way in which transactions were made in Havana, George distrusted all merchants and believed that they were all out to cheat him. It was customary to bargain for everything in Havana to the extent that merchants would first demand prices that ranged between 25 and 50 percent and sometimes up to 300 percent above what they expected to get for a given article. It should not have taken anybody long to figure out that Cuban society was one of negotiation, and that everything from the price of a bunch of bananas to the color of one's skin to the salvation of one's soul had a price and it was subject to negotiation.[30]

George's writings contain several allusions to what he perceived to be the merchants' generalized penchant for dishonesty. "The unconscionable dishonesty of tradesmen here is incredible," he wrote home on one occasion,

> Yesterday an ironmonger's Bill was brought to me by a young fellow. . . . In the Bill was included an Article made of copper & lined with tin, called a 'paila,' for boiling clothes in; the ironmonger had agreed to let us have the thing for 20 dollars (£4), & we heard, after we had ordered it that we could have it at another place for 15 dollars; the Bill was a long one, & in it was put down this said copper vessel for 22 dollars, which we luckily detected before paying.

"The young swell," continued George,

> had no hesitation, on detection, to take off the two extra dollars; whether he had authority to do this, & what defence could be set up for such an impudent attempt at fraud I could not take the trouble to inquire, the young fellow's language being Spanish. There seems to be no general principle among tradesmen except that of shirking their engagements if you will let them.

Upon returning from another shopping excursion George complained about the "tradesmen whose dishonesty & manners were disgusting."[31]

Havana and its outskirts was also a notoriously dangerous place, where robberies and murders were commonplace. Roving gangs of criminals committed robberies almost on a daily basis, sometimes murdering their victims. In 1841 there were 372 robberies and 74 murders. Eight years later there were 609 robberies and 66 murders. Many of these crimes remained unpunished for a variety of reasons, ranging from police corruption, to an ineffective judicial system, to the protection that members of the elite offered to ruffians working on their behalf. The high incidence of crime notwithstanding, George felt secure in the outskirts of Havana, as attested by his assurances to a visitor that it was not necessary to fasten doors and windows at night.[32]

On balance, the process of settling in El Cerro and getting used to the setting and its people turned out to be traumatic and full of surprises for the Backhouse family. Shortly after their arrival, George and Grace began to signal their disillusionment. "This place," wrote George, "is by no means so beautiful as I had expected." A few weeks later, and in much harsher terms, he said of Cuba: "there are plenty of sights here disgusting & disgraceful to the Nation that can produce them." Grace also became increasingly impatient with her new surroundings and more homesick with each passing day. About three months into their residence in suburban Havana, Grace sent home a letter in which she dubbed Cuba "this obscured Island"; she expressed concern about their future and hoped to be able to go to England—at least for a visit—in four to six years.[33]

# III

## The Mixed Commission and Cuba's *Emancipados*

S oon after his arrival in Cuba, George assumed his official responsibilities as Her Britannic Majesty's Judge at the Havana
Mixed Commission for the Suppression of the Slave Trade. At
noon on March 26, 1853, he arrived in the Captains-General's palace
where he placed his hand on a Bible and swore that he would "faithfully judge, [and] would not show partiality toward the apprehended or
their captors."[1] On that occasion George first met the Spanish Captain-
General Valentín Cañedo, whom Crawford scorned as "a partizan of
the slave Traders" and whose complicity in the trade was repeatedly
denounced by other high-ranking British officers.[2] Cañedo had previously inquired about George's record and character and had been
assured by the Spanish minister in London that the new judge was
known for his "moderation and conciliatory character."[3] Indeed
George's heart did not harbor the flame of abolitionism; this would

From Luis Martínez-Fernández, "The Havana Anglo-Spanish Mixed Commission
for the Suppression of the Slave Trade and Cuba's *Emancipados,*" *Slavery and
Abolition* 16, no. 2 (August 1995): 205–225. Reprinted by permission of Frank Cass
Publishers.

have made his appointment to the Mixed Commission intolerable to Cuba's Spanish officials and those segments of society profiting or depending on the continued importation of slaves. Although there is little evidence suggesting that George was a committed abolitionist, an extensive record supports the contention that he took his responsibilities very seriously and that he was beyond the reach of bribes and similar pressures. The slave-trading interests did not welcome that.

Perhaps not fully aware of it, George stepped into a very difficult and controversial position. As a foreign representative with judiciary powers over captured slave ships, he became probably the only resident in the island with some power to curb the odious trade in human beings. His duties had very serious implications since they aimed at abolishing a trade that, given the slave population's incapacity to reproduce itself, would, if successful, necessarily translate into the eventual demise of slavery itself. And slavery was, simply put, Cuba's economic backbone. The slave trade was a colossal source of profits for its investors as well as for colonial officials who drew hefty bribes. It was estimated that a five-hundred-slave expedition could net close to a quarter-million pesos profit to its investors and an additional $100,000 disbursed among a wide assortment of bribe recipients.[4] Planters, merchants, colonial bureaucrats—in short, the island's most powerful and influential people—deemed the preservation of the slave trade vital to their economic interests. Such were the forces that George would face over the next few years.

Due to a complex web of mutually reinforced reasons ranging from humanitarianism, to the desire to protect British colonial agriculturalists, to seeking to make Cuba less attractive to United States expansionists, the abolition of the transatlantic slave trade and eventually the end of slavery itself became central goals of Britain's Caribbean policy beginning in the 1810s. As early as 1817, and with the mediation of a large cash indemnification—some have referred to it as a bribe—Britain forced Spain to sign a bilateral treaty for the suppression of the slave trade. The treaty included provisions for mutual searches of ships suspected of slave-trading and the establishment of mixed courts in Cuba and Sierra Leone to decide on such cases. The Havana Anglo–Spanish tribunal that George eventually joined and its sister court in Freetown, Sierra Leone, were established in 1820.[5] The fact that some 250 years earlier the Elizabethan corsair John Hawkins raided the coasts of Sierra Leone to capture slaves whom he then smuggled into the Spanish Caribbean

**Enslaved man on the shores of Africa.** (Reprinted from Lydia Milagros González and Ángel G. Quintero Rivera, *La otra cara de la historia*.)

remains one of the greatest ironies of Atlantic history. According to treaty stipulations, Spain and Britain were equally responsible in supporting and staffing the Mixed Commissions of Havana and Sierra Leone. Both nations were also supposed to receive equal amounts of whatever was gained from the sale of condemned slave-trading ves-

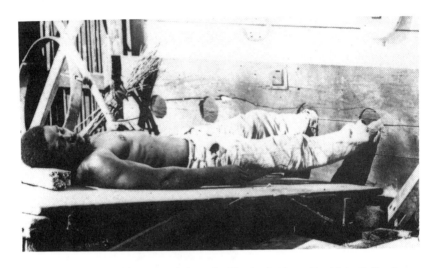

**Slave posing in stocks.** (Photograph from the Charles DeForest Fredricks Collection, courtesy of Keith de Lellis Collection, New York.)

sels. Whenever the court determined that a given vessel had been illegally detained, however, it was the responsibility of the capturing nation to indemnify the ship's owner for any losses and inconveniences.[6]

The slave trade suppression treaty of 1817 remained a dead letter and the Havana Mixed Commission quite ineffective, as attested by the fact that an estimated 169,000 slaves were illegally imported into Cuba between 1821 and 1835, an average of 11,266 a year.[7] The abolition of slavery in the British West Indies in 1834 provided Britain with greater moral force to further pursue its self-appointed role as international crusader against the slave trade. The persistence of slavery in the Spanish colonies, furthermore, provided these territories with an additional edge over their British counterparts, whose sugar industries now depended on more expensive waged and indentured labor. Thus, in 1835 the British forced Spain to sign yet another bilateral treaty for the suppression of the slave trade, this time with more teeth in it to effectively put an end to the growing trade in bonded human beings. The new treaty established severe penalties for those involved in the slave trade and added a new equipment clause, which stipulated that in the absence of actual slaves, equipment such as shackles and large quantities of water and other provisions would suffice as evidence of involvement in the trade.[8]

The 1835 treaty also reflected a renewed interest among British statesmen in the welfare of the *emancipado* class, those slaves liberated by the Mixed Commissions. It stipulated that emancipados would henceforth come under the authority of the capturing nation rather than under that of the nation in whose territory the court was located, as heretofore. Spanish officials also came under the obligation to provide the Havana Mixed Commission with updated registers of emancipados every six months.[9] It is significant that at this juncture, which coincided with the abolition of slavery in the British colonies, the British government ceased to hand over emancipados to the Spanish authorities and began paying for the relocation of hundreds of them to several of its Caribbean possessions.[10] Early on, the British island colony of Trinidad figured as the preferred destination, with 1,173 emancipados sent there in 1833–35 alone.[11] In 1840 at least one shipment of 327 emancipados arrived in labor-hungry Belize. By the late 1840s and early 1850s the dwindling flow of British-liberated emancipados shifted to Jamaica. Almost 200 emancipados left Cuba for the neighboring island under the auspices of the British government between 1849 and 1853.[12]

Britain's abolitionist pressures in Cuba reached a peak in 1840–42 during David Turnbull's concurrent tenures as British consul-general and superintendent of liberated Africans. Turnbull's anti-slavery activities backfired, however, and Great Britain's influence in Cuba eroded as a result of the Turnbull crisis, culminating in the bloody repression of the actual or fabricated slave conspiracy of La Escalera in 1844. In the light of mounting controversy, Turnbull was recalled from his consular post in February 1842. Later in the year his other post, the Superintendency of Liberated Africans, was abolished after Spanish authorities arrested him, executed some of his black Anglophone associates, and ordered him to leave and never return. Turnbull had reason to believe that his abolitionist activities had placed his life in jeopardy and he was fortunate to have left the island alive.[13] Aware of the diplomatic consequences of extremist abolitionism, Lord Palmerston's successor at the Foreign Office, Lord Aberdeen, appointed Crawford, a moderate and pragmatic abolitionist, to replace the controversial Turnbull.[14] Throughout the decade following the Turnbull crisis, the Havana Mixed Commission maintained a very low profile, reflecting Britain's reduced interest in forcing an abolitionist agenda. The opposite posture had not only done little to benefit the slaves and emancipados and had failed to stop their continued importation, it had also activated both United States–based expansionism and Cuban annexationist filibustering, activities that peaked in 1848–51. A dangerous upsurge of anti-British sentiment was another result of Britain's activist role against the Cuba slave trade.[15]

The Anglo–Spanish Mixed Commission that George joined in the spring of 1853 had been a dormant institution for over a decade. Between 1840 and 1850 it had dealt with only seven cases. It condemned three vessels, freed three others, and was unable to adjudicate another case. No cases reached the Havana court in 1843, 1844, 1845, or between 1847 and 1850.[16] The inactivity of the Mixed Commission drew severe criticism from various quarters. One British subject scorned it as a "shameful farce"; another criticized it for not having "much if any business" beyond simply watching "the iniquities of Cuba." Yet another critic left the island "mortified" at the sight of the "poor figure" England made regarding the slave trade.[17] At one point, Cuba's corrupt Captain-General Federico Roncali called for the tribunal's abolition, stating that no vessel suspected of slave trading had been condemned since 1835.[18]

Several factors limited the Mixed Commission's reach and effectiveness. First, it brought into frontal conflict two very distinct legal traditions: the more decisive and inflexible English common law tradition and the more lenient Spanish tradition with its roots in Roman law.[19] The Mixed Commission's structure and composition did not allow it to function properly. The treaties that established it stipulated that the court be composed of two judges, one Spanish, one British. Whenever a case came before the court, both judges had to agree on a verdict of either lawful prize or unlawful seizure. Agreement, however, was seldom, if ever, achieved because in practice the British judge almost always played the prosecuting role while his Spanish colleague defended the suspected slavers' case. Two arbitrators, one from each nation, were also supposed to be part of the court, their task being to decide the verdict whenever the judges reached a split decision. To determine which of the arbitrators would break the tie, dice were cast or lots were drawn. Following the death of the British arbitrator Campbell J. Dalrymple in 1847, however, the British side of the court was put at a disadvantage and no lots were to be drawn in the case of tied decisions. Consul-General Crawford sometimes played the role of acting British arbitrator and he persistently maneuvered to get the actual appointment. George later received instructions "to claim the right in certain cases in the absence of the British Arbitrator to call in as arbitrator any British consul or Vice Consul who may be resident at any Port of the Island of Cuba."[20]

Another factor that made the court ineffective was that it had juris-diction only over Spanish or British vessels suspected of participating in the slave trade and their cargoes. It had no authority to determine guilt or punishment for either the ships' owners or masters or for vessels flying the colors of other nations. The fact that during this period most of the slave trade was carried out under the protection of the United States flag made the Havana court's efforts against the trade quite inef-fective.[21] Not until the 1860s, with a civil war raging in the United States, did Lincoln's government agree to cooperate with Great Britain in the struggle against the commerce in African chattel laborers.[22]

Spanish officials were not interested in turning the Mixed Commis-sion into a functioning institution, as attested by the backgrounds of the Spanish judges appointed to the court. José María Herrera y Herrera, the Count of Fernandina, served as Spanish judge in the 1840s while figuring as one of the largest slave masters of the island. José Buena-ventura Esteva, the Marquis of Las Delicias, was the Spanish judge when George arrived and would remain in that position until his retire-ment in 1855. Before a Parliamentary committee, Kennedy described Esteva as "perhaps the largest proprietor of slaves . . . [and] the great-est hirer of slaves in the island." He was not only one of the largest slave holders, he also received hundreds of emancipados liberated by the court for his private use. This Galician-born planter of reputedly low social origins became one of the island's wealthiest and most influential men. His palatial home in El Cerro was considered a must-see sight for foreign visitors, although Grace said of it, "I could not discover at all [its] boasted beauty."[23]

There were also problems with the British half of the Mixed Com-mission. Not only did it operate at a disadvantage because it lacked an arbitrator, it also lacked a full-time judge with full powers between James Kennedy's departure in August 1851 and George's arrival in March 1853. Even when fully staffed, the British half of the Mixed Commission left much to be desired. One critic of the court testified that Kennedy devoted "his whole time" to the study of ornithology and that the senior Dalrymple was a "*poor man . . .* too simple to do good, and too innocent to do harm." By his own admission, Kennedy spent some of his tenure pursuing another hobby, archaeological investigations in the Yucatán for a book he planned to write. One British critic of the court denounced that its commissioners got "very handsome salaries, and, by all accounts, do rather less than nothing for them."[24] There had even been a problem of actual slave-holding among British officers and commissary judges. Dalrymple, R.B. Jackson, and Kennedy all at one point or another owned slaves or made improper use of emancipados. Kennedy, who served fifteen years as the island's top British official entrusted with putting an end to the slave trade, technically participated in it when he took his slave, Pancho, to England, where he automatically would become a free man, and later returned him to bondage in Cuba.[25]

Although George was committed to turning the Mixed Commission into a more aggressive and functioning body, during his tenure he continued to face many of the court's long-standing problems: the insufficient patrolling of Cuba's long, jagged coastline; Spain's lack of cooperation and even obstructionism; a partially staffed court; the hostility of the city's elite; and tensions with the office of the British consul.

George was involved in only three slave-trade cases: the *Arrogante Emilio,* the *Casualidad,* and the *Grey Eagle.* These cases provide an excellent window to the kinds of obstacles that British officials faced while trying to put slave traders out of business.

Three months before George's arrival in Havana, Captain Hamilton's HMS *Vestal* captured the *Arrogante Emilio* five miles off the mouth of the Havana Bay, suspecting that it was involved in the slave trade. According to Hamilton's sworn statements and the accounts of other witnesses, the *Arrogante Emilio* was equipped with hidden beams and boards for the construction of slave decks, carried a large sum of gold doubloons, and included among its equipment charts and maps of Cape Verde and the African coast. For their part, the captured vessel's crew and captain complained of having been mistreated by the British officers, whom they accused of themselves fabricating the incriminating evidence. They maintained that they were on their way to Buenos Aires to pick up a cargo of jerked beef, a staple of the slaves' diet.[26]

Following weeks of depositions and the preparation of voluminous reports by teams of experts, the Mixed Commission proceeded to issue a verdict. Crawford, who at the time was acting as British judge, voted to condemn the *Arrogante Emilio*. Esteva, as expected, declared it not guilty and thus unlawfully searched. Since there was no British arbitrator, the split decision went automatically to the Spanish arbitrator, Brigadier Francisco Yllas. Claiming ill health, Yllas yielded to the Spanish Regent of the Real Audiencia, Pedro Pizarro, who not surprisingly voted with his fellow countryman, declaring the ship a lawful commercial ship. The *Arrogante Emilio* was declared free on the very day that George arrived in Cuba.[27]

The verdict of the *Arrogante Emilio* had many ramifications that George would have to deal with during his judgeship. A year after the initial verdict, George moved to have the case reconsidered. Judge Esteva, however, declined to meet with his British colleague over this issue, reminding him that all Mixed Commission decisions were final and unappealable. George insisted and told Esteva that he had orders to do so, but to no avail. Some time later the owner of the *Arrogante Emilio*, the notorious slave-trader José Joaquín Correa, demanded and eventually received a 3,080-peso indemnification for the losses he claimed he suffered while the ship remained in the court's custody.[28]

The first case in which George was actually able to make a determination was the one involving the vessel *Casualidad*, which was seized by Captain Dobbie's HMS *Buzzard* on April 17, 1853. On the same day, James Dalrymple, the court's eyes and ears and son of the late arbitrator Campbell James Dalrymple, brought news of its capture to his boss. The *Casualidad* had come to the island with an undetermined number of slaves, all of whom were safely landed prior to the ship's capture. The case came to court on April 20 and George and the Spanish judge boarded the vessel a week later to examine its cargo, which consisted of an unusually large number of water casks (twenty-one) and "large hatchways fitted for laying a slave deck." Following a tedious and protracted process of depositions and further investigations, on May 31, George issued his opinion that the *Casualidad* was indeed guilty of slave trading. George's written closing statement was not ready on time but he was able to present it later in the day thanks to the help of one of Crawford's clerks. Esteva delivered his verdict verbally and as George anticipated the "[t]wo sentences [were] totally opposed." Lots were drawn and the Spanish arbitrator won and proceeded to vote with Esteva. The *Casualidad* was released and its owner, Juan Coll, received from the court 600 pesos in damages.[29]

On June 27, 1854, the man-of-war *Espiegle* captured another vessel suspected of slave trading off the coast of Bahía Honda, about fifty-five miles west of Havana. According to the Spanish governor of the district, the deserted and flagless *Grey Eagle* had brought a cargo of 205 slaves, all of whom came under the custody of the diligent local authorities. The British investigation, however, revealed that the cargo actually had consisted of around 670 slaves and that following the disbursement of 32,000 pesos in bribes more than 400 slaves were allowed to disembark. George reported that the bribe money had been "divided between all the local authorities without exception."[30]

In the case of the *Grey Eagle* it was evident that the vessel had been involved in the slave trade. Even the corrupt local officials acknowledged that. The central issue in this case was, instead, whether the ship's nationality allowed the Mixed Commission to have jurisdiction over it or not. Here too, after a long examination that produced a mountain of redundant documentation, lines were drawn along national alliances: George concluded that the *Grey Eagle* was Spanish and therefore condemnable by the court, Esteva declared it a United States ship over which the court had no authority. A final determination was made on May 26, 1855. The vessel was not adjudicated but instead it was turned over to Captain-General José de la Concha to dispose of as he saw fit. Not satisfied with the case's outcome, George argued that the ship should at least be handed to its captors, the British. The Foreign Office later ordered him not to pursue the matter further.[31]

By virtue of its powers over condemned slave-trading vessels, the Mixed Commission had authority to supervise the process whereby slaves from captured ships were liberated and declared *emancipados*. According to the Anglo–Spanish treaty of 1835 and other legislation, *emancipados* were supposed to fall under the custody of the nation whose ship recovered them; in practice, however, this was not always the case. Other laws established that *emancipados* remaining under the custody of Spain would be registered, issued tin tickets for identification, and made to serve, ostensibly to ease their transition to civilization, five-year labor terms under some responsible trustee. These terms could be legally extended, however, to a maximum of three more years, and other mechanisms existed to extend the periods of servitude indefinitely. Spanish colonial law also established that *emancipados* be fed, clothed, and given medical attention by their trustees; they were also supposed to receive religious instruction and training in some trade as part of their transition to full freedom. Many of those who had served their terms were kept in servitude and paid nominal monthly wages.[32]

Many if not most emancipados in the hands of the Spanish colonial state fell victim to corrupt practices of labor allotment and were made to fill in for the chronic labor shortages of the period. During the first decades, emancipados were either exploited directly by the colonial government or were consigned to individuals, as political favors, in return for pecuniary donations. There were reports that during the 1830s Spanish officials were selling emancipados at nine gold ounces, or about one-third of the cost of a slave.[33] In the early 1850s, Captain-General Concha tried to bring some order to the emancipado affairs by setting up the Junta de Emancipados and by establishing fixed rules to regulate the ways in which they were to be consigned.[34] Although Concha insisted that the Junta was composed of "people that were characterized by and possessed all the necessary guarantees to oversee the good treatment of the emancipados," it was evident that the Junta had close ties with the island's slave-trading interests. Its composition according to British officials was "very objectionable." It included one nephew and one close friend of Joaquín Gómez, a reputed head of the slave traders, and Francisco Aguirre, who according to British intelligence was personally involved in the illicit trade of human chattel.[35] Quite significantly, George denounced one of the clerks of the Junta de Emancipados, José Sávates, who lived luxuriously on a $60–70 monthly salary and upon retirement bought a 100,000-peso sugar estate.[36]

Most individual trustees directly exploited their emancipados' labor whether they paid for their consignment or got them for free as a political favor. Those who rented emancipados from the state were still getting labor at quite a cheap rate even after the consignment fees and wages were deducted. Such arrangements also provided greater flexibility than outright ownership of slaves, which required large outlays of cash and the risk of loss in the case of the slave's death or escape to freedom. Rental of emancipados was also an ideal arrangement for those seeking a reliable, short-term, or seasonal supply of hands. Moreover, emancipados represented a more vulnerable and therefore more exploitable form of labor that could be coerced to a greater extent than free wage laborers, who could, and often did, move about within the free labor market. In Havana free labor was not only very expensive, it was also very mobile and unreliable.[37]

Some emancipados were exploited in yet another fashion. Their trustees would allow them to hire themselves out as long as they sur-rendered part of their income to them. These practices were declared illegal in 1854, when charitable institutions and widows retained the exclusive right to sub-consign emancipados; the establishment of 100-peso fines in 1867 and reports to that effect suggest that the practice of sub-consigning emancipados continued long after it was declared illegal.[38] Under such arrangements an emancipado, even if *ladino* (serving beyond the first five-year term with a trustee), would not receive a wage from his official trustee but rather from his direct employer. The case of Gabino, one of the emancipados whose rights Consul-General Turnbull fought to protect, reflects this practice. Gabino's trustee hired him out as a water carrier and forced him to give her one peso a day. After two decades of toil, Gabino reportedly generated 5,228 pesos for his trustee, who paid only 612 pesos to the government for the right to exploit the emancipado's labor.[39] A similar case was that of Marcelino Urrutia, whose trustee allowed him to work at the cigar factory of José María Montero, where he earned 10 to 12 reales a day. Marcelino was at first obliged to pay one peso a day, almost all of his earnings. After some negotiation the surrendered amount of his salary came down to 5 reales, still about half of Marcelino's income. What Marcelino got to keep was above the le-gally stipulated emancipado monthly salary of 6 pesos, but still way under the going salaries for free skilled labor.[40] Demetrio Lucumí, tin ticket 95, had a similar arrangement with his trustee. He too was forced to surrender 5 reales per day to his trustee and according to his testi-mony he was under continuous threat of being sent to the cane fields if he failed to produce that amount. When Demetrio came forward to George's office with his grievances, he claimed to have fallen behind in his payments and to owe his trustee about eight pesos.[41] What made this type of arrangement all the more difficult and oppressive was that if for illness or some other reason an emancipado lost his job or was unable to continue working, his trustee still expected to receive an income from him.

As the cases described above demonstrate, up to three parties could benefit from the labor of emancipados. First the colonial state, which paid nothing to acquire them, allotted them either for money or as political favor. The trustees who received them had access to their cheap labor or could profit by illegally sub-consigning them to third parties and taking a substantial cut of the emancipados' wages. Those directly employing and those getting the emancipados in sub-consignment were exploiting labor at below-market rates and avoiding the long-term commitments, preoccupations, and maintenance costs associated with slavery. As if all this was not enough, the colonial state levied confiscatory income taxes of 18 or 24 pesos per year depending on the emancipado's sex, a rate equal to 33 percent of an emancipado ladino's minimum salary.[42]

In the worst of cases, emancipados were abused to such an extent that some of them were illegally enslaved. Declared dead by their trustees, and certified buried by conniving priests for a small fee, many emancipados—as many as 3,000–4,000, by Crawford's estimate—were brought back to life in slavery with new identities and false documents to cover for dead slaves.[43] This type of fraud was widespread beginning in the 1820s, when Captain-General Francisco Dionisio Vives was forced to establish 500-peso fines against those who sold their emancipados, falsely claiming that they had either died or escaped.[44] This was apparently the case of Pedro Alejandrino, tin ticket 273, who claimed that he had arrived on the island in June 1832 on board El Águila and that he was subsequently declared emancipado. Colonel Mariano Romay, however, insisted that the black man's real name was Congo Mateo, that he purchased him as a slave in 1830, and that he had purchase and birth certificates to prove this. Three shipmates of Pedro Alejandrino testified that they had arrived with him more than a decade earlier, that he was a fellow emancipado, and that they recognized his distinctive ritual scars.[45]

Emancipados like Pedro Alejandrino found themselves in a limbo status, not free and not slave. Their legal condition was best summarized by a contemporary historian who stated that emancipados constituted a class that "was neither enslaved nor could be freed."[46] Indeed, their day-to-day existence combined the worst of two worlds. Emancipados certainly did not enjoy the freedoms and much higher wages of the free population of color nor did they enjoy the few legal and material protections that most slaves could reasonably expect. Their status was further damaged by their isolation from the larger slave community, which devised solidarity mechanisms for survival, resistance, and the pursuit of freedom. There is some evidence suggesting that emancipados were the object of contempt of both free blacks and slaves; the term emancipado, in fact, was used by blacks as a derogatory label.[47] Of all aspects of the emancipados' existence, perhaps the worst was the uncertainty about their status. Slaves knew they were slaves and many fought to resist and escape that condition in a variety of ways. Legal institutions like the *coartación* and the post of the *procurador síndico,* despite their shortcomings, also existed to protect the slaves' right to seek freedom and other basic human rights.

During his tenure in Havana, George became actively involved in looking after the welfare of the emancipado class in a way that no other British official had since the days of Turnbull, a decade before. Though not a trenchant abolitionist, he was a truly responsible man who displayed much care and integrity while carrying out his official tasks. His Spanish colleague, on the other hand, did not accept emancipado claims as part of the Mixed Commission's business. Soon after his arrival George scheduled a meeting with Judge Esteva to discuss the matter of the emancipados. Esteva did not show up. "No man keeps his word in this Country," wrote a disappointed George later that day.[48] Captain-General Cañedo also proved callous toward this matter as he did in relation to the slave trade. He refused to allow George any jurisdiction over this unfortunate class and ignored all of his petitions on their behalf. He insisted that those with grievances come to see him directly. Emancipados, however, did not stand a chance with this notoriously corrupt official who would consider liberating an emancipado only if he could use the occasion to teach a lesson by proceeding to deport him or her. Those emancipados who went directly to the Spanish officials were treated harshly and made examples of for their courage to stand up for their rights. In the spring of 1853, for example, Cañedo ordered the deportation of Mamerta, tin ticket 290, Lugardo, tin ticket 184, and four of their children, Petronila, Ysabel, Juana, and José. Another daughter, Leonarda, was fugitive and like her parents did not wish to leave the island they came to consider home.[49]

Prospects for emancipados improved temporarily with the arrival of Captain-General Juan de la Pezuela in December 1853, who upon arrival issued several decrees to guarantee their freedom of employment and to limit the power of the state and their employers over their labor. George welcomed these measures and viewed Pezuela's intentions as sincere. When Pezuela left the island in September 1854, however, his successor, Captain-General Concha, reversed most of the earlier decrees aimed at protecting the emancipados.[50]

Pezuela, through his controversial decrees against the slave trade, managed to alienate virtually all the powerful elements of Cuban society. They were eager to see him leave and made a point of humiliating him upon his departure. Crawford's official reaction was regret at the removal of "this honest Governor," but he also expressed hope that Pezuela's successor would follow a similar path. George was one of the few white men on the island who truly regretted Pezuela's departure.[51] After being introduced to the new captain-general, George took a carriage to Pezuela's country home to say goodbye and to thank the departing official for his bold steps against the slave trade. Pezuela's wife greeted George and told him that her husband was ill in bed and could not get up to see him. Contemporary sources described Pezuela as looking unusually pale on the days prior to his unceremonious departure, when he was forced to march through the same arc of triumph that had been erected a few days earlier to celebrate Concha's arrival. Grace described Concha's welcoming celebrations as "quite a nuisance to quiet people." "[F]or 3 days," she explained, "you heard nothing but the poppings of small guns of all sorts from morning till late at night; and the people made fools of themselves in various ways."[52]

George and Crawford came across many dramatic cases of emancipados who sought protection for their rights under the British flag. Emancipados and slaves learned about Britain's position with regards to their plight for freedom and the word soon spread among them. Many emancipados came to view George as their advocate. Crawford, on the other hand, appeared to pay more lip service to their cause rather than care to do something on their behalf. Although in his correspondence with the British Foreign Office Crawford presented himself as a champion of the emancipado class, his actions reveal a different sentiment toward them. While on the one hand he referred those who came to see him to Backhouse, on the other, he recommended that George not take any action on their behalf. Word soon spread about his hypocrisy to the point that by January 1854, Crawford openly prided himself on having "had no more visits from those negroes."[53]

George learned of many cases of emancipados who were being held under forced labor contracts long beyond the expiration of their labor terms. Such was the case of Ángela, tin ticket 57, a woman belonging to the Lucumí ethnic group who was officially declared emancipada in October 1843 following her rescue near Matanzas. She was consigned by then Captain-General Leopoldo O'Donnell to her first trustee; following the expiration of her legal term, she was assigned to another trustee, Mrs.

Díaz, for five more years. Once her second term expired, Ángela was illegally forced to continue working for her second trustee. In her statements to George, Ángela admitted receiving four and a half pesos per month in wages from Mrs. Díaz but longed to gain full freedom for herself and her two children.[54] Another heartbreaking case to reach the desks of Britain's officers in Havana was that of Mamerta, tin ticket 290, who had five children and had served under four different trustees over the past quarter-century.[55]

Several other cases reflect the extent of the practice of keeping emancipados in servitude long beyond the legally established terms. One emancipada, Escolástica, whose ship had been detained way back in 1828, should have been freed in 1836 at the very latest; she was still toiling as an emancipada in 1853. Another emancipado, Demetrio Lucumí, arrived in 1832 on board *El Negrito.* Following the vessel's capture by the *Victor,* Demetrio spent the next twenty-one years working for a dozen different trustees. Originally consigned to Don Manuel de Armas, then alcalde, Demetrio also worked for a police commissary, for a man surnamed Correa, and for Don Eustaquio Rebuelta. Demetrio changed his last name almost as often as he changed trustees; he finally settled for the name Demetrio Correa. His last trustee, Rebuelta, allowed Demetrio to hire himself out but insisted on keeping part of Demetrio's earnings while refusing to provide him with food, clothing, and other essentials.[56] Yet another case of extended servitude to reach George's office was that of emancipado Marcelino Urrutia, a Mina from Africa's Gold Coast whose ship was captured in 1828. Marcelino first worked for Doña María de Jesús Urrutia, under whom he learned the well-remunerated trade of cigar-making. At the end of his first labor term, Marcelino's fortune slipped further, being assigned to work on a sugar plantation. He later worked for Miguel Cabello, the colony's political secretary, who allowed him to hire himself out to a local cigar factory. A quarter of a century after he first set foot on the island, Marcelino was as unfree and helpless as when he first arrived.[57]

George's good offices proved helpful in the liberation of several emancipados. On December 20, 1853, the newly arrived Pezuela liberated Demetrio and Escolástica, whom he also ordered to leave the island. George and Crawford intervened on their behalf so that they could stay on the island where they had spent most of their lives. While George pleaded Demetrio's case, the poor man remained behind bars using an alias, Pablo Correa, to avoid being found by his trustee with whom he was in debt. In the end, with the help of George, Demetrio and Escolástica were allowed to remain in Cuba as free laborers. After a lifetime of servitude, however, they now faced the prospect of years of unproductive old age without even the mild legal guarantees and social solidarities afforded to slaves.[58]

Perhaps the most dramatic of the emancipado cases to reach the desks of the British officials in Havana during the turbulent mid-1850s was that of John Baptiste Dasalu, a Yoruba converted to Christianity, who was captured and sold into slavery in 1855 by the Dahomeans who had invaded the city of Abeokuta in present day Nigeria. British missionaries had aided and the British government had armed the city's Egba population against the invading Dahomeyan army that had the rare distinction of including women warriors among its ranks. According to the official correspondence, "Admiral Bauce and Captain Heseltine while on that station made every effort with the King of Dahomey to procure his release but without effect." Dasalu's friends, relatives, and the missionaries of the English Church Missionary Society had perhaps lost all hope of ever seeing or hearing from him again until the day in which they received a strange letter in seemingly broken Spanish that Dasalu had dictated to a man named Martín Garro in Havana. It is not clear how the letter reached its intended destination in Lagos, possibly other returning emancipados brought it with them.[59]

Dasalu had ended up in a slave ship bound for Cuba that was later intercepted by a British man-of-war. He was fortunate not to have been thrown overboard alive along with the rest of the human cargo, for many slave traders did this to avoid being caught with incriminating evidence of slave-trading activity.[60] As established by law, Dasalu immediately became an emancipado, was renamed Nicolás Lucumí, and received the tin ticket number 50. Since the letter dated June 16, 1855, had been written by Garro in the residence of the Count of Fernandina, one of the island's wealthiest men and recipient of scores of emancipados, it is probable that Dasalu, like many others, had been allotted to the count. The letter was addressed to Dasalu's relatives, whom he assured "ge no mi es mueto toabia Gracia al dios" (I have not died yet thank God). A few months later, the letter reached Lagos, where Reverend Samuel Crowther, a Yoruba prelate of the Church Missionary Society, relayed it with a note of his own to the society's secretary, Reverend H. Venn. Crowther's communication informed the society's officials that John Baptiste Dasalu had been one of their first converts and that he would gladly pay for his passage back to Africa if the British consul at Havana could determine his whereabouts. By the end of 1855 several high-ranking British officials were aware of the case, and on December 29, Lord Clarendon wrote to Crawford with instructions to seek Dasalu. Meanwhile, Dasalu prayed and waited, toiling in bondage 5,000 miles away from home.

Throughout his tenure as judge in the Havana Mixed Commission, George had to deal repeatedly with problematic situations created by his assistant James Pilgrim Dalrymple, a thirty-two-year-old fellow Briton whose behavior was the exact opposite of the ideal Victorian ethical code. The son of the late former arbitrator of the Havana Mixed Commission, Dalrymple began serving as clerk to the British judge while still a teenager in 1842. When George took office he inherited the services of this most naughty of the tropical Victorians. Grace's first impression of Dalrymple was very negative. A week later, after Dalrymple had offered to get the Backhouses' laundry done, George, quite upset, jotted in his diary, "Some things brought home very carelessly, & badly washed." "We have suspicions," continued George, "about Dalrymple's interest in taking charge of our dirty linen. We may be mistaken."[61]

After only two months of supervising Dalrymple's work, George decided to confront his aide. George brought up Dalrymple's many absences and his failure to give notice of them. Dalrymple became infuriated and left in haste. George remarked in his diary that during this discussion Dalrymple had been "very stupid & disagreeable." The very next day, on Saturday, May 21, 1853, as the Backhouses were preparing for dinner, Dalrymple's concubine, María Guadalupe Quintana, and an unidentified man showed up to tell George that Dalrymple had been arrested in connection with a robbery at the British consulate. She pleaded with George to intervene on her companion's behalf.[62]

As soon as the robbery was discovered, police authorities were notified and the investigation began. The servants were searched and the consulate's employees were interrogated. The building's porter proved most helpful in the determination of suspicion of guilt. According to his testimony, Dalrymple returned to the consulate at between four and five in the afternoon of May 20, which would have been shortly after his row with George, and remained inside the office for about fifteen minutes.[63] The investigation determined that the perpetrator used a false key to open a secret drawer in the consul-general's desk and extracted $3,664, most of which belonged to British citizens who had entrusted their money to Crawford for safekeeping. There were no savings banks in Cuba and keeping his compatriots' cash and valuables was one of the responsibilities that Crawford took on as the island's highest-ranking British official. Three years earlier the consulate had been the target of another robbery, one that resulted in the murder of the building's old black porter. On that occasion the office was ransacked and some jewelry stolen. Two blacks and one mulatto were suspects but there was not enough evidence to convict them. By the time they were to be released from custody, however, one had died of cholera behind bars.[64]

On the basis of the preliminary investigation, Dalrymple was arrested as chief suspect in the most recent robbery. He denied having returned to the consulate on that Friday afternoon but there were serious discrepancies between his testimony and that of María Guadalupe. The day following the incident, Dalrymple was transported to a detention center near la Puerta de Monserrate, where he spent the night behind bars. Dalrymple scorned the place as "a miserable dungeon."[65]

On the next day the suspect was escorted to the notorious and purposely conspicuous Tacón Jail, a large two-story yellow stone building with an imposing neoclassical facade, whose dark, fetid interior, according to most observers, afforded the most Dantesque scenes imaginable.[66] Inside the Tacón Jail, Dalrymple spent the next three days and two nights incommunicado in one of the dungeon-like *bartolina* sections of the compound living on bread and water. He was then transferred to one of the *galeras,* sections of the compound popularly dubbed "the infernos." Scores of convicts remained in prolonged storage in structures resembling cages and smelling of sin. A few years earlier, a British officer attested to having witnessed there "scenes of disorder and horror, unparalleled . . . in any other prison." Dalrymple complained that he was in the company of 133 dangerous inmates and that he was at one point wounded in a stabbing fight between two other prisoners. The galeras were segregated by race and in them were rum shops for the pleasure of those inmates who could afford the numbing spirits. Payment of two reales per day allowed inmates to transfer to the better galeras, and six reales opened to them the doors of the so-called *salas de distinción.* No food was provided for the inmates,

**The Tacón Jail.** (Contemporary sketch from José García de Arboleya, *Manual de la Isla de Cuba.*)

which meant that it was their relatives' responsibility to bring them meals. María Guadalupe faithfully delivered Dalrymple's daily meals.[67]

George regularly visited his subordinate while he remained behind bars. In their many conversations Dalrymple maintained his innocence and insisted that he was the victim of Consul-General Crawford, who was going out of his way to seek punishment for the unfortunate clerk. As it turned out, Crawford was not even pressing charges; from the beginning, the prosecution was entirely in the hands of the Spanish *fiscal*. Dalrymple continued fixating on the idea that it was all Crawford's doing and repeatedly threatened to complain directly to the Foreign Office. "I tried to set him right," wrote George in his diary, "but as usual he did not appear to hear a word I said." George continued to visit Dalrymple in jail and to advance him money so that he could meet his prison expenses. Following one such visit, George described the deteriorated physical state of his imprisoned aide: "He looked very wretched today. A handkerchief round his head for a headache. Has not shaved lately. . . ." In the meantime, George hired a temporary assistant to deal with the Mixed Commission's mounting paperwork, a very reliable Irish Catholic man named Thomas Callaghan, at 2 pesos a day.[68]

Following his acquittal on the basis of insufficient evidence fifty-one days after his arrest, Dalrymple continued his attacks on Crawford, whom he insisted on blaming for his misfortunes and alleged wrongful imprisonment. In his correspondence with the Foreign Office, Dalrymple presented himself as a victim of Crawford's vengeance, a vengeance that he argued had profound roots. According to him, Crawford held a deep grudge ever since Dalrymple's mother accused the consul-general of depriving her and her family of the house rent that her deceased husband had received as member of the Mixed Commission so that Crawford could claim the benefit for himself. In another communication Dalrymple presented himself as a poor but honest man and stated that all he had left was "his character."[69]

Crawford denied ever having deprived Dalrymple's mother of a roof over her head or having pressed charges against Dalrymple. The senior official responded that he had even bailed him out of jail in 1844 and 1845 and that he had always "assisted and befriended" him. Crawford counterattacked Dalrymple's charges by denouncing the clerk's pattern of misconduct. Information surfaced about Dalrymple's misrepresentation toward a young English woman, Miss Belling, whom he contracted to come to Havana "under the belief that he was a married man and that she had obtained a situation as a Governess in a respectable family." According to Crawford the unsuspecting woman "very soon discovered the deceit practiced upon her and through the influence of Mrs. Crawford . . . obtained another situation." Crawford's letters to the Foreign Office also raised accusations of Dalrymple's problems with alcohol, his neglect of official duties, and his "almost total disregard of truth."[70]

Dalrymple's family affairs also stood a far cry from the ideal Victorian domestic model. Crawford reported, and other sources confirmed, that Dalrymple lived in adultery with María Guadalupe Quintana, who remained legally married to a man named Pollo, who was still alive—it is not clear whether this man's surname was actually Poyo or whether Pollo (Chicken) was his nickname. According to Crawford, Dalrymple's many problems stemmed from his association with María Guadalupe and with "those by who the poor man is surrounded in consequence of that connexion [who] are notorious for everything but their honesty." It was not clear either what relation he had with the woman's many children, or even how many of them there were altogether. Dalrymple reported having five children in 1851 when he returned from a trip to England. During the cholera epidemic of 1853 he requested an advance on his salary allegedly to face the extraordinary expenses of having to bury two of his children. A few months later Dalrymple requested another advance, now claiming that he had seven children to feed. A much puzzled Crawford, his superior at the time, wrote to the Foreign Office: "two of his children had . . . died of cholera which must have reduced the number to three at that time, and how there can be seven now, is hardly possible."[71]

On July 13, the day when Dalrymple was released following his acquittal by the Real Audiencia, he showed up at the Backhouses' residence and asked George to grant him two or three days of leave. George granted the request, but Dalrymple continued to absent himself from work during the balance of the month and during the following month, sometimes three days in a row. Dalrymple became involved in other disreputable activities after his release from jail. He went around asking for money, stating that during his imprisonment he had been deprived of his salary, which was not true. Not only had he received his regular clerk's salary but several loans and advances as well.

In his desperate quest for cash he approached the Catalan Francisco Marty y Torréns, the notorious former smuggler who had twenty years earlier turned himself in to Captain-General Miguel Tacón so that he could claim the reward for his own capture.[72] His close association with Tacón and his successors thereafter awarded Marty several special concessions, among them monopolistic rights over the sale of fish and theatrical productions in Havana. Marty was also deeply involved in slave-trading activities and in the kidnapping and importation of laborers from the Yucatán. At one point during the incumbency of Captain-General O'Donnell, Marty lobbied for and was granted an 11 P.M. curfew for taverns and other places of entertainment not associated with his Teatro Tacón. When the patrons of a nearby café challenged O'Donnell's orders, troops were deployed only to face a shower of bowlsful of milk liqueur. This confrontation was immortalized in Havana lore as la Batalla del Ponche de Leche. Marty's earlier capital, his own and other rewards, fishmongering, and theater productions turned the former smuggler into one of the island's wealthiest and most influential men. This self-described "honest Spaniard who managed to acquire fortune with hard work and sacrifice" was deeply involved in the slave trade.[73]

Dalrymple also took his sad stories to Marty's son and even to

Esteva, the Spanish judge of the Mixed Commission. He reportedly asked Esteva to sign a blank sheet of paper for a subscription on his behalf. In George's estimation, Dalrymple was way out of line and his actions were seriously compromising the image of the Mixed Commission. On September 9, 1853, George decided to suspend his problematic clerk. Dalrymple asked for a written notification, which George gladly produced: "I have to state to you that, on my own responsibility, I suspend you from the exercise of your official functions."[74]

Dalrymple's misfortunes continued during the balance of 1853. In December, Captain-General Pezuela issued an order forcing Dalrymple to leave the island for having slandered the government of Spain. Crawford and George, both of whom had been victims of Dalrymple's calumnies before, intervened on their naughty compatriot's behalf and secured from the island's top authority Dalrymple's right to remain on the island without having to apply for permanent domicile. Following their mediation, the problematic Dalrymple was allowed to stay in Cuba. Lord Clarendon, the top man at the Foreign Office, later instructed George to reinstate Dalrymple as the court's clerk but not without first giving the controversy-prone clerk a serious warning and pointing out to him that "it is not becoming that any person holding a situation in a foreign country under H M Govt. should go about, as you have done, soliciting money from the foreigners amongst whom he resides."[75]

Dalrymple had a long history of financial problems dating back to at least 1843, when he went bankrupt. In 1844 he landed in jail for his mounting debts. His money problems caught up with him again in 1849–50, when he returned to prison in spite of Judge Kennedy's pleas on his behalf. At the time, Dalrymple owed a considerable 3,904 pesos to some 42 different creditors. Kennedy made up excuses for his underling's incapacity to pay back the staggering debt and eventually arranged for 31 of the creditors to agree on receiving installment payments of 240 pesos every three months.[76] Dalrymple's money problems did not abate but rather got worse. He fell behind in his rent for the house in which he lived at la Calzada de Belascoaín, in the working-class neighborhood of San Lázaro. In April 1854, George paid Antonio Llarena, the owner of the house, $204—the equivalent of six months' rent. A few months later Dalrymple decided to request a salary increase directly to the Foreign Office. He now claimed to have eight children to support and that the workload at the Mixed Commission had greatly increased. Dalrymple supported his case by enclosing a certified document with the signatures of eleven British merchants who attested that his salary was not sufficient for the expenses of Havana. He was currently making around £350 a year and was scheduled to receive yearly increments of £10. There were reports that he complemented his salary by teaching English, and his earlier dealings with the Backhouses suggest that his *compañera* probably washed clothes on the side.[77] Only God knows how else they earned money, but their association with Marty and other slave traders leaves open endless possibilities, including misinforming George about slave trade matters in exchange for bribes.

George agreed with Dalrymple's assessment of the inadequacy of the clerk's current salary. But he also relayed further complaints to the Foreign Office; this time he accused Dalrymple of showing up drunk for work. Dalrymple's untimely request for a salary raise was denied, and he received instead a severe warning that the next time similar accusations were made he would be fired. Dalrymple responded "never having been in my life intoxicated either in or out of office."[78] Throughout the balance of George's tenure as judge, Dalrymple would continue to be a problematic and unreliable aide. He was certainly an obstacle in the way of the Mixed Commission's tasks.

# IV

## Life in a "Male City"

Nineteenth-century British and North American travelers who shared a Victorian Protestant culture, for the most part, found Havana to be a most inhospitable town. Dozens of them have left vivid accounts of their visits to Cuba's capital that are peppered with mostly negative assessments and recountings of painful experiences on an island that to them was as unbearable as it was beautiful. To many of these travelers, Havana was the best example of a natural paradise corrupted by Spanish population, culture, and institutions.[1] If anywhere in the world the Anglo-Saxon Protestant, abolitionist culture clashed frontally with the Spanish Catholic, slave-holding culture, it was in Havana, where colonialism and the tropical context magnified the already marked cultural differences. During the convulsed middle decades of the nineteenth century, marked by slave insurrection scares and by filibuster invasions or threats of invasion, Havana reached one of its peaks of inhospitality. North Americans and Britons, in particular, were perceived by Spanish authorities as undesirable guests, un-

"Life in a 'Male City': Native and Foreign Elite Women in Nineteenth-Century Havana" by Luis Martínez-Fernández, from *Cuban Studies* Volume 25, Louis A. Pérez, Jr., Ed., © 1995 by University of Pittsburgh Press. Reprinted by permission of the University of Pittsburgh Press.

welcome bearers of the contagious germs of abolitionism, republican-
ism, and Protestantism. It was not uncommon for colonial officials and
other Habaneros to scorn the most inoffensive Londoner or New York-
er as a *filibustero*.[2]

Female visitors and long-term residents from Europe and the United
States faced by virtue of their sex an even harsher reception upon
arrival in Havana, and they endured many particularly alienating experiences from which their male counterparts were spared.[3] Foreign
women were subjected to seclusion and other prevailing forms of discrimination whose causes they did not really understand and whose
logic did not include them. The system in place was one that, notwithstanding its pernicious nature, included alongside the stern restrictions
on native women's behavior, provisions for what was construed to be
their own protection. It also made young white women the objects of
male *caballerosidad* (chivalrous attitudes and behavior), which were
quite obviously welcomed by most Habaneras. In the case of foreign
women, whose societal roles were being reshaped in their own countries, all the restrictions were meant to apply but they were for the most
part neither the recipients of "protection" nor the objects of gentlemanly gallantry. As alienating and limiting as the results were for
native Habaneras, there was a place for them within society; foreign
women did not fit in society and therefore did not exist. This was the
Havana into which Grace Backhouse stepped in the spring of 1853.

Havana, with the phallic Morro Castle as its gatekeeper, was characterized by nineteenth-century travelers as a "male city," likened to the
mythical "Rome of Romulus." "Where are the women and where are
they to be found in Havana?" inquired one concerned visitor. According to another traveler, "the absence of the female form" constituted
one of Havana's "most striking features."[4]

Indeed, there were considerably fewer women than men in Havana
as well as on the island as a whole. According to the 1861 census there
were 149 men for every 100 women in Havana and its environs, while
the ratio for the entire island was a milder 134:100.[5] Although the
overall sex imbalances were in great measure the result of slave-trading
practices favoring males over females at a ratio of between 4:1 and 5:1,
similarly striking sexual imbalances were found among the white population, and particularly among whites residing in Havana. On the
island as a whole, the white male–white female ratio grew steadily
throughout the nineteenth century from 114:100 (1827) to 127:100

(1846) to 150:100 (1862). The sexual imbalance among whites was even sharper in Havana, the island's administrative–military–mercantile center to which the exclusively male population involved in such activities gravitated. Havana was also a city of immigrants and transients, most of whom were men. In 1861, according to census figures, there were 1.8 men for every woman among Havana's residents of European descent.[6]

Women in nineteenth-century Havana were not only a numerical minority, they were also subjected to seclusion, discrimination, limited options, and gross double standards of acceptable social behavior. The seemingly obsessive desire on the part of society to protect and seclude women of the upper and middle classes appeared—was, in fact— stronger in Havana than in any other western society, colonial or metropolitan. In other societies, England and the United States among them, women faced similar forms of restriction, segregation, and exclusion, but to a much lesser degree. What, then, accounted for Havana's more restrictive codes of female behavior than any other city in the west? The answer to this question lies in the particular structure of its society: its slave base, the imbalance of its male–female ratio, its population of color constituting a majority, the strong correlation between color and class, its highly hierarchical social structure, and the very limited opportunities for social mobility. Sexual codes were thus intimately linked to issues pertaining to demographic patterns, class, color, and restrictions on social mobility.[7]

Otherwise disempowered white Habaneras were, for example, forced to carry the burden of controlling access to society's white elite. As Verena Martínez-Alier concluded in her now classic *Marriage, Class, and Colour in Nineteenth-Century Cuba*: "the device through which the purity of the group was achieved was virginity, that is female purity. By controlling the access to female sexuality, control was exercised over the acquisition of undesirable members of the group." Through seclusion, high regard for female virginity and chastity, and legislation obstructing interracial marriages, society "protected" white women and their race—and by extension their class—from what was perceived as "racial pollution."[8]

Interestingly, the same central tenet that shaped the Cuban elite's political postures during the middle decades of the nineteenth century—fear of the black man—also shaped, to a great extent, social rules regulating female behavior as they pertained to virginity, courtship, and marriage. Some of the island's political figures of the mid-century justified the desired annexation of Cuba to the United States on racial and sexual terms. The annexationist editors of *La Verdad,* for example, referring to events in Venezuela, denounced "the most lamentable spectacle, the most repugnant liaisons to our instincts, the most shocking to our present state of civilization and public opinion, the most degrading and shameful to our race, marriages between white women and blacks, mulattoes, *zambos,* and *mestizos.*"[9] Note that the editors' concern was not with miscegenation per se—a long-accepted way of dealing with Cuba's "racial problem"—but specifically with men of color having sexual access to white women. Another contemporary observer hiding behind the title of "Yankee" but suspiciously familiar with Cuban ways, referred to the seclusion of Havana's "ladies" (meaning white women) as a "necessity" to spare them the "risk of meeting blasphemous, *odorous,* and drunken negroes." At one of the moments of highest racial tension, stemming from a temporary suspension of laws interdicting interracial marriages in 1854, a critic of the suspension pointed out that this and other reforms had encouraged blacks to salute Havana's ladies and to pay them "compliments in impudent and audible commendations of their beauty." He added that such "insolence . . . carried alarm into the bosom of every family." Prison terms and other penalties were applied against men of color who dared approach white women in obscene or intolerably familiar ways.[10]

Clearly established social rules designed both to "protect" and subdue women contributed to keeping white Habaneras under seclusion. According to the prevailing etiquette, "ladies" were not allowed to walk even two blocks on the streets. A contemporary woman observed that even when crossing a narrow street to visit a neighbor, Havana's ladies would dash as "fearful doves that flee from the sound of the lumberjack's ax." Arriving in Havana in 1848, the wife of Captain-General Federico Roncali sought to put an end to female seclusion by herself walking the streets of Havana. It was to no avail; her bold steps were not followed by other women of the local elite.[11]

Women of color and others not pretending to the title of lady, however, walked about as they pleased, sold fruits and other goods out in the open, and frequented places like cockpits, which were completely off-limits to white women.[12] These privileges granted to Havana's women of color reflect a paradoxical situation resulting from the overlapping and somewhat conflicting logics of a slave-based and male-dominated society. The most evident distortion of these conflicting yet mutually reinforced power structures was that women of color, slave or free, appeared to enjoy greater liberties than the women of the master class. Needless to say, Havana was still first and foremost a slave-based class society and not a few black or mulatto women would have gladly given up the right to walk up and down Obispo or O'Reilly streets in exchange for the standard of living and privileges of the women of the elite.

Nonetheless, the highly visible "freedoms" enjoyed by black and mulatto Habaneras appear to have been a point of friction between women of different classes. The Countess of Merlín, in her famous epistolary travelogue, scorned the almost snobbish pride with which Habaneras of color walked the streets, "cigar in mouth, almost naked with their round shining bare shoulders." The tone of the countess's comments reflects a degree of jealousy directed toward black women, who by virtue of their physical mobility and more revealing attire were made more visible, and therefore more accessible, to men of all races, including whites. Other contemporaries also noted a degree of rivalry between the secluded white Habaneras and their sable sisters and commented on the proud and "jaunty" air that the latter displayed while walking in Havana's streets. One observer described black women as walking nonchalantly, allowing their low-cut garments to "slip with picturesque negligence from their dusky shoulders." A mid-century moralist criticized Havana's women of color for seeking the status of white women by using bleaching devises and by luring "men of all classes."[13]

Foreign visitors often expressed their dismay at the sight of homebound white Habaneras clinging to the iron bars of their glassless windows from which they gazed at the forbidden world of the outside "like captives in durance." One obviously amused visitor recorded in his travelogue that he had seen "[m]any a bright lustrous eye, and fairy-like foot ... through the wires of her cheerful cage." It was believed that there was a relation between the Habaneras' celebrated prodigal small feet and their not being able to walk outside. Another traveler likened Havana to a "zoological garden, in which the insiders and the outsiders have changed places." A Bostonian feminist found less to joke about and scorned the practice as a form of "Oriental imprisonment." Havana folklore had it that one visitor from the United

**Free *mulata*.** (Painting by Víctor Patricio Landaluze.)

States on passing threw a few coins through an iron-barred window thinking that the sad-looking woman behind it was a convict, her home the city jail.[14]

While behind bars, Habaneras struggled to remain visible to those outside; custom could keep them from stepping outside but not from keeping their windows wide open. The compromise, thus, was to remain out of reach but not out of sight. A variety of contemporary sources attest that most windows were kept open and that the women came "freely . . . to the windows to chat with passers-by." According to one visitor accustomed to Yankee privacy, wide-open windows made it "nearly impossible to avoid glancing in upon domestic scenes that frequently exhibit the female portion of the family in déshabillé." Another *observer* reported that "one has the inspection of the interior

**Habanera behind bars.** (Drawing by Samuel Hazard from his book *Cuba with Pen and Pencil.*)

arrangement of all the front parlors of Havana, and can see what every lady wears, and who is visiting her." Passersby complemented the women with witty *piropos*. Every night, after sundown, an army of bachelor Habaneros—*lechuzos* (night owls) one visitor called them—proceeded to call on the single, captive Habaneras, whom they courted, "like monkeys," through the iron-barred windows that extended from the floor to ceiling of their homes. According to the description by two keen observers of Cuban social life, gentlemen callers positioned themselves at an angle outside the window to avoid being seen by their lovers' families. William Henry Hurlbert, a visitor from the United States, hinted that bars did not keep lovers from engaging in the most intimate expressions of tenderness.[15]

For the otherwise imprisoned white Habaneras—at least for those whose families could afford it—there was an "angel of deliverance": the *volanta*. "Ladies" could move about freely throughout the streets of Havana only when riding on volantas, *quitrines,* and other horse-drawn carriages, whether these belonged to their families or were rented at a fixed fare. They were not, however, allowed to ride by themselves or accompanied by men, but instead could ride with one or two female

**Courting through bars.** (Ramiro Fernández Collection.)

friends or relatives. Volanta cabins were set up for two passengers but a third seat—significantly called "el de la niña bonita" (the one for the pretty girl)—could be added in front for a third passenger. Men rarely rode on volantas, preferring instead to walk or ride horseback.[16]

Because of the mobility and visibility that such vehicles allowed them, Cuban women were particularly fond of volantas and appear to have exerted considerable pressure to make them household budget priorities. Indicative of the centrality of carriages was the fact that they were usually parked inside the houses, right before the living room, for all to see. The wealthiest families were said to own a volanta for each

**Cuban *quitrín* carriage.** (Print by Federico Mialhe from B. May, *Álbum pintoresco de la Isla de Cuba.*)

marriageable daughter and even kept an extra one for occasional female visitors. Middle-class families would go out of their way to purchase one such vehicle, setting aside for this purpose the household's very first savings. One traveler remarked that middle-class Cubans "would sooner live on beans and cold water, dress in rags, and lie on straw . . . than go without a volante."[17] Given the exorbitant cost of purchasing and maintaining a volanta, however, most middle-class families could simply not afford to own such vehicles.

The ownership of a volanta or similar type of carriage was a visible sign of social and economic status in the highly hierarchical city of Havana. Carriages also served to mark class boundaries in a society obsessed with maintaining rigid distinctions between its classes. Such vehicles, along with palatial homes and a coterie of domestic slaves, became the trademarks of Havana's urban and suburban elites. The richer the family the more carriages it owned and the greater the extent of their ornamentation, including fancy woodwork and gold leaf, with postilions and horses dressed to match.

The hour of the *paseo* in the volanta was the daily high point for upper- and upper-middle-class Habaneras. According to one observer, most women belonging to these classes spent their mornings and after-

**Women riding on a *quitrin*.** (Drawing by Samuel Hazard from his book *Cuba with Pen and Pencil*.)

noons "killing time" in rocking chairs, fanning themselves in their dishabille in anticipation of paseo time. "It is for their hour on the Paseo," wrote the British novelist Anthony Trollope, "that the ladies dress themselves." According to another account, young women preferred to go without food rather than skip the paseo. During evening paseos, women of the upper classes displayed their charms and fancy clothing and elaborate coiffures from their volantas for the pleasure of the scores of gallant Habaneros who, either walking or on horseback, saluted the ladies whom they passed over and over again. At paseo time the covers of the carriages were pushed back to allow maximum visibility. Over the cabin's side panels were spread the ends of the occupants flowing skirts. According to one observer: "The full, flowing skirts of these ladies were spread carefully out at each side of the volante, hanging nearly to the ground, and giving the vehicle, when viewed from the rear, the appearance of being furnished with wings."[18]

Volantas served another important function: they allowed white Habaneras to go shopping. So strict were the norms regarding not walking on the streets that upper- and middle-class women engaged in shopping expeditions on the basis of a curious predecessor to the drive-by shopping or window service. As custom had it, "ladies" would order their carriages halted in front of a given shop; then the shop's clerk would jump over the counter and proceed to walk outside carrying a handful of goods for the inspection of his prospective costumers. Shoes and other items were tried by women while on their carriages parked outside the stores. This system allowed the mostly Spanish-born, mostly male retailers to force on their female customers their slower merchandise as well as their higher-priced, lower-quality articles. The fact that the entire transaction transpired outdoors and in what had to be a hurried manner must have also put female customers at a disadvantage given the bargaining fashion in which purchases were usually made. Women also had their carriages driven to the portals of the city's famous cafés, *La Dominica* and *El Louvre,* where they were not welcomed to sit at the tables but could place orders for ices and other refreshments to go from the *mozos* serving the drive-by customers. Another shopping fashion not violating restrictions consisted in merchants sending articles for home inspection. Servants were used in these transactions, which could take a whole day of back-and-forth bargaining before an agreement on the price was finally reached.[19]

Another place where Habaneras created their own spaces that allowed them some mobility and visibility was the interior of the city's many churches. Given its conservative stance on most matters, it appears rather paradoxical that the church was the one Cuban institution where white women found freedom, comfort, and a space to call their own and where there were no segregated spaces on the basis of gender or race. In some ways the church was a more progressive institution than either the state or the general population. Canonical law, for example, did not differentiate between male and female adultery as did Spanish legislation and social custom. A quite revealing episode demonstrates these postures. In the summer of 1852 the members of the lay all-male Real Archicofradía del Santísimo Sacramento of the church of Nuestra Señora de Guadalupe wrote to Queen Isabel II, patron of the Catholic Church in Spain and its possessions, requesting permission to erect railings to segregate the sexes inside the church in order to "maintain the composure and decorum required in the Lord's House . . . and to avoid the distractions with which the common enemy would try to disturb devotion and concentration." Both the bishop of Havana and Captain-General Valentín Cañedo had prohibited the use of the railings, the latter scorning it as "a disagreeable distinction in the House of the Lord."[20]

Under the umbrella of the church, women of the elite were also able to take upon themselves the responsibilities of charitable work and of raising funds for and taking care of the vestments of their church's female saints and virgins.[21] Since it was considered sacrilegious for any man to touch or even lay eyes on an undressed statue of a female saint or virgin, only women could fulfill the task of taking care of their vestments. This exclusively feminine activity allowed some women to come together and establish yet another area of activity they could call their own. Grace and other women from the United States or England sojourning or residing in Havana, because most of them were Protestant, could find little consolation in the spaces that church ceremonies provided for Cuban women.

Church attendance was almost exclusively female; most accounts agree that less than 10 percent of attendants to Havana's thirty-odd churches were male and that most of the men seemed to be more interested in the devout Habaneras than in either mass or the saints that lined the naves and side chapels. One woman visitor commented in her travelogue that she "could count on the fingers of one hand, all the males that [she] had seen, during [her] whole stay in Cuba, engaged in any voluntary act of devotion." Another remarked that men appeared to have "no religion at all."[22]

Yet another place where white Habaneras were able to become socially visible were the special upper boxes at the city's theaters, which were specially designated for women unaccompanied by either a husband or a father. There they sat "in full dress, décolletées, without hats." Although highly visible, the box sections were separated by gates zealously guarded by older women and armed male guards. Along with the glances and messages of the "telegraphic fan," handwritten notes were passed back and forth between the balconies and the exclusively male pit section, carried by servants of color. Here again, Havana's white women settled for being out of reach as long as they did not remain out of sight.[23]

Female travelers and long-term foreign residents of Havana like Grace faced the dilemma of either complying with the roles and behavior expected of native women or challenging them and facing the consequences. They were for the most part shocked by the prevailing odious restrictions but also faced considerable pressures to conform with the norms, particularly if they were planning on an extended sojourn. According to one contemporary observer, foreign female travelers who challenged the social mores by walking the streets of Havana faced passing remarks, "annoyance and even insult" that in the end forced most to comply. One United States traveler recounted an incident in which a female compatriot of his was momentarily left alone in her volanta by her husband and was soon approached by a dashing Habanero who "with the greatest familiarity [proceeded] to take a flower from her hand." The woman responded by smacking the man, who immediately left the scene shouting obscenities of all sorts. Another recorded incident described an episode in which several men and boys chased a group of North American women while shouting insults at them. Yet another instance of harassment included the gathering of a laughing and insulting mob provoked by a daring North American woman who went for a drive with a local male resident. Interestingly, license to harass women appeared to cut across class and color lines as attested by an incident in which "a couple of half-naked, horrible looking negroes," harassed the Swedish writer Fredrika Bremer.[24]

As one United States consul put it, his female compatriots would try walking once or twice but would eventually conform to the restrictions and "be quite miserable." A woman from the United States reported that even "the hardiest American or English woman will scarcely venture out a second time without the severe escort of husband or brother." In a humorous tone she added that the North American woman who was usually very jealous of her own space and time alone in the United States "suddenly becomes very fond of her husband" on whom, while in Cuba, she comes to depend as saving escort and bodyguard. As to the general rule of female seclusion, this North American woman ended up rationalizing it by saying that in a place like Cuba where "the animal vigor of men is so large in proportion to their moral power . . . women must be glad to forgo their liberties" for their own protection.[25]

Not all foreign women complied with Havana's strict norms about not circulating in the streets. For example, one woman from the United States, Rachel Wilson Moore, and her friends, while recognizing that walking was not considered safe, stuck to what she called their "republican habits" and tried to ignore the stares and remarks that were thrown at them. Another woman traveler got tired of being able to walk only up and down the halls of her hotel and decided to go shopping "after the American fashion." Her daring move attracted a storm of long and mean stares but she went on.[26]

Some foreign women challenged other restrictions on female behavior. There were several women dentists with Anglo surnames who practiced their trade-profession in nineteenth-century Cuba. Another foreign woman, the Swiss Dr. Enriqueta Faber Caven, passed for a man (Enrique) so she could practice medicine on the island; to maintain her false sexual identity she even went to the extreme of converting to Catholicism and marrying another woman, Juana de León Hernández, in 1819. Thirteen years into the marriage, however, Dr. Faber Caven's wife denounced her to the authorities and she landed in jail. She was sentenced to twenty-four years in prison but was released sooner to be banished from the island.[27]

Walking or not walking the streets of Havana was just one issue within a broader clash of cultures that was played out around various aspects of female behavior. English and North American women visiting or residing in nineteenth-century Havana simply looked, dressed, acted, and thought differently, and their mere presence was perceived by many Habaneros to be a dangerous influence on Cuban family and social life. According to one contemporary, general opinion held that women from the United States made "rather inconsiderate" wives.[28] One of the most visible signs of foreign origin was the use of bonnets, virtually unknown in Havana, where women wore their hair uncovered, with ribbons or flowers, or perhaps with a veil. As one traveler put it, "[t]he bonnet, which forms so important a part of a lady's costume in Europe and America, is rarely worn by the Creoles, and strangers who appear on the streets of Havana with the latest fashion of this ever varying article are regarded with curiosity." Indeed, women wearing bonnets complained of being constantly stared at. One British visitor, Amelia Matilda Murray, recorded in her travelogue that in order to avoid the unwelcome stares she stopped wearing her bonnet, substituting it with a cap and black veil. Most foreign women, however, continued to wear theirs, as symbols of defiance and cultural affirmation. One woman referred to them as "audacious bonnets," which, coupled with more assertive voices and louder laughs, attracted stares in the few public places that tolerated the presence of foreign women.[29]

Like the Backhouses, most long-term foreign residents chose—and could afford—not to live within the city limits of Havana, where the seclusion of women was more strict, but rather in suburban villages outside Havana. Life in the suburbs spared foreigners, particularly women, the direct and continuous policing of their actions that prevailed inside the city. Thus, in contexts such as El Horcón or El Cerro foreign women were better able to establish their own spaces and networks of fellow women around which they organized various activities that helped them cope with the alienating life that Havana offered.

Grace, because of her status as a long-term resident foreigner and because of her husband's position, complied with the norms regarding not walking in the city streets although she ventured out in the suburbs in the company of other European women. She also walked into stores and dashed from store to store when shopping in Havana.[30] A good Victorian English wife that she was, Grace followed restrictive codes of her own. The Victorian woman of the middle classes was expected not to have a life of her own but rather to find delight and accomplishment by promoting and supporting her husband's goals and aspirations.[31] As Grace herself put it, referring to George's brother's fiancée, "If she loves him as she ought China or the world's end would make no difference to her." Grace expressed no qualms about defining herself as the Royal Judge's wife. She supported wholeheartedly George's decision to take the Havana appointment and thereafter dutifully supported his endeavors, which on occasions such as during Dalrymple's sprees of absenteeism included helping him with the copying of official letters and documents, in what George described as "a most beautiful & very official looking & legible hand."[32]

Their family life and relations with long-time friends disrupted by their relocation to Havana, Grace sought a new network of friends and acquaintances and engaged in social activities in the company of other middle- and upper-middle-class foreign women, mainly the women of the Crawford clan of El Cerro and its environs. This group, described by a contemporary as "a circle of intelligent Englishwomen," included a dozen or so women of the long-term resident British and German elite, whose families were linked to trade, commercial agriculture, and diplomatic service. This somewhat cliquish group of women, to which, according to one observer, Consul-General Crawford held the key, included the consul-general's wife, Sally; her sister Fanny Runge; his daughters Mrs. Wille and Mrs. Scharfenberg; his mother-in-law, Mrs. Tolmé; Mrs. Brown; and Grace Backhouse, among others. Sally Crawford, Mrs. Scharfenberg, and Mrs. Runge were particularly welcoming and of help while the Backhouses' were settling in.[33]

Most women of the Crawford circle lived outside of Havana proper, and because of their status they afforded either slave or waged service, which liberated them from most domestic manual tasks. Servants took care of the cooking, cleaning, and washing while white European or Cuban nursemaids fed, bathed, and watched over the small children. The only manual domestic tasks that Grace ever recorded in her diaries and correspondence were organizing the contents of drawers and baking cakes for birthdays and other special occasions.[34] Overseeing the usually unsettled service staff, however, appeared to be a full-time occupation by itself.

Grace and other women in her social circle enjoyed plenty of leisure time. They sought each other's company, exchanging visits over tea and snacks or on occasion more formal dinners. Grace and her neighbor, Mrs. Runge, became particularly close, visiting each other on more than a daily basis for some time. At one point the British and German women of El Cerro and El Horcón organized a reading club around which they met once a week in different homes to read articles from European magazines such a *Punch* and *Illustrated News.* On January 12, 1854, for example, Mrs. Runge, Mrs. Scharfenberg, Mrs. Brown, and Mrs. Tolmé came to the Backhouse residence for reading club day.[35]

Grace and her friends also organized hikes and volanta trips to places of recreation in El Cerro and beyond. On several instances Grace, Mrs. Runge, and other friends walked to El Cerro's celebrated Paseo de Rosas, to Judge Esteva's palatial home, and to the renowned Bishop's Garden at the end of la Calle Tulipán.[36] Formerly part of the Bishop of Havana's private resort home, the Bishop's Garden now belonged to the Count of Peñalver, who kept the magnificent garden open for public use. The garden's luscious vegetation included countless fruit trees. One visitor wrote that there "you find shade which you find nowhere else." "[T]he trees are planted in straight alleys," continues the account, "and the water-roses, a species of water-lily of immense size, fragrant and pink-colored, grow in a square tank." By mid-century, the Bishop's Garden had developed a natural appearance of neglect as if nature had taken control over what originally was a well-planned and groomed garden. Dozens of mutilated statues, silent casualties of earthquakes and storms, dotted the magnificent landscape. Sally Crawford was fond of organizing picnics at the Bishop's Garden. Grace and her friends enjoyed countless hikes to the gardens, where they took their children to see the caged lions, peacocks, crocodiles, and other animals.[37]

Grace and other women of her small circle of friends spent many mornings shopping in Havana's retail establishments and having ices or other refreshments before returning to the quiet life of the suburbs. They also frequented the sea baths that lined the coast just west of the city's walls. These sea baths consisted of square, solid limestone structures that sat right on the rocky coast, measuring about twenty square feet and three to eight feet in depth. Large holes on the sea side of these structures allowed the circulation of clear, warm, Gulf Stream water into and out of the baths over which hung wooden planks to protect the bathers from overexposure to the sun. Havana's public sea baths, of which Los Campos Eliseos was the finest, remained open throughout the year and were segregated by race and sex.[38]

Grace also sought distraction and escape from the monotony of life in suburban Havana by engaging in crafts and other domestic hobbies. She spent some of her free time playing the piano and maintaining her voice. Grace also drew sketches in a small room they set aside especially for that purpose. Once she made an ottoman out of a wooden box and a remnant of fabric. Another contemporary foreign woman residing in El Cerro avoided boredom by "drawing, painting, working in wax, stuffing birds, [and] polishing the different varieties of wood."[39]

Writing letters to, and reading letters from, her loved ones were among Grace's most cherished activities. Corresponding with those who were dear to her and to George became an important source of connection that helped alleviate the pain of separation from loved ones and home. Once a month, around the twenty-third day of each month, the Backhouses received correspondence from England. Their mail usually arrived in bundles of seven to fourteen letters, which took between four and seven weeks to arrive via the English mail ship; there was usually one letter from Grace's widowed father, one from George's widowed mother, and several others from relatives and friends. They also received occasional packages with gifts of clothing, books, fruit preserves, and toys for the children. Grace's anticipation of the correspondence's arrival and her spirited reaction attest to the vital emotional link that the letters helped her maintain with the London she never quite left. "Hurrah! The English Mail came in," she wrote in her diary on June 22, 1853, upon the arrival of "a charming packet of letters." Grace's diaries and correspondence are peppered with similar reactions; she referred to her letters as "dear things," a "delicious packet," and "delightful letters," "a refreshment as usual to us."[40]

Writing letters absorbed a great deal of Grace's time. She wrote letters at a rate of about one every other day and started letters and then added on to them on successive days, as if they were diaries, until the English mail packet was scheduled to depart, around the ninth or tenth of each month. She also took on the responsibility of maintaining the correspondence with George's side of the family. Only on special occasions, particularly when he had business matters to discuss with his mother and sisters, did George write home. His letters were usually shorter and more to the point. Most of the time he counted on Grace to maintain the correspondence flowing and asked her to excuse his poor writing habits. "George told me to make excuses for him not writing," wrote Grace to his mother once. In another letter to George's mother and sisters Grace interrupted the epistolary flow with the following dialogue:

> (Grace to George) 'Do you send your love to your family?'
> (George to Grace) 'Yes, very much.'

George himself was often apologetic for the inconsistency and brevity of his correspondence.[41]

Even with the help of nursemaid Hilton and her nurse assistants, most of Grace's time and emotional and physical energy were spent with her children, Alice, who was only eight months old when they arrived in Havana, and Johnny, born seven months after their arrival.

Little Alice was a jolly, active girl. Her mother described her as a "*tomboy*" who climbed "on all the chairs & stools and trunks she can find." On another occasion George described her as noisy and high-spirited. Before bathing her, Grace and Hilton usually allowed her to run around for a while "in a *state of nature*" until she was tired enough to be manageable. Physically, her own loving mother admitted, Alice was "not in the least pretty" but explained that she had "a merry little face" and was funny and utterly amusing. Alice was fat, according to her mother, and had curly hair.[42]

Culturally, little Alice was an amusing creolized product of British, Spanish, and African influences. Like other children growing up in a household that uses a foreign tongue, Alice was "backward in talking, [though] not in noise." In August 1853, when she was fourteen months, George reported that Alice's vocabulary consisted of only two words: "yes" and "pretty." Her mother, however, insisted that she knew about twenty words. Since in her household English speakers were outnumbered by Spanish-speaking servants, Alice learned quite a bit of Spanish early on. According to Grace, she was "inclined to mimic" and spoke Spanish in the same tone that it was spoken to her. By the time Alice was two years old, Grace was reporting that she "understands Spanish quite as well as English, and says quite as many words in Spanish as English." Alice mixed both languages in what was described as a "most comical" way. Grace relayed a transcribed sample home: "[S]he says 'Dolly, kean (i.e. clean) Pancha, Sucio' which *means* 'Dolly has got nice clean clothes on and Pancha the washer-woman must have her dirty (sucio) ones.' "[43]

Alice picked up other things besides the broken Spanish of the black servants. She spent a lot of time under the care of Martina and other under nurses after the birth of Johnny, whose health problems required special attention from Grace and Hilton. Grace reported that Martina was "quite a blessing to Alice," whom she fed, played with, and took for long walks; Hilton, in the meantime, retained the responsibility of giving the toddler her daily baths. The little girl picked up Martina's fashion of wearing her shoes "down at heel." She also learned to dance in a way her mother described as "Nigger style" and took to the "elegant accomplishment" of spitting.[44]

Grace found enormous satisfaction purchasing an occasional toy for her daughter. She confessed in a letter to her mother-in-law that she was "*very* weak" when faced with the opportunity to buy toys for Alice. In another letter she revisited the topic: "Alice has just seated herself in her wheelbarrow and coaxed Hilton to give her a drive. This wheelbarrow I bought at the Havana—you know George's ideas about too many toys—but he is very lenient, and I *smuggle* them occasionally for instance when we stop at some shop, say a *grocers,* and I see opposite a Toy shop I let George go *alone* to the grocer's, and when he is safe in there I step out and make a *little* purchase in the Toy shop. They ask exorbitant price. Fancy giving a dollar, at least 4s[,] for a small box of nine pins!"[45]

In her children, in her husband, in keeping connected with their loved ones in England, and to a lesser extent within her small circle of friends, Grace found meaning, consolation for her homesickness, and soothing comfort to face the many alienating experiences that came with being a foreign woman in the "male city" of Havana.

# V

---

# Leisure and Pleasure

U pon moving to the outskirts of Havana, the Backhouses soon
joined a small, closed circle of Europeans made up mostly of
British and German families that revolved around the patri-
archical figure of Consul-General Crawford. The Crawfords, Tolmés,
Runges, Scharfenbergs, Willes, Browns, Rittemeyers, and a few other
families belonged to the long-term resident foreign elite that enjoyed
high social and economic status. The Backhouses, because of their
official status, were soon drawn into this circle's very active, demanding, and expensive social life.

The Crawfords lived in a splendid mansion, whose proportions
matched the extent of the consul-general's patriarchal pretensions. One
contemporary described it as "one of the most beautiful houses I have yet
seen here." It had a stone staircase, continues the description, "leading
first to a music-gallery; besides other rooms, a splendid drawing-room
and ante-room, the one with an ornamental marble floor, the other *en
parquet,* of a pattern elaborately worked in various woods; Pompeian
ceilings; a beautiful ornamented dressing room, a bedroom beyond-
recherchées, and in good taste." Several years later, when Crawford retired and moved back to England, he sold most of his house furnishings,
including a 500-volume library, fine English and French china sets, and
numerous pieces of furniture and assorted ornaments.[1]

This European social clique remained closed not only to Cubans and Spaniards, with whom its members had minimal social interaction and whom they deemed inferior, but also to North Americans, whom they invariably regarded as unrefined. The Backhouses shared these sentiments of cultural superiority. To them, Yankees—a term they incorrectly applied to all North Americans—were repulsive, unreliable beings, too vulgar to warrant any proper social attention. Grace recorded in her diary some remarks on a dinner gathering at the Runges's with the King family from the United States. She described them as "not remarkable people in any way. Mr. King a vulgar Yankee as usual." Most probably Grace was referring to the family of the late William R. King of Alabama, owner of the Ariadne plantation. King was elected vice-president of the United States in 1852; being too ill to attend the inauguration ceremonies in Washington, DC, he took the oath of office in Matanzas but never served in that capacity.[2] If these are the Kings alluded to by Grace, they were certainly not Yankees, and their vulgarity would have been a matter of personal interpretation. In a letter to his mother, George revisited the topic, commenting: "There are heaps of Yankees here, male and female," he wrote, "& I dare say some will be at the pic nic. There is a Yankee war steamer here; and it is said (I won't answer for the truth) that a fast American Lady here has pronounced her compatriot officers not gentlemanly enough to be invited. I heard yesterday one of them having broken a bottle of brandy on the head of another in a quarell."[3]

Doubtless the social antagonism between Britons and North Americans living in Havana had much to do with the escalating tensions between their respective governments precisely over the island of Cuba and the issue of the slave trade. John A. Quitman was organizing a massive filibuster expedition in the United States, and Britain's government would have perhaps responded militarily to avoid the island passing to the hands of such forces. The Backhouses had their own more profound and ancestral motives to dislike the citizens of the United States. George's grandfather and great grandfather owned a Liverpool-based commercial firm that had endured confiscations during the American War of Independence. For decades the family tried to collect pre-revolutionary debts in the amount of £12,000, but to no avail.[4] It is possible that the Backhouse mercantile house, like so many others in eighteenth-century Liverpool, was linked to the slave trade, that hemorrhage of bonded human beings flowing out of Africa's coastal wounds.

Spaniards and Cubans were even less welcome to the closed endog-amous European social circle. Only on rare occasions did the Back-houses interact socially with Spaniards; there is no mention of any Cuban or Spaniard ever being invited to their home for lunch, dinner, or even tea. With her Creole neighbors, Grace, who spoke no Spanish, only exchanged bows and polite smiles.[5]

Neither she nor George had much good to say about Cubans and Spaniards. They found them loud, dishonest, lazy, and unreliable, too given to flash and excess, and too Roman Catholic for their taste. Spanish and Cuban men, the Backhouses believed, smoked too many cigars and were too indolent; the women wore too much makeup, wore dresses that were too tight and too low cut, and behaved in infantile ways. Cubans and Spaniards, in the eyes of the Backhouses, as well as in those of many other Britons and North Americans, were as far as one could get from the ideal Victorian man and woman. One United States official, trying to understand this obvious cultural clash, de-scribed the relations between Spaniards and his fellow countrymen as "antipodal."[6]

George and Grace participated in many of the social gatherings of El Cerro and El Horcón's European elite. Their social events ranged from picnics at the Bishop's Garden to formal dinner parties and gala recitals. Sally Crawford was the events' chief organizer and had the power to invite whomever she pleased and to leave out those she did not care to see. In August 1853, Mrs. Crawford coordinated a ball at the Rittmeyers' in El Cerro to which she did not invite Grace and George. "Strange to say," wrote a puzzled George in his diary, "Grace & I were not invited we don't know why."[7]

Sally Crawford was fond of music and song; she often organized recitals at her home with guest musicians with whom she sang along. After one such occasion, George wrote his sister that at the party sang "a bad tenor singer (professional I think) whom Sally Crawford had held out to us as bait to come, she of course sang besides." At the Runges's and other suburban Havana residences the European social circle enjoyed evenings caressed by the melodies of Beethoven, Men-delssohn, and other classical composers. Dancing to the rhythms of the Cuban contradance and other tropical musical forms was another com-ponent of the foreign elite's social gatherings.[8]

Adequate music was such an important aspect of social intercourse that the Backhouses felt compelled to acquire a piano at great financial sacrifice. The second-hand French Erard piano they eventually bought at 18 gold ounces (306 pesos) was small and in need of tuning but was "very well supplied ... with keys" and had handles on each side. Grace considered the purchase "a great deal." At the time when they bought it, a time of serious financial constraints, George explained in a letter to his mother: "I don't consider our purchase of a piano a wanton piece of extravagance as it might appear for persons in difficulties generally: without it we felt we could not be quite as hospitable as we ought to be. Of course our own pleasure in such a matter & under such circumstances ought not to weight much; all the same I won't deny it is to me (& I hope to Grace too) a great pleasure. Grace has most agreeably surprised me by her musical performances after being so long without practice; she has been charming me with them very much this Evening. I think our piano a much better bargain than we should generally have been able to make here."[9]

Most of the Backhouses' social gatherings gravitated around food, whether these were picnics or formal dinners. The enormous cost of gastronomical entertaining proved draining to their economic resources. After hosting a dinner party at their place to which they invited the Runges, Crawfords, Mr. Tolmé and his son, Mr. Scharfenberg, and John V. Crawford, Grace jotted in her diary: "Dinner went off well. Things from Dominica good but *very* expensive." An inventory of the Backhouses' liquor cabinet provides a good indicator of the extent and the expense of the hospitality they were expected to dispense. It included four dozen bottles of ale, six dozen bottles of sherry, twelve half bottles of champagne, eight dozen bottles of Claret St. Julien, twenty-two-and-a-half dozen bottles of claret, and thirty-two-and-a-half dozen empty bottles. In all, nearly 500 full bottles and close to 390 empty ones. The inventory also registered seventeen pounds of tea and a beer bill of $75.[10] Besides their social role, alcoholic beverages and boiled drinks like tea and coffee were safe to drink, which was not the case with water in either Havana or London.[11]

Social gatherings also included games like chess and table turning, a predecessor of the Ouija board. Grace took note in her diary of one afternoon of table turning: "I tried table turning with some others. They began calling upon a *spirit to manifest itself* in German, French, Spanish & English. The table did not stir in the least, and as to the *spirit* I do not quite approve of that *amusement* & made Mrs. Sharfenberg [*sic*] take my place. George joined afterwards, but got too tired, & knocked the table to make it move, thereby breaking the charm to the annoyance of some of the party, then 4 tried intently, wishing much to find out what reality there might be in it, but no, the table was thoroughly obsticiate & nothing came of it all."[12]

Because George was one of the two highest ranking British officials in the island, he and Grace were expected to generously dispense their hospitality by hosting the officers of British vessels, particularly those of the anti–slave trade squadron with whom George worked closely. British naval officers were regular guests at the Backhouses' for lunches, afternoon teas, and dinners. The Backhouses were particularly fond of Commander Baile and the other officers of the man-of-war *Medea,* the ship that brought them across the Atlantic. They enjoyed such visits but Grace noted that the young officers paid no attention to Hilton, who remained single and frustratedly desirous of a family of her own.[13] The British naval officers reciprocated in kind by hosting the Backhouses and other British subjects on board their vessels, usually on Sundays with lunch following on-board services of the Church of England. British naval officers also demonstrated their affection for the Backhouses with sporadic gifts, mostly pets like Jason, a cat presented to them by Commander Baile, and Linda, their beloved white-and-liver English Spaniel.[14]

By the spring of 1855 the Backhouses were showing signs of being both emotionally and financially drained by the intensity of their social life. "I begin to be almost tired of exchanges of hospitality with our Naval Officers," George wrote home in a letter complaining of the expense of it all. And in a letter home dated May 11, 1855, he remarked: "I have lots of English Society now in the Navy, not always the best specimens."[15]

Attending formal and gala balls were other social responsibilities of Her Britannic Majesty's Judge and his wife. Some of the gala events took place at the Crawfords' palatial home, others at the Villanueva or Tacón theaters, whose orchestra sections could be covered with boards to convert them into elegant ballrooms; yet others were held at the Captains-General Palace. George and Grace, who during their London years had been graced with at least one invitation to a ball at Buckingham Palace, found little appeal in the tropical versions of such events. Commenting on a ball given by Captain-General Pezuela in honor of the French Admiral Duquesne, Grace remarked: "[I]f there had been more ladies, more light & more refreshments it would have been a much less shady affair."[16]

George's light and flexible work schedule (10 A.M. to 2 P.M.) allowed him plenty of time to engage in leisure activities with his children and wife. They took afternoon strolls around the neighborhood and took drives to downtown Havana to shop, have lunch, or enjoy ices of countless exotic flavors. They also found plenty to do in Havana during the night, from dinning at fine French restaurants, to attending balls, to enjoying world-class opera and theatrical productions.[17]

Because the Backhouses lived outside Havana proper, many of their leisure activities required them to reach the city's downtown, where most of the services, shopping establishments, and places of entertainment were to be found. They found themselves in a difficult position with regards to the transportation challenges posed by life in suburban Havana. On the one hand, they enjoyed a relatively high social ranking that made walking not an option—this was certainly the case for Grace—yet on the other, they faced financial difficulties that did not permit them the luxury of owning their own carriage. They had originally intended to acquire one such vehicle and George attended a carriage exhibition where he found United States–made vehicles to be the best. Soon they dropped their plans because of the carriages' "generaly enormous" price tags. Apparently they were interested in acquiring a four-wheeled carriage of the kind that cost more than $1,000, rather than a cheaper two-wheeled volanta or quitrín of Cuban manufacture. The horse required to pull the carriage cost an additional $85 to $120, plus the cost of the animal's maintenance and care. In addition, most types of carriages paid road taxes of one peso a month and registration and other fees.[18]

Because of their circumstances, the Backhouses' options were limited to public and hired modes of transportation. Fortunately, they lived just off the thoroughfare that linked El Cerro to the old part of Havana, a location that afforded them a variety of transportation options. The Intramuros section of Havana and the village of El Cerro were connected by *guaguas,* horse-drawn omnibuses, and by horse-drawn trolleys that rode over rails placed in the middle of la Calzada del Monte and la Calzada del Cerro. The guaguas, which began serving the Plaza de Armas–El Cerro route in 1840, rolled by every 5 to 15 minutes and cost only one real. Drawn by three-horse teams, guaguas could transport ten to twelve passengers. In June 1855, El Cerro was linked by omnibus service with Marianao, a suburban village west of Havana

that the Backhouses were particularly fond of; for some reason
Marianao reminded them of England.[19] George and Grace patronized
the guaguas early on, but soon became "much disgusted with the spitting herein." Upon another trial, they became convinced that they
would no longer patronize them, as attested in a letter of Grace to
Mary Backhouse: "I am getting quite disgusted with Omnibuses . . .
there was so much spitting, and it was so full of *snobs* that George said
it should be the last time we managed an expedition in that way." It
was not the last time, however.[20]

Another transportation alternative was to hire volantas or other
types of carriage cabs.[21] Volantas were peculiar-looking carriages of
Cuban invention that elicited obligatory comments—mostly critical—
from most everyone encountering one for the first time. This type of
carriage, described by United States Consul James W. Steele as "a
cross between a mule-litter and a wheelbarrow run backward," consisted of a low-cut chaise-like body, sometimes ornamented with precious metal trimmings, which rested on a pair of disproportionately
large wheels that measured about six feet in circumference. Volantas
had room for only two or three passengers. From the vehicle's body
emerged two long shafts, sixteen to twenty feet long, that were attached to the sides of one or two small horses with their tails tightly
braided and tied back to the saddle or harness. In all, from the end of
the wheels to the horse's nose the vehicle extended a distance of
around twenty-two feet.[22] On the horse, separated from the passengers,
sat the postilion, usually a black man dressed in a most colorful costume that would have outshined the most decorated of Napoleon's
generals: a buckled top hat, a tailed scarlet jacket trimmed with a
generous dose of silver or gold braid, and leather jackboots ornamented with oversized spurs and bright silver buckles. One contemporary observer ridiculed the entire costume, describing it as "three
parts jack-boots and one part silver-laced jacket." There was a sharp
distinction between the postilions who drove the for-hire carriages and
those who drove the private ones. The former were reportedly filthier,
less well-mannered, and worse drivers than the slaves who drove the
carriages of the upper class. One contemporary source states that the
elite's postilions constituted a sort of aristocracy among the slaves. The
attire of postilions working for some of the wealthiest families could
cost several thousand pesos—more than the slaves themselves.[23]

Most foreigners visiting the island were quick to criticize the ubiquitous volanta as odd-looking and impractical. One contemporary referred to it as "very comical" and another dubbed it a "queer vehicle." Yet another observer described the volanta as the "oddest vehicle conceivable." "Grotesque" was perhaps the most commonly used adjective in reference to the Cuban carriage. The closest comment to a compliment was made by a United States woman who said that it had a sort of "barbaric splendor."[24] Foreign visitors, the British in particular, seemed obsessed with the carriage horses' welfare. One commented on the cruelty of tying their tails in a way that kept them from protecting themselves from mosquitoes and other insects. Others were critical of the fact that the small Cuban horses were forced to carry the weight of both the carriages and the drivers.[25]

Most foreign critics failed to understand, however, that this peculiar Cuban invention reflected the particular needs and structure of the society that created it. First and foremost, volantas afforded mobility and visibility to the city's elite, particularly its women of marriageable age. At the same time, given the volantas' proportions and their elevation from the road, they allowed a considerable distance between the passengers, mostly female, and the pedestrians, mostly men. Like bars in house windows, volantas kept the city's women of the upper and middle classes out of reach but not out of sight. Given the narrowness of the streets inside the walled city of Havana, the length of the volantas' shafts, which made turning difficult, appeared senseless. This characteristic, however, secured a considerable separation between the white passengers and the black postilion and the horse(s). The nature of the postilions' attire, which matched the extravagant ornamentation of the volantas and horses, further established them as objects that were far removed from the human and individual qualities of those they transported.

The much criticized volantas also responded to specific climatological and topographic needs. They were well ventilated—the tops of quitrines could be pulled back for maximum air circulation and visibility. The poor condition of most of Havana's roads also explains some of the volantas' features.[26] The disproportionately large size of the wheels, the separation between them, and the separation between the cabin and the horse(s) made volantas virtually turnover-proof even in roads with holes two feet deep that filled with mud during the rainy season. The volantas' construction also allowed for a very comfortable ride even over some of Havana's worst roads. The South Carolina physician John George F. Wurdemann celebrated the vehicles' easy motion while the Swede Fredrika Bremer, who disliked the vehicles' appearance, described riding in them as being "rocked on a cloud."[27]

A good proportion of the few thousand volantas and quitrines that crisscrossed Havana's thoroughfares and narrow streets were public vehicles for hire.[28] These were regulated and taxed by the colonial government and their fares supposedly establish by law. According to government stipulation, hired volantas should provide transportation within the city for a distance of a mile or less for a mere peseta (20 cents). They could also be hired on an hourly basis, as the Backhouses often did, for a regulated flat fare of about one peso. Four-wheeled carriages and rentals during rainy days cost more. In a letter home, Grace explained the cab fares: "There is a fixed rate of prices here for hired carriages if you have the carriage any time between 12 & 3 o'c, either all that time or for half an hour only you pay just the same, i.e. a 4 dollar[s]. . . . We order it at 5 o'c & may keep it till 8 o'c at the same rate."[29]

The reality of cab fares was a bit more complicated, fluid, and subject to negotiation. Most postilions were free blacks and some were slaves and emancipados who worked for the owners of the cabs and came under the obligation of producing a fixed amount of money each day; whatever the postilions made above that amount, usually not much more, was theirs to keep.[30] The increasing demands of the vehicle owners and the stagnant fares as stipulated by law forced postilions to find creative ways to maintain their livelihood. Unsuspecting foreign visitors were the easiest targets of the creativity of Havana's cab postilions. Many recently arrived foreigners, like George on his first day in the city, made the mistake of asking "how much?" rather than handing over their smallest coin at the end of the trip. The travel literature is full of accounts of incidents in which cab patrons were charged many times the legally established fares. The author of one travelogue described an incident of a postilion insisting on the payment of $4.25 for a mile-long ride that should have cost one peseta. After an exchange of insults the postilion got two pesetas for the ride and moved on. Another visitor described an incident whereby the cab driver insisted on a higher fare and when the patron refused to pay more he "refus[ed] to take it, and jabbered away."[31]

Besides their creativity with fares, cab postilions had a reputation for being dirty, raggedly clothed, foul-mouthed, unreliable, impolite, hard drinkers, and reckless drivers. Unlike their well-attired, well-behaved brethren who drove the private carriages of the elite, public volanta drivers were poorly dressed. One contemporary described them as wearing broken hats and patched jackets, and being dirtier than the horses.[32] Grace recorded an instance of a postilion being very drunk when he came to fetch them at the end of a ball. On one occasion George ordered a cab for five o'clock. The driver showed up an hour late and with the wrong kind of cab. Upset by the lateness and the inadequacy of the vehicle, George offered the cab driver 2 pesos instead of the usual 4 pesos. The postilion declined the offer and left. Later that night the right carriage, with space for all, finally arrived and the Backhouses headed to Havana for some refreshments and a little shopping. That night Grace bought two toys for her daughter's birthday—"one a white curly lamb the other a gay young gentleman with an internal whistle."[33]

Shopping excursions to Havana were among the Backhouses' favorite activities; shopping helped them escape or at least cope with the cultural alienation that they endured as it allowed them to purchase imported English products like beer and tea, and familiar English-language publications. Like others, the Backhouses did most of their shopping in the commercial district, in the old part of town.[34] To reach the commercial district the Backhouses had to take la Calzada del Cerro and then Calzada del Monte until they reached el Paseo de Isabel Segunda, which ran parallel to, but outside, the city walls. Once they reached Marty's monumental Teatro Tacón, they had to turn right toward the bay and proceed to penetrate the walled city through la Puerta de Monserrate that led into la Calle Obispo; la Calle O'Reilly, next to it, was for the outgoing traffic exiting the Intramuros section. Crossing these two streets at right angles were Oficios, Mercaderes, San Ignacio, Cuba, and several other commercial streets.[35] A continuous canopy of bright-colored awnings sheltered several of these streets from the crushing tropical sun, giving Havana a distinctively Turkish air.

Many of the streets and shops in Havana's commercial district were specialized. The larger warehouses and dry goods stores were on la Calle Mercaderes. Closer to the bay, la Calle Oficios was, as its name suggests, lined with the establishments of tailors, shoemakers, and the like, trades in which free black and mulatto Cubans were conspicuously overrepresented. La Calle Ricla was known for its jewelry stores and well-stocked dry goods stores. The main commercial streets of Obispo, O'Reilly, and Obrapía were lined with an uninterrupted suc-

**Plaza de Armas and Captains-General Palace.** (Print by Federico Mialhe from B. May, *Álbum pintoresco de la Isla de Cuba.*)

cession of small shops. One visitor described Obispo as "one of the liveliest streets in town, its sides lined with the most attractive stores all the way out to the old walls of the city." Most stores were specialized. La Flor de La Habana and Lombard's sold nothing but furniture; El Sol specialized in cosmetics; and El Esmero sold but mosquito nets. Other establishments specialized in other particular items such as matches, ribbons, and fans. There were also fine clothes stores, well-stocked pharmacies, cigar shops—which George regularly patronized—and book stores like B. May & Co., which specialized in the sale and publication of English-language books. There were also plenty of physician's and dentist's offices on Calle O'Reilly and Calle Cuba.[36]

Most visitors and foreign residents from Britain or North America were amused by the names of Havana's commercial establishments. Used to a commercial tradition whereby stores usually carried their owners' names, most foreigners found Havana's commercial names to be quite amusing. They deemed names like El León de Oro, Las Delicias de las Damas, La Cruz Verde, and Las Ninfas to be senselessly funny. One visitor found it appalling that seemingly dishonest merchants would give their commercial establishments such righteous

**La Calle Obispo.** (Drawing by Samuel Hazard from his book *Cuba with Pen and Pencil.*)

names as La Rectitud, La Integridad, La Probidad, La Buena Fe, and La Conciencia.[37]

The critics of these naming practices, one of whom concluded that "Spanish people are always prodigal in names," failed to understand some of the basic tenets of Spanish culture and particularly Havana's commercial culture. Commercial activities, especially at the retail level, such as artisanal tasks, were not traditional sources of social pride in Spanish society but rather motives of contempt, sometimes associated with plebeian and even religiously impure backgrounds, certainly not the kinds of activities that elite families wanted their surnames associated with. Furthermore, Havana's retail merchants were a predominantly foreign and relatively transient crowd made up mostly of Catalan,

Basque, and Asturian immigrants who viewed Havana as a place to become wealthy before returning to their ancestral homes. These circumstances made naming one's store after oneself impractical. Las Ninfas could remain Las Ninfas after its owner decided to sell it to a *sobrino* or *paisano*. Peninsular Spaniards, who for the most part led frugal lives, dominated retail business. It was customary for them to live in small rooms located above their commercial establishments. Hard work, cunning, and sometimes unscrupulous business practices allowed many of them to amass huge fortunes that they channeled toward money-lending, slave trading, and on occasions to penetrate commercial agriculture. Spanish businessmen were so visibly dominant in the commercial districts of Havana that one contemporary concluded that "a Creole found in those streets is to be considered an exotic plant."[38] Peninsular control over commercial activities was yet another source of friction between Cubans and Spaniards.

The bargaining fashion in which most retail transactions were carried out became a source of frustration and irritation to many European and North American visitors to Havana. Foreigners not used to this style of business were at a disadvantage and usually ended up paying more than native customers would; not understanding the system, they blamed the raw deals they received on the arbitrary and dishonest nature of Havana's merchants. The author of one travel guide warned his compatriots: "Let the novice take care how he offers one-half the price asked for an article, if he does not wish it, for that, not unfrequently, is its real one; in almost every case one fourth will be deducted." Another contemporary, a British woman, advised how to proceed: "Three times the price intended to be taken is often asked in the first place; then the buyer offers three times less than she intends to give, and at last, after many objections and remonstrances on both sides, the bargain is struck."[39]

Havana offered a multitude of other shopping options including its ubiquitous street vendors and colorful and well-supplied open markets. The main market, located in la Plaza Vieja, included scores of booths with bananas, piles of oranges, pineapples, coconuts, and countless varieties of fruits and vegetables, as well as live poultry, meats, spices, and other dry goods.[40] Canary Islanders, Chinese, and women of color dominated street market activities as vendors, dispensing fruits, vegetables, sweets, and spices. Milkmen delivered milk to Havana's urban

**Milk delivery in Havana.** (Photograph from F. Tennyson Neely's *Greater America*.)

and suburban residences "on the hoof," milking their cows right in front of their customers, thus assuring the fresh and unadulterated quality of their product.[41]

The city's most colorful and famous market was the fish market located at the end of la Calle del Empedrado next to Havana's cathedral. Built and owned by Marty, the infamous former smuggler turned slave trader and entrepreneur, the fish market had a 150-foot-long neoclassical facade ribbed with an imposing colonade; inside, an equally long marble table displayed an incredible variety of seafood and fish. Marty's private quarters were located on the second floor. By virtue of a special decree, Marty enjoyed a monopoly over the sale of fish; no one else could sell it anywhere else in the city. By most accounts, the fish market was a must-see sight. "Whoever goes to Havana," Dr. Wurdemann wrote, "should not fail to visit the fish-market." According to several contemporary accounts, the market offered more than 1,000 different varieties of fish and seafood including sharks, porpoises, rays, flounder, and snake-like eels. It was a most colorful combination of sea creatures of all sizes, colors, textures, and shapes.[42]

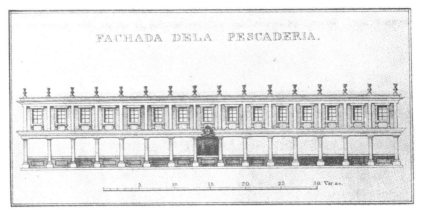

**Plan for Marty's fish market.** (Reprinted from Felicia Chateloin, *La Habana de Tacón*.)

Numerous world-class restaurants and cafés dotted Havana's downtown. A well-traveled British visitor reported that "in no town of France or Italy [had he] ever seen so many, or, proportionately, such sumptuous and constantly crowded *cafés* and *restaurants*." The city, indeed, offered a wide array of cosmopolitan gastronomical experiences to its wealthier residents and transients, including fine French restaurants, seafood restaurants, and establishments specializing in Spanish and Creole cuisine. Among the Backhouses' favorites were the spacious Le Grand's, in El Prado #124, and the famous La Dominica, at the busy corner of Mercaderes and O'Reilly streets.[43]

A combination café–confectioner–bakery, J. Costa's La Dominica was the Backhouses' favorite refreshment and snack stop. They visited this establishment for the first time on their second night in Havana. George and Grace's diaries and correspondence reflect that they patronized La Dominica almost every time they drove downtown.[44] They were not alone as the café was a favorite stop of Cubans and foreigners alike. One contemporary recorded in her travelogue that "All the day long it is full of people of all nations." Although Cuban patrons predominated, it indeed attracted a cosmopolitan crowd, and most foreign visitors apparently followed a travelogue writer's recommendation that anyone visiting Cuba's capital "must not omit seeing 'La Dominica.'" Most of La Dominica's patrons were male, but a few foreign women ventured into the famous establishment in the company of their husbands or an appropriate escort. Even if properly escorted

**Café La Dominica.** (Drawing by Samuel Hazard from his book *Cuba with Pen and Pencil.*)

they had to be "prepared to endure any amount of eyeshot." It appears from the Backhouse records that Grace and her friends did not set foot inside the café without a proper escort, but instead ordered to-go ices and other products that were delivered by La Dominica's waiters to the carriages parked outside the popular café.[45]

Centrally located next to the Captains-General Palace and across from the Dominican Convent, La Dominica was described as "one of the best ordered and most elegant cafes in the world." Its large main entrance door led to its main lounge. Tightly packed marble-top tables of different shapes crowded the stone floor whose epicenter was marked by a small gilded fountain that produced a refreshing sound that drowned the patrons' loud conversations and strident laughs. Its mostly male crowd of guests puffed a wall of thick tobacco smoke through which filtered the café's dim golden illumination; this, according to one observer, gave the place a "Rembrandtic tinge." Several travelers' accounts attest to the fact that Havana was a city of smokers, where men, women, and even children five and six years old were addicted to tobacco. Foreign observers noted, however, that they saw very few intoxicated people during their sojourn in Havana.[46]

Its privileged location and attractive ambiance aside, what made La Dominica famous was the quality and variety of its products. It was best known for its ice creams of countless flavors, its colorful sherbets, and its icy-cold fruit juices. Guava, guanábana, and other flavored ices and ice creams were served "pyramidally in an overgrown wine glass. On the plate under it lay a long brown coil [*barquillo*], looking like a cigar, and tasting like a baked combination of brown sugar, well-beaten eggs and flour. This is designed as a spoon to eat the towering cream." The Backhouses' favorites were those flavors that they were most familiar with, strawberry, raspberry, and peach; they failed to develop a taste for the sweeter tropical flavors. Grace once criticized the confectionery as being "generaly nasty . . . too ugly taste & much too sweet." Another contemporary visitor from the North described some of the ices as nasty and advised her readers "not [to] buy the syrups, for they are made with very bad sugar." La Dominica's marmalades, preserves, and fruit juices were also in great demand by natives and foreigners alike. Guava jellies were among the most popular; of them one traveler wrote: "It is good, it is cheap, it will keep (with proper care) till the end of time." Lemon and orange *granizadas* and other refreshing drinks, some of which were named after U.S. presidents, were among the place's many attractions.[47]

By most accounts, Havana had a lively and animated nightlife that offered Cubans and foreigners a vast array of entertainment options. Following the quiet siesta hours of the afternoon the city came alive with bustle and noise at around 5 or 6 P.M. After sunset the city's gas lighting system, in place since 1846, illuminated the Intramuros section as well as some of the main thoroughfares outside the city walls. In the sky above, bright stars formed what to foreign eyes were "strange constellations" shinning "with planetary splendor." The cool breezes of the evening contributed to the enjoyment of Havana's outdoor nightlife.[48]

**Paseo de Isabel Segunda.** (Print by Federico Mialhe from B. May, *Álbum pintoresco de la Isla de Cuba*.)

The most popular of Havana's late afternoon and evening rituals was the promenade. A network of wide paseos, which one writer described as a "mixture of street and pleasure-ground, whose use is peculiarly a Cuban institution," crisscrossed the Extramuros section of the city. The most important of these paseos was el Paseo de Isabel Segunda, which connected with el Paseo del Prado north of la Puerta de Monserrate. Likened by more than one traveler to London's Hyde Park, el Paseo de Isabel Segunda consisted of a wide central avenue for carriage traffic, lined by two narrower malls for pedestrians to walk on. Large marble statues, flower beds, stone benches, and four colonnades of royal palms added to the splendor of el Paseo de Isabel Segunda, which Fredrika Bremer described as "the finest promenade anyone can imagine."[49] Perpendicular to el Paseo de Isabel Segunda and in a direction away from the bay, la Calle de la Reina lead into yet another important paseo, el Paseo Tacón, later renamed Paseo de Carlos Tercero, and more recently renamed Avenida Salvador Allende. This was a scenic road with fountains and monuments, and two double rows of royal palms, one on each side. One visitor described a drive over it as being "as smooth as [over] a pebbly beach."[50] Smaller and exclusively for pedestrian promenades was la Cortina de Valdés, an elevated esplanade behind the cathedral, which overlooked the bay.[51] Grace and George, often with their children, took promenades on la Cortina de Valdés and enjoyed drives on hired carriages to see the lights and hear the music.[52]

It was on thoroughfares like el Paseo de Isabel Segunda that Habaneros and Habaneras of the upper classes carried out their daily paseos. Promenade time started at around five or six in the afternoon, when unending convoys of horse-drawn volantas, with their women passengers, converged on the city's grand paseos. In the meantime, men on horseback or on foot arrived on the scene; there they exchanged glances with the women, who responded with their "telegraphic fans."[53] The classist nature of the paseo was made patent by the prohibition against hired volantas circulating on the paseos during paseo time. According to the novelist Cirilo Villaverde, if any rented carriage slipped by the paseo's armed guards the upper-class participants expressed their indignation with mocking laughter.[54] Later, at around eight or nine on some evenings, many of the vehicles and pedestrians entered the walled section of the city and reconvened at la Plaza de Armas for the ritual's next stage, *la retreta.* At that time the city's regimental band began to play for the pleasure of the crowds that gathered under the main plaza's majestic canopy of royal palms. One visitor described la retreta as producing "a scene of hilarity and mirth so Oriental and fairy-like as almost to bewilder European eyes."[55]

At the other end of O'Reilly and Obispo streets, beyond la Puerta de Monserrate and just across the north end of el Paseo de Isabel Segunda, stood one of Havana's grandest buildings and one of the elite's favorite places of entertainment, El Teatro Tacón. Inaugurated in 1838, the building was named after Captain-General Tacón, who granted Marty the concession to build and operate it. The Tacón, with the capacity to seat 3,000 spectators, was the largest theater in the Americas and one of the world's most spacious and elegant. It consisted of five levels of boxes and galleries and an orchestra section with 600 red leather armchairs. Its walls were painted white and lavishly decorated in gold. Above it all hung a majestic glass lamp hovering over the large pit. The original structure was designed by Antonio Mayo and later served as the base for today's Gran Teatro Nacional.[56]

The quality of opera, zarzuela, and theater productions staged at El Teatro Tacón matched the splendor of the edifice. The early to mid-

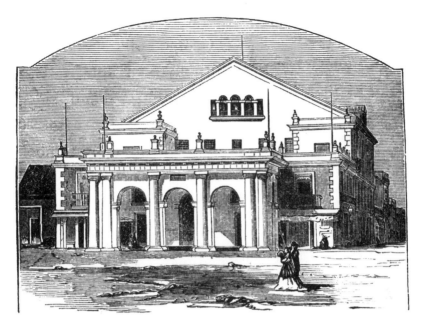

**El Teatro Tacón.** (Drawing by Samuel Hazard from his book *Cuba with Pen and Pencil.*)

1850s were in fact the high point of world-class opera in Havana. The city attracted artists of the caliber of Albini, Fornasari, Montresor, Mussati, La Rosi, Salvi, Bachiali, and Mariani. Opera deteriorated somewhat after the departure of Salvatori in the mid-1850s.[57] The very demanding Grace passed good judgment over one operatic performance in Havana, which she described as "well acted, well said, well sung, dressed good, & scenery not bad." In the company of her husband and their friends she also enjoyed lighter theatrical entertainment at the Tacón. One night's program included the zarzuela "El Tío Canillitas" followed by a tragedy "Il Guiramento" followed by a duet with Linda de Chamouri.[58]

El Teatro Tacón also served as the city's main stage for the enjoyment of one of the Habaneros' greatest passions, dancing. The floor level of the Tacón could be raised to the level of the stage, producing a majestic ballroom that could accommodate 7,000 stumping guests. A contemporary of the Backhouses concluded that in the city everybody danced from "the little child who is learning to walk, to old women . . . and even those who are lame."[59]

**Interior of El Teatro Tacón.** (Drawing by Samuel Hazard from his book *Cuba with Pen and Pencil.*)

The city of Havana, indeed, was full of distractions and entertainment options for those who could afford them and those who were allowed to participate in them. With a demanding social life, both official and private, the Backhouses found plenty to do with their spare time. Yet with all the expense of their social life, a year into their stay in Havana, Grace reported home that they had no real friends there. George and Grace basically had each other and the children they shared.[60] As a family they tried their best to find distraction and repose while away from the place they called home.

# VI

## Protestants in Roman Catholic Cuba

The Backhouses were people of faith and active communicants of the Church of England. While in London they regularly partook of Sunday mass at St. Paul's Church in Knightsbridge, where they rented a pew. Grace usually attended two or three other services during the week. George, who had an uncle in the ministry, the Reverend Thomas Henry Backhouse, was a very devout man and a voracious reader of religious literature. Interestingly, one of the very first arguments between George and Grace was prompted by his untimely reading of a religious article. It happened during their honeymoon, when one night George "staid up some time reading a pamphlet ... about what churchmen ought to do in opposition to the Pope." Grace soon brought George to his senses and convinced him to join her in the nuptial quarters.[1]

As it eventually became obvious, the article on how to confront the Pope, which George probably did not have time to finish reading, constituted poor preparation for Anglicans relocating in Roman Catholic Cuba. In the Spanish colonies Catholicism was the official faith of the state to the exclusion of any other religion. There was not a single Protestant place of worship on the entire island of Cuba. Neither was there a Protestant minister to serve the several thousand resident and transient Protestants who lived in or passed through Havana each year.

Even the exercise of Protestant worship in the privacy of one's own home could be punished under Spanish law.[2]

Religious exclusivism and intolerance got worse during the middle decades of the nineteenth century as religious purity matters became intimately tied to the defense of slavery and the preservation of colonial rule over the island. Spanish authorities were convinced that Protestant presence and propaganda spurred slave agitation during the late 1830s and early 1840s. In 1838 they arrested James Thompson of London's Bible Society for his distribution of Bibles and his alleged abolitionist activities. A few years later, Consul-General Turnbull and his associates also endured persecution for their allegedly "anabaptist" abolitionist propaganda.[3] New laws in 1848 and a concordat between Spain and the Vatican in 1851 confirmed the exclusion of other faiths and prescribed harsh penalties for those engaging in non-Catholic worship and proselytizing.[4] As a British Protestant entrusted by his government with fighting the continuation of the slave trade, George found himself at the uncomfortable and potentially dangerous intersection of political, social, and religious controversy.

As Cuba's commercial ties with the Protestant North Atlantic became stronger, religious exclusivism became an increasing source of tension between local ecclesiastical and state authorities and the growing foreign Protestant population. Just prior to the arrival of the Backhouses, the Church of England and the British government made a forceful push to secure the freedom of worship of Britons and other Protestants residing in Cuba. The Anglican bishop of Jamaica failed in his quest for permission to perform services in Havana; Captain-General Cañedo had been warned ahead of time of Jamaica's Protestants' alleged schemes "to unsettle the public peace" in Cuba.[5] Official British attempts in the early 1850s to secure the religious rights of British subjects were rejected by Spanish statesmen, who underscored the need for more severe restrictions in Spain's remaining colonial domains. In 1855, during one of the peaks of filibusterer threat against Cuba, further restrictions on immigration were put in place along with a law banning the importation and distribution of Bibles.[6]

Since early colonial times, religious purity—meaning Catholicism and Catholic ancestry—had been prerequisites for residence in Spain's colonial domains. Similar requirements remained in vigor during the nineteenth century, when the relaxation of immigration laws allowed foreigners to settle in the Spanish islands. Spanish legislation prescribed that any foreigner establishing domicile or seeking to practice a profession or to own property in Cuba had to take an oath of catholicity.[7] According to one contemporary observer from the United States, "You were immediately galvanized, electroplated and made a Roman Catholic." Foreign officials like George, however, were spared from this requirement. "I know George would have refused to do it if he had been required," Grace wrote home. A short-term visitor from the United States boasted that rather than take the oath, "I shall demand my passport, shake the dust from my feet, and leave this natural Eden to its serpent."[8]

There is plenty of evidence suggesting that the catholicity oath was more of an obnoxious inconvenience than a real obstacle keeping Protestants from settling on the island. Contemporaries commented that few foreigners actually took the oath. Many of those who did, quibbled their way through it by omitting the word Roman, thus acknowledging alliance to a more encompassing Apostolic and Catholic Church. George reported that this omission satisfied "the consciences of Protestant Foreigners who take the oath." Some foreigners avoided the matter altogether by hiring agents to handle their domiciliation procedures. Yet others avoided presenting actual proof of catholicity by paying a fee. Still, despite the myriad ways of getting around these regulations, British officials continued to attack the catholicity oath for being "as hurtful to the commercial development of Cuba as it is obnoxious to the consciences of Foreigners."[9]

The Backhouses, like most other Protestant visitors and residents, had their first brushes with Spanish colonial Catholicism not long after their arrival. Most travelogues include accounts of visits to Havana's many Catholic churches. Some foreigners were drawn by curiosity or lured by the sacred music being played within. Others soon learned that church services afforded one of the few opportunities to see elegantly attired native women; yet others were moved by a sincere desire to find a temporary alternative to Protestant worship.[10] Grace and George paid their first visit to a Havana church three days into their stay, on March 24, 1853; it was Holy Thursday. It turned out to be a complete disappointment, as attested in their diary entries. "Went into a church," wrote George, "Grace I believe rather shocked at the behavior of the people there. Church looked more like a show than anything else." On the same day Grace recorded her perceptions thus: "The High Altar was a blaze of candles, and a wax figure of our Lord

**Havana's cathedral.** (Drawing by Samuel Hazard from his book *Cuba with Pen and Pencil.*)

lying in the grave was on the Altar step. To us there was a shocking tawdriness about all the display. There were many other pictures & images in the Church, and great talking & staring and apparently but little devotion amongst the crowd." A few days later George and Grace ventured into another church, San Felipe's. Grace remarked that they were "not pleased with what we saw & heard there." She found the service "very noisy."[11]

Not far from la Plaza de Armas stood Havana's cathedral, the most visible symbol of the city's religious life, whose erection dated to the mid-1700s. This massive edifice, in whose interior supposedly rested Admiral Columbus's remains, produced mixed reactions among those who came within sight of its imposing baroque facade.[12] While some described the cathedral's outward appearance as "venerable," "majestic," and "splendid," others said that it was "tasteless" and "not worthy of description." Several travelers commented on the temple's seemingly decaying state and its aged appearance. One described "arborescent tracings of coral branches and shell impressions" that marked the building's facade.[13]

The cathedral's portico, which faced la Calle del Empedrado, led into the main nave with its floor covered by an endless succession of alternating black and white marble tiles. Throughout the cathedral's interior stood or hung dozens of carved or painted representations of Jesus Christ, the Virgin Mary, and countless saints and biblical characters. There was a fine painting of Saint Christopher, Havana's patron saint, and a statue of the martyrdom of Saint Sebastian, which one Protestant resident remarked looked "like a pin cushion." The same iconoclastic observer described the rest of the saintly images with great irreverence: "all bald, all clad in red and purple gowns, all having the general look of having been made in the same factory, after the same general model, and all producing the vague impression that if they are in heaven and look like that, one does not want to go there."[14]

Above the cathedral's main altar hung a figure of Christ that struck observers from the Protestant North as being shockingly realistic. This life-size statue of the crucified Christ was, as one Protestant clergyman put it, "the countenance of death—the nails through his hands, knees and feet—the blood gushing over his limbs, and down his side." Grace found these images "painful to behold & such a dreadful tawdriness, and disgusting attempts at bringing the actuality of our Lord's sufferings before our bodily eyes." Most other Protestant observers agreed that the altar decorations were tawdry, puerile, and in bad taste. In Richard Henry Dana's estimation, Cubans had "a childish taste for excessive decoration. Their altars look like toyshops."[15]

Neither the cathedral nor the rest of Havana's churches were well attended, according to most accounts. It was reportedly not uncommon for priests to outnumber parishioners during some services. As already mentioned, Church attendance was overwhelmingly female, as women found inside the city's temples a space in which they could move about freely, display their charms, and meet other people. The fact that Havana's churches had no pews facilitated mobility, as Habaneras were able to set up camp almost anywhere within the church's interior. Those who could afford it were usually accompanied by servants of color who carried pieces of carpet and folding chairs for the comfort of their mistresses; prayer books, profuse jewelry, rosaries, fans, and other paraphernalia completed the devotional equipage. White women attended church dressed in black, their heads covered with black mantillas, while black and mulatto women wore white dresses. Much to the surprise of visitors from the United States, churches were not segregated according to race.[16]

Church was the best place for foreign visitors and Havana residents to catch an unobstructed glimpse of the proverbial beauty of the elusive Habaneras. Several sources state that this was in fact the only place to see white women. Some travel accounts written by men include detailed and somewhat lusty descriptions of native churchgoers of the opposite sex "whose graceful, voluptuous figures, bent down before the shrines." One visitor referred to the sight of a church filled with "pretty women" as a "source of amusement"; another described it as "a beautiful sight": "their necks and arms bare, and often resplendent with jewels; their dark glossy hair ornamented with pearls and flowers, and their exquisitely wrought fans, inlaid with gold and precious stones, 'glittering in their hands like so many butterflies.' "[17] Another traveler described female behavior inside a Havana church as disorderly and quite irreverent: "She kneels, but in the course of a few minutes sits. An ill-bred person would say, squats. Tired with the course of the ceremonial, she at length reclines. In the middle of the service the floor is strewn with a choice assortment of ladies' dress-goods with the ladies inside of them. At certain places in the ceremonial, it is necessary for everybody to place themselves again in a kneeling posture, and there is a general struggle to attain this end. To see two or three hundred women scrambling at once from a reclining to a kneeling position, has a tendency for the moment to destroy the solemn feeling one should have under these circumstances." Yet another observer described church as a rendezvous place of "gayety, and flirtation" where women communicated with the opposite sex via the "telegraphic fan."[18]

The few male "worshipers" to be found anywhere near a church remained, for the most part, strategically positioned either behind the interior columns or preferably just outside the doors, where they could catch "a glimpse of the pretty ankles ascending the steps of the *volantes*." According to one account, their actions and grins showed that they were "neither believers, nor ashamed of their unbelief." Another chronicler recounted that many of the men "merely come within the door, drop one knee, with their faces towards the principal altar, and utter a short, but scarcely audible prayer." Church authorities denounced the irreverent and disrespectful crowds of young men who habitually gathered outside the city's churches to see and talk to the young women before and after mass.[19]

Most Protestant foreigners, even those familiar with High Anglicanism, reacted negatively to what they perceived to be the excessive ceremony and senseless ritualism that went on inside Havana's places of worship. They could not find within the practices of Roman Catholicism the source of spiritual enrichment and fellowship they were used to having in their respective home congregations. They were particularly alienated by the fact that Roman Catholic priests read—or murmured—mass in Latin, in a seemingly hurried way, and with their backs toward the worshipers. They were also highly critical of several Roman Catholic practices and beliefs that clashed with their own, specifically the keeping of images, confessions, the infallibility of the Pope, the existence of a purgatory, and the intercessory role of the Virgin Mary and the saints.[20]

The Backhouses' arrival in Havana coincided with the culmination of the Christian calendar and the high point of the city's religious activity: Holy Week. This not only enhanced the visibility of Catholic fervor and public ritualism, it also heightened the Backhouses' sense of alienation and their longing for a Protestant place of worship. On her first Good Friday in Havana, only four days after their arrival, Grace dolefully wrote in her diary: "Friday—Good Friday—and no Church for us to go. Alas!" Two days later, on Easter Sunday, she jotted: "Happy day, would we could have spent it happily by going to Church." Grace and George continued to long for a Protestant church throughout the remainder of their stay in Havana.[21]

It was extremely difficult for anyone in Havana not to notice the advent of Holy Week. Beginning on the morning of Good Thursday, all business came to a halt and all carriages were banned by law from circulating in the city's streets. Even church bells remained silent as the entire city sunk into a doleful state of mourning. A woman from New York described Havana during Holy Thursday and Good Friday as having an "almost oppressive atmosphere of stillness and gloom."[22]

Holy Week was the time of year when Havana's churches, including the female portions of their congregations, overflowed torrentially into the city streets. As one traveler put it, it was the "only day of the year when dainty Havanese female feet press the pavements." Many men and women participated, and many more observed the processions that traversed Havana's unusually quiet streets. The processions served multiple purposes besides the obvious religious ones. For one thing, they helped reinforce the hierarchical nature of Cuban society. They also served the seemingly contradictory purposes of allowing role reversals and providing escape valves for women and other marginalized groups.[23]

Several contemporary observers, among them George and Grace, have left detailed accounts of Havana's Holy Week processions. There were a number of different processions scheduled throughout the religious calendar, and these were modified over the years. They usually included music, a funeral march dominated by the mournful beat of muffled drums. A few dozen black men wearing turbans and large scarfs carried torches at the head of some processions. Then followed priests and prelates, their robes indicating their order affiliation and rank. Some processions included someone representing Pontius Pilate, usually a tall black man "in tail coat and cocked hat." Then followed the hated Judas who shook a ten-foot pole crowned with a box containing the infamous thirty pieces of silver. Toward the end of Holy Week processions came a state bed with an effigy of the dead Christ, followed by a weeping image of the Lord's mother.[24]

Despite the solemn and gloomy nature of the entire affair, several observers recorded instances of irreverent and profane behavior, both among those who marched in the processions and within the crowds of spectators that lined the streets. Fredrika Bremer, who visited Cuba in the early 1850s, witnessed a procession in which, according to her, "not a particle of seriousness was observable." On the city's thin sidewalks, in the meantime, stood several hundred elegantly dressed Habaneras, some of whom wept inconsolably at the sight of the reenactment of Christ's martyrdom.[25]

Grace and many other contemporary foreign-born observers found much to criticize about Havana's religious processions. One Good Friday the Backhouses came across a procession that Grace scorned as "sadly idolatrous looking and strongly repulsive to our religious feelings." "There was no solemnity about it," she continued, "and the villagers & others who thronged the road were in holiday attire & holiday spirits." George described another procession, one in honor of Nuestra Señora del Pilar, as "a mixture of twelfth-cake, pantomime, & ballet."[26] One contemporary visitor criticized the "poverty of the materials" used to reenact scenes of Christ's death, which he insisted failed to create a reverent atmosphere. Another Protestant denounced the "*theatrical* representation of the crucifixion" as something "profane." Even foreign Roman Catholics were critical of what they saw. "A procession in Popayán, Seville or Rome is sumptuous, magnificent; in

Havana," explained a Colombian visitor, "it is the most ridiculous thing imaginable."[27]

Despite many visible signs to the contrary, the Roman Catholic faith in Cuba endured a profound crisis. The Catholic Church's wealth, political influence, and credibility among the general population deteriorated dramatically during the nineteenth century. This was part of a worldwide crisis aggravated in the Caribbean by the secularizing demands of agrarian capitalism. The wholesale confiscation of land and buildings belonging to religious orders during the late 1830s and early 1840s contributed further to the impoverishment of the church in Cuba.[28] A well-traveled Briton who visited Havana while the Backhouses lived there concluded that "Roman Catholic worship seems to be at a lower ebb in Cuba than almost any country in which I have ever seen it." Most other chroniclers left similar descriptions. Bremer emphatically remarked that "religion was dead in Cuba," while a British traveler reported that it had "no hold whatever on the masses."[29] Most Cubans reportedly avoided attending church and going to confession. They were said to have little faith in church doctrine and to hold the predominantly Spanish-born clergy in very low esteem. "Sabbath breaking, profane swearing, uncleanness, irreligion, and infidelity, are awfully prevalent," wrote the Englishman James Mursell Phillippo. Cubans, he concluded, "are practical atheists."[30]

For Grace and George and many other Protestants, one of the clearest indicators of Cuban irreligiosity was the widespread blatant inobservance of the Sabbath. One visitor from North America observed jokingly, "If any American were dropped suddenly down in Havana on Sunday, without being told what day it was, he would, likely as not, pronounce it Fourth of July." Sundays were indeed days of heightened frolic and fun. Sundays broke with a blast of noise, the city's many church bells tolling, and cannon firing from the forts and the Spanish men-of-war anchored in the bay. Stores opened soon after, and the city's residents embarked on a day-long pursuit of profit and pleasure.[31]

What offended devout Protestants the most was the fact that on Sundays, Habaneros engaged full throttle in worldly activities of the most profane and hedonistic kinds. Sabbaths were the big days of drinking, card playing, cock fighting, bull fighting, and mascarade dancing.[32] As a United States consul later put it, on Sundays, even during Lent, "everybody may dance, sing, eat meat, trade horses, and fight cocks with a clear conscience." On one occasion, the Backhouses declined an invitation to attend a gala ball at the Captains-General Palace on account of it being Sabbath. That night Grace recorded in her diary that Crawford and her Protestant neighbors, the Runges, went anyway.[33]

Young, devout, and idealistic as they were, upon their arrival in Roman Catholic Havana, George and Grace decided to work toward the establishment of a resident Church of England minister. On Easter Sunday, 1853, less than a week into their stay in Cuba, Grace and George bound themselves to donating £20, which an aunt of George's gave them, toward a subscription to bring an Anglican minister to the island.[34] It did not take long for Grace and George to learn of previous failed subscriptions and of the intransigent stance of local authorities, who would not permit non-Catholic services to take place. "I am quite down hearted on that subject," Grace wrote Mary Backhouse, "for the more enquiries I make the less I find reason to hope." Grace became so frustrated with the matter that she once confided in her aunt that "when the Bishop passes our house as he constantly does in his drives I feel quite inclined to stop him and appeal to his compassion."[35]

For hundreds of Protestants residing in Havana the presence of a resident minister would not become a reality until the arrival of the Reverend Edward Kenney in 1871. Even then, because of the convulsed state of political affairs, government and church authorities limited and closely monitored non-Catholic services. For the time being, Grace, George, and other Protestants had to settle for home services, occasional services on board British or United States ships, and the rare occurrence of an illegal private service held by a visiting clergyman.[36]

The many obstacles notwithstanding, Grace and George sought to cultivate their spiritual life in a context they perceived to be a spiritual wilderness of Godlessness and empty ritualism. Almost every Sunday, George and Grace, by themselves and sometimes with Hilton, held services in the privacy of their home. Usually they held one family service in the morning and another in the evening, including the reading of the scriptures, prayers, and sermons. Grace recorded in her diary each time they held home services and included information on special occurrences such as interruptions by unexpected visitors or the crying of one of their children. It was obvious that their home services were not an adequate substitute for the type of service they were used to attending at St. Paul's Church: "George & I read it together in the Eveg. How earnestly I wish we had a Church & Clergyman here!"[37]

Still, these private services and their prayers remained an important source of spiritual and emotional strength.

The calling of a British man-of-war was usually a source of joy for the Backhouses because it represented the arrival of a floating Anglican temple. During their sojourn in Havana, Grace and George, sometimes with Hilton and their children, attended Church of England services on board Her Britannic Majesty's ships *Boscawen, Vestal, Buzzard, Argus,* and others. The tense international climate surrounding the island of Cuba made for an almost continuous presence of British and U.S. ships of war. On-board Sunday services usually began by 10 A.M., and were well attended by resident communicants from Europe and the United States. A non-ordained chaplain, usually the ship's captain, officiated the services, which could include the reading of sermons and prayers, and communion. Some crews were more musically talented than others. The sailors of the *Argus,* for example, had a fine choir that sang hymns accompanied by the accordion of the vessel's first lieutenant. Another British vessel, *The Powerful,* had a large and "fine" band that played along with the ship's "full and effective choir."[38]

On-board services also provided a context for the gathering of Havana's spiritually neglected Protestant community. These were, perhaps, the only activities in which British subjects and citizens of the United States participated together in some harmony. With some contempt, however, Grace wrote in her diary that in a February 1855 service on board the *Vestal* there were "a great many Yankee ladies." The ships' captains usually displayed ample hospitality toward visitors coming on board for services, including tours of the vessel and in some special instances hearty lunches.[39]

A few of Her Majesty's vessels calling in the port of Havana had ordained naval chaplains who could perform the sacramental ceremonies of the Church of England. Three months into their stay in Havana, the Backhouses learned of the visit of Naval Chaplain Hannan on board the *Alban.* "My heart beat high with hopes that he would say the prayers on board the Buzzard," Grace wrote home, "but alas! I was disappointed for Captain Dobbie officiated himself."[40] The following Sunday, Hannan officiated a private service at the Crawfords' residence; he said prayers, delivered a sermon, and baptized the son of businessman Charles Tolmé, Sally Crawford's brother. The Backhouses missed that service too, because in Grace's words they "were not positively invited to join them." They planned to go anyway but torrential rains kept them home. Grace wrote home that the chaplain's visit to "this obscured Island" "resulted in no benefit to us with regard to the services of our Church." Referring to another chaplain who visited the port, Grace wrote that he was "a sad subject!"[41]

As far from ideal as they were, for many Protestants residing in Havana the occasional visiting Protestant clergymen were the only source of sacraments. The Catholic Church held firm control over baptisms, marriages, and burials and reserved those ceremonies exclusively for Catholics; there was no such thing as civil birth registration, or civil marriage, and the state church controlled access to the island's burial grounds. As Consul James W. Steele eloquently put it, the Catholic Church "begins at the beginning, and sends the infant into the world with a ceremony and accompanying documents without which it is impossible at any time thereafter to prove legitimacy. She afterward solemnizes a marriage for him, which no other has the power to do," "[A]nd with out her," Steele added, "you had better not die."[42]

Protestants residing in Havana had few options regarding these most vital milestones in their lives. Parents waited months or years before having their children christened by a passing clergyman of their own faith. Couples lived in concubinage either because they rejected Catholic matrimony or because it was denied to them. Dying Protestants passed on unceremoniously, their minds tormented with images of inadequate burials in some gruesome unconsecrated potter's field.

Soon after their arrival in Havana, the Backhouses began to worry about baptismal arrangements for the child they were expecting. Their second child, a baby boy, was born on October 26, 1853, seven months after they arrived in Cuba. Coincidentally, the HMS *Vestal* called in Havana on October 28 with a naval chaplain on board, Mr. Henry Parmister. George made arrangements on the very next day to have his son christened. The Backhouse family physician, Dr. Charles N. Belot, gave orders that the four-day-old infant "on no account" leave his room, so George arranged for the chaplain and the guests to come to their house. On Sunday, October 30, at noon, Parmister officiated a service at Crawford's house, where he married a couple and christened eight children; he then proceeded up la Calzada del Monte to the Backhouse residence in the company of Crawford and Mrs. Scharfenberg. Grace, who was waiting at home, had prepared the ceremony's setting. She set aside a little white and pink glass vase to be used as the baptismal tank and arranged the participants' placement so that the clergyman stood facing east. George, Grace, and Crawford stood in the place of the absent and unsuspecting sponsors, who were John Mullins Sandham, Grace's father, Clara Catherine Belcher, an aunt, and James Nicholson, an uncle. Hilton held the baby's older sister, while the chaplain christened her brother with the name John Sandham. Unbeknownst to them, George had been christened on October 30, thirty-five years before.[43]

Roman Catholic intolerance followed Protestants all the way to their graves. As one traveler from the United States put it, "[t]he charities of the Cubans, such as they are, do not extend to the bodies of dead Protestants." One United States consul summarized the predicaments of moribund Protestants on the island when he bluntly advised his compatriots: "Don't die in Cuba."[44] The Catholic Church in Cuba held firm control over funeral services, burials, and cemeteries. In the words of one critical contemporary, "[t]he Mother Church is the mistress of ceremonies of all kinds. She owns the cemeteries practically, is interested in the sale of coffins and management of hearses, buries the dead, licenses the inhuming and exhuming of all bodies." Crypto-Protestants and nominal Catholics who either avoided Catholic rites or received Protestant sacraments were well aware of this situation and, not surprisingly, many of them either converted to, or returned to, the Catholic faith during their final days.[45]

North Americans and Europeans from Protestant countries were denied funeral ceremonies and burial in consecrated ground unless their surviving friends and relatives could produce evidence of catholicity. Since licenses granted by local curates were required before corpses could be interred in the cemeteries, the authority to determine who could and could not be buried lay strictly within the Catholic Church.[46]

Most foreigners suspected of not being Catholic were buried in so-called potter's fields, unfenced makeshift cemeteries in desolate and remote locations. A host of North American and British residents and visitors have left poignant testimonies about these inadequate burial grounds. One described a potter's field near Havana in these terms: "Here the space for burial is so limited that the defunct have even but a temporary occupancy of this channel-house, and a new incumbent cannot be deposited without turning out previous occupants. As a consequence, therefore, the ground is strewn with the bleaching relics of mortality, and in one corner is a heap, most of skulls, several yards

**Funeral procession.** (Drawing by Samuel Hazard from his book *Cuba with Pen and Pencil*.)

high." Another visitor described similar scenes: "Thousands of bones lie either in heaps or scattered over the burying grounds, exposed to the scorching rays of the sun, or bleach in the dews of night." The controversial British Consul-General David Turnbull once complained directly to the captain-general, describing the Protestants' burial grounds as a place "where dead bodies are left exposed . . . and where the Vulture contends with the worm for his share of the human spoil." Of Protestant burials, yet another contemporary observer wrote: "Uncoffined and unshrouded, for the most part, the dead are flung into shallow graves, whence they will soon be jostled by their successors in the endless procession."[47]

Relatives of Protestants who died unexpectedly sometimes made efforts to have the remains of their loved ones transported to the United States or Europe for burial there. Many obstacles, however, were thrown in the way of such efforts by the Spanish colonial state and the Catholic Church. Those bodies already buried with Catholic rites had to be disinterred also with Catholic rites at great expense if relatives sought their relocation. Other provisions stipulated that corpses could not be disinterred before the elapse of a two-year period, unless the body had been embalmed at the time of burial, and that no other remains could be disturbed in the process. Surviving relatives of some who died in Cuba opted to have their remains embalmed for shipment abroad. In 1860 physicians charged the exorbitant amount of $500 for embalming a cadaver.[48]

Quite understandably, religious intolerance was one of the main sources of friction between visitors from predominantly Protestant countries and their Catholic hosts in Cuba. This remained a continuous source of anxiety and longing for Grace and George, who strove to keep their faith alive. Many foreigners found enormous relief when they left Cuba and returned to their own congregations under the spiritual care of their clergymen. "As we passed the Morro Castle," wrote an embittered contemporary of the Backhouses, "I thought of the dishonesty, bigotry and cruelty practiced in the place we had just left, under the sanction of Roman Catholicism."[49]

# VII

## A Land Flowing with Milk and Pestilence

If George's predecessor's statement about having lived thirteen years in Havana and not being sick a single day was true, it was certainly not the norm, particularly among foreigners. Havana was by most standards an unhealthy place. Insalubrity and sickness reached a fatal peak just prior to the Backhouses' arrival as attested in the official correspondence between Havana and London. In the fall of 1852, Crawford reported to the Foreign Office that yellow fever was "in abundance and of the most malignant description. Cholera also prevails to a great extent and the small pocks have recently made their appearance with great virulence and fatality." Some 30,000 people, mostly slaves, died during the cholera epidemic of 1850–54, producing a larger than usual demand for illegally imported slaves. On December 16, 1852, the day before offering George the Havana post, Under Secretary Addington sent Crawford a dispatch stating that as long as yellow fever prevailed in Cuba no British subject should be sent there on Royal Mail Ships.[1]

Unacclimated immigrants and transients from higher latitudes were particularly vulnerable to the onslaught of tropical diseases prevailing in the Caribbean during the warm and rainy seasons. Paradoxically, during the winters Cuba was a favorite health resort for invalids from North America. Doctors advised European migrants to become acclimated first in the Canary Islands, and upon their arrival in Havana to abstain from "excesses in drinking, romantic pleasures, insomnia, violent or depressing passions, exposures to the cold, and eating." In Havana mortality rates among recently arrived foreigners reached appalling levels of between 260 and 400 per thousand. Urban Havana was, according to contemporary statistics, one of Cuba's most insalubrious districts, with a mortality rate of 36 per thousand, almost 40 percent higher than the rate in the rural districts of the Diocese of Havana.[2] One United States consul referred to mid-nineteenth-century Havana as one of the "foulest" ports in the world. Another foreigner, Robert Francis Jameson, a British official during the early days of the Mixed Commission, blamed Havana's proverbial unhealthiness on the fact that the city's fortifications obstructed the free circulation of air currents, creating "a stagnant cloud of fetid vapour, exhaled from a crowded population and the marshy shores of the harbour." Jameson concluded that no other place in the Caribbean was "so replete with the seeds of mortality as the *Havana*."[3]

The most dreaded foe of the unacclimated foreigner was yellow fever, a virus transmitted by mosquitoes that thrive in stagnant water. The source, however, was not known then, as the scientific knowledge of the time attributed the disease to atmospheric miasmas. The link between yellow fever and mosquitoes was not established until later in the century, when during the early 1880s the Cuban scientist Carlos J. Finlay began to put forth the hypothesis that yellow fever was transmitted through mosquitoes. Mid-century folk medicine prescribed several ways to avoid contracting yellow fever, including avoiding exposure to the moon and sun, not eating fruit at night, and keeping one's stomach covered at all times. During the 1850s experiments were carried out in Cuba to develop a vaccine against yellow fever; scientists involved in the project erroneously believed that they had extracted and isolated the virus from morning dew.[4]

Yellow fever, or *vómito negro* as Cubans used to call it, was responsible for the vast majority of deaths among the newly arrived and was also responsible for numerous deaths among the native population. Data collected in the Diocese of Havana in 1843 show that yellow fever was the second most common cause of death among the population of Havana and its outskirts (8 percent) after pulmonary consumption (19 percent). Similar data for 1871 indicate that more than 10 percent of deaths in Cuba's capital were the result of yellow fever.

This disease was particularly deadly among white adult males. Yellow fever caused about one-third of deaths within this group. More specific data from hospitals serving colonial troops (almost exclusively Spanish-born) and foreign sailors point to the fact that between 50 and 70 percent of those dying in such facilities were victims of yellow fever. These proportions are corroborated by an 1857 register of fatalities in three Havana hospitals and on board U.S. ships calling at the port, which included 114 dead, all but four of whom died of yellow fever.[5]

Yellow fever epidemics, like the region's other curse, hurricanes, had their peaks during the hot, rainy months of the year. June, July, August, and September were particularly deadly. Alexander M. Clayton, a U.S. consul, stated that upon his arrival in the middle of July 1853 he found "yellow fever raging as an epidemic, in an unusually malignant form, and attacking every unacclimated person, in a very short time." Consul Clayton lost a dear friend during the sickly season of 1854 and returned to the United States soon after that, asserting that he was "unwilling either to live apart from [his] family, or take them to such a climate." In an August 1856 dispatch, United States Vice-Consul Thomas Savage reported that within "the last six or seven weeks almost every one of our vessels has had a greater portion of the crew in the Hospital." He added that three masters, eleven mates, and thirty-four seamen had died during that period.[6] Unacclimated Europeans were advised to arrive in Cuba between early October and February, preferably either in October or November. Arrival during the hot rainy season was to be avoided altogether. Those foreign residents who could manage and could afford it left Cuba each year after the middle of May. Even the British warships, reported Grace, "keep quite aloof from this unhealthy harbour" during the summer months.[7]

The Backhouses reached Havana in the last week of March 1853, not the sickly season yet, but only two months away from it. George had most probably heard about the previous season's yellow fever epidemic and must have become very concerned about the health of his loved ones as well as his own. Within three days of their arrival, Grace got sick. The Backhouse documents do not specify any of her symptoms but it is possible that they were related to her entering her second month of pregnancy. With Crawford and Dalrymple's assistance, George sought the services of Dr. Charles N. Belot, the English-speaking physician who served many among Havana's foreign resident elite. Grace and George had a good first impression of Dr. Belot. "We liked what we saw of him very much," George wrote home. From that day on and for the remainder of their stay in Havana, Dr. Belot served as the Backhouse family physician, the man who more than anyone else in Cuba got to know their bodies and their minds, the man who shared in the Backhouses' happiest and saddest moments. While in Havana, the Backhouses also recurred to a foreign-born dentist, Mr. Biddle from the United States.[8]

A Spaniard by nationality, the New Orleans–born Dr. Belot sported degrees from the universities of Paris, Leipzig, and Madrid. He tended to the medical needs of many among the foreign population from the British consul-general to penniless dying sailors of U.S. merchant ships. He made home and on-board visits, had an office in the Intramuros section of Havana, and owned a three-hundred-bed private clinic across the bay in Regla, which served mostly foreigners.[9]

Later in his career Dr. Belot became the center of a professional controversy, when he expanded his services to provide burials in a cemetery not far from his clinic. Dr. Belot, it so happened, managed not only to bury his mistakes, he was also able to make a profit on them.[10] In 1858 the U.S. consul denounced the practices of the lowland clinics, stating that their proprietors obtained "a large part of their profits" from burying the dead. He pointed out quite caustically that patients were better clients dead than alive, for each death produced a net profit of seventeen pesos. The consul's successor, Charles Helm, also expressed concern over this matter. In a letter to Dr. Belot, he "represented the evil growing out of the charge of $25.50 for the burial of a destitute seaman," underscoring "the effect upon the mind of the patient, the impression that it was more profitable to kill than cure him, and specially the injury which might result to his own reputation." Dr. Belot finally yielded to the mounting pressures and promised to "surrender all profit in the futur [*sic*] from the private cemetery attached to the hospital." He agreed "only [to] exact the church fee $7.50, the charge for digging the grave $2 and cost of intermens [sic] and ground $2, making in all $11.50, the coffin to be furnished by the ship master or the [consulate]." Dr. Belot later developed a health insurance scheme that eventually became the model for Cuba's mutualistic medical insurance plans, the quintas, whose name derived from the lowland quinta (resort home) where Dr. Belot had his clinic. The section of Regla, across the bay from Havana, in which the clinic stood is still referred to as Belot.[11]

The Backhouses recurred to Dr. Belot dozens of times for treatment of their ailments and those of their servants. During their first sickly season in Havana, George and Grace came down with what appeared to be yellow fever. Dr. Belot began treating them on September 16; he sent them to bed and prescribed "[l]ots of Castor Oil" and lemonade. On September 19 a bed-ridden George jotted in his diary: "Dr. Bellot [*sic*] found Grace getting better. He said I was attacked worse than she, & considered me very feverish and nervous. I felt very irritable. Had 44 leeches in the afternoon, the application most tedious; the whole business occupied more than 2 hours, I lying most of the time in one position wh[ich] became excruciatingly painful. Lost a great deal of blood. Could scarcely stand. Tried to sit up for a foot bath. Turned faint & was obliged to lie down without the foot bath, after an injection. A mustard plaster to the & small of my back to relieve the pain I had been suffering there. Bad night." The next day George reported having no more fever, and having had "weak chicken broth," the first source of nourishment since he had fallen ill four days earlier.[12] Caroline Langley, the maid who arrived at the Backhouse household from England that week, fell ill too and became very nervous. At around the same time Hilton contracted what Dr. Belot diagnosed to be yellow fever and was treated with a mustard plaster. In an official dispatch to the Foreign Office, George wrote: "Sickness here generally by yellow fever has been, I believe, unusually great this season, and has attacked very strongly the ships in the harbour."[13]

At the beginning of the sickly season of 1854, the Backhouses again had a bout with the tropical fevers. Late in April, Dr. Belot confirmed Grace's suspicion that she was "in the family way," and estimated that she was in her fourth month. On May 13, he diagnosed George with either smallpox or scarlet fever. Three days later Grace fell ill and had a miscarriage while at home. Grace's fever symptoms continued until the end of the month.[14]

Some of Dr. Belot's remedies placed his craft closer to the art of gourmet cooking than to the science of medicine. He applied plasters of mustard, bread, oil, vinegar, and pepper, which elicited one contemporary to remark that he seasoned and stuffed his patients "with herbs, fit for roasting." Dr. Belot also prescribed quinine to fight fevers, administered calomel—a paste of mercury and chlorine—to soothe the digestive track, and gave injections of unspecified concoctions to combat other maladies. He was a strong believer in leeching, a treatment that doubtless hurt more than it helped given that anemia accompanied many of the fevers affecting his clientele.[15]

There were some complaints that Dr. Belot did not take his female patients seriously enough. When Caroline Langley got sick, he cured her by simply laughing at her, reported Grace. Grace believed that Dr. Belot did not take some of her own symptoms seriously. "Dr. Belot is a funny man," she wrote, "when he has reduced you to an extreme of weakness he calls you *quite well* and pays very little attention to you."[16]

Of all the family's illnesses none was more excruciating, prolonged, and emotionally draining than the one endured by little Johnny Backhouse. No topic in the Backhouse correspondence, particularly in Grace's, took more attention than Johnny's seven-month-long battle with a digestive disorder.

Johnny was born on October 26, 1853. On that night, after what must have been a particularly long and tiring day, the baby's proud father recorded in his diary: "Just ten Minutes after Midnight consequently this Morning, came into this World a little Boy with a very large head & face, our Son & Heir!!!" Like most parents, George and Grace rejoiced at the arrival of their perfectly normal and healthy child. As she had done for Alice, now sixteen months old, Grace dutifully breast-fed little Johnny right from the beginning.[17]

A few weeks into lactation Grace began to signal some problems. She referred to Johnny as "a very hungry baby," and in a letter to her mother-in-law confided: "I am not such a good nurse as I was with Alice." When Johnny was a little over three months old, Grace was seriously considering weaning him and placing the little native on a diet of arrowroot from which source, she reported, he got "his chief support." Johnny seemed to be getting along well and healthy and Grace attested that he was "very good . . . at night."[18]

By the last week of February 1854, Johnny was close to being weaned. He was then four months old and consumed mostly cow's milk and purees of assorted tubers. On February 20, the baby fell ill, was restless, and vomited most of what he ingested. Grace attributed the baby's symptoms to her own milk and weaned him at once. That day George went to get Dr. Belot. The doctor feared that Johnny had contracted brain fever, "an illness," he said, "infants are very subject to in this country." Upon further observation he realized that the child suffered a digestive disorder, probably an allergy or gastrointestinal reflux, and prescribed him a gram of calomel and some castor oil. For the next ten days Johnny's symptoms persisted. Dr. Belot visited him every day, usually twice a day, and experimented with different doses of castor oil and calomel. He also ordered the little patient's stomach rubbed with almond oil, *aguardiente,* and quinine. Dr. Belot ordered milk eliminated from Johnny's diet and prescribed a new one based on barleyed water.[19]

During the first two weeks of March, Johnny continued to be ill, throwing up most of his meals. On the night of March 10, Dr. Belot came to the Backhouses and placed Johnny on a new diet, "bread boiled and the bread well squeezed and Baby to drink the water." He told Grace that it might become necessary for her to arrange for a wet nurse. On the next day Grace wrote in her diary: "Baby very ill all night, digested nothing, Dr. Belot came."[20] That day, one of Mrs. Runge's servants delivered a note for Grace. "Dear Mrs. Backhouse," Mrs. Runge wrote, "I feel so very sorry about your baby, an idea has just struck me which I must communicate to you immediately, perhaps he could digest my milk as it is so very young & perhaps we could get him to suck me, you know woman's milk is more easily digested than anything send me word and I will come immediately or if you wish to ask the Dr. first do so & let me know, you know if he takes the breast you can afterwards get him a wet nurse, *do* not wait to decide till it is too late. Do not be offended or think me officious for I have not considered a moment as soon as the thought rose in my brain I have put it to paper so do you answer as frankly[.] y[ou]rs F. R[unge]."[21]

Mrs. Runge's note caught Grace by surprise; her first reaction was to wait to hear what Dr. Belot had to say about the matter. Later that day, Mrs. Runge, who had a four-week-old baby of her own, walked to the Backhouse residence and convinced Grace to let her feed Johnny right away. Grace agreed. Once inside the nursery Mrs. Runge uncovered her milk-swollen breasts and gently pulled Johnny into her bosom. Twice more during the night Mrs. Runge returned to feed little Johnny. That night Grace jotted in her diary: "I cannot express my full sense of her *great* kindness. Dear Baby was better for it." On the next day, a Sunday, Mrs. Runge came over four times. Little Johnny was taken to her twice on the following day. Grace wrote home that "poor Baby was delighted to be nursed in such a way again, from that time he certainly began to mend."[22]

Feeding two babies, her own and Johnny, and walking back and forth between nurseries proved to be an exhausting task. Mrs. Runge complained of headaches and hinted to Grace that she could not continue feeding Johnny much longer. Mrs. Runge breast-fed the Backhouse baby less than four days; enough, however, for his parents to remain forever grateful to her. In their correspondence with England, Grace and George credited Mrs. Runge with having saved their baby's life, and as a token of their gratitude they presented Johnny's "foster sister" with a silver cup and saucer set. From that time on Grace and Mrs. Runge developed a very special close bond.[23]

The Backhouses sought new alternatives to Johnny's nourishment right away. Sally Crawford called to suggest the Backhouses hire a wet nurse, an Irish woman whom she believed was available. They soon found out, much to Grace's sorrow, that the wet nurse was already engaged.[24] George, who followed up on another of Dr. Belot's suggestions, came home with a black goat, not very tame. There were very few goats around Havana. The one they got belonged to an Englishman who was kind enough to lend it to the Backhouses. Someone else had earlier tried to exact an exorbitant £34 for another goat. Dr. Belot gave orders that Johnny suck directly from the animal but Grace described the task as a great misery. They eventually settled for feeding him two spoonfuls of freshly milked goat's milk every two hours and an occasional sip of sugar water to quench Johnny's thirst. By March 23, a more calmed Grace reported that Johnny, though still thin, was improving and was "more hungry, and more lively. Yesterday he took to laughing quite in his old way."[25]

George jokingly described his struggles with the black goat thus: "[Mother], [y]ou will have heard from Grace how entirely a Goat was made afterwards to take the place of a wolf to this little 'Romulus' of ours; that classical mode of proceeding did not suit his taste though strongly advocated by the doctor; & now the goat is milked several times a day & the milk put into a bottle for him to suck. I flatter myself I have become rather a good hand at milking a goat. Grace thinks I manage to get more at a time than anybody else. The little boy for whom this is done is improoving very steadily but not quite fast enough to please Grace. His appetite increases, & milk sometimes runs short." On April 4, George brought a new goat, this time a white one; the other one was running out of milk and this one had a plentiful supply.[26] Later in the month, Dr. Belot allowed some more food, three tablespoons of weak arrowroot and four drops of sherry to be followed by a tablespoonful of orange peel tea. Johnny's diet still centered around goat's milk, which did not prove to be entirely satisfactory; diarrhea and vomiting continued to torment the infant. Dr. Belot insisted, and little Johnny would have certainly agreed, on the benefits of woman's milk.[27]

A Victorian mother, who viewed feeding her child as her own obligation, Grace disliked the idea of a stranger feeding her child, particularly a native woman of color. On a letter dated March 19, Grace wrote to her mother-in-law that she "would *much* rather not have a wet nurse." A few weeks earlier, she had expressed "horror" at the mere thought of another woman's breasts feeding her child. Cándida, a native of the Canary Islands, started working at the Backhouses' shortly after Johnny's birth. Grace wrote a letter home expressing her disgust when Cándida gave her "ocular demonstration . . . of having lately had a baby to nurse. This baby she told me was dead, a horror came over me that she would be feeding my boy some day so I quickly gave strict orders to Hilton on no account to leave her alone with him." Grace interrogated Cándida further and learned that she had lost her baby, had had seven other children, only two of whom were still alive, had never been married, and led what Grace deemed a "sadly immoral life," a characteristic she attributed to all Canarian women. In an earlier letter she had expressed qualms about hiring a black under nurse. "I intend setting aside my dislikes," she wrote Mary Backhouse, "and if possible engaging a *clean tidy blackie* to act as under nurse."[28] The idea of hiring a wet nurse was intimately tied to notions of race and class and to profound emotional issues of physical inadequacy and domestic control. To the Backhouses, the whiter the nurse the sweeter the milk, and this held true for goats as well. In their view it all went downhill after Mrs. Runge, who was acceptable as a European woman of their own class. The Irish wet nurse whose breasts never came close to little Johnny, for she had already been hired, would have also been acceptable.

Johnny's deteriorating condition forced Grace to consider milk from other sources. He was still very thin and weak; in his mother's words he was "quite a painful object to look at."[29] There were many slave and free women of color who were rented out or rented themselves for such purposes. Prolonged lactation was a common practice among them and the high mortality among their own children made their breasts for hire available to the hungry children of the master class. In some instances slave women were forced to prematurely wean their own infants to begin feeding their masters' children. Among some West African ethnic groups it was considered a source of extraordinary talents when a child was breast-fed by many women.[30]

On May 27, Grace learned of an available wet nurse from a newspaper advertisement: "For rent or for sale[,] a black Creole woman of around 20 years of age who has just given birth, with her infant boy; has good and abundant milk, is a good cook and excellent presser of men's clothes, very loyal, humble and loving of children, . . . [has] no blemishes or diseases. Arrangements will be made in Calle de Villegas #17 between calles O'Reilly and La Bomba."[31] Grace immediately sent her servant, Manuel, off to the city to fetch the woman. Manuel returned home with a black woman who carried a two-month-old baby. "[N]ot strong enough" to suck the woman's breasts, Johnny was given spoonfuls of the white rays of milk that spurted out of the woman's dark and seasoned nipples. Later that night, Dr. Belot delivered a new set of instructions: the wet nurse was to sleep in the nursery and give Johnny two tablespoons of her milk every hour. Hilton was not happy with the idea of sharing the nursery with this "savage" woman, whose pendular breasts had become the center of all attention. She smoked and spat freely, besides. The very next day Grace sent off the black wet nurse, who remained nameless in her diary and correspondence. "[S]he would give all her milk to her own child," Grace complained, "& starve my poor darling Baby."[32]

After having noticed some improvement since the latest doses of woman's milk, Grace decided to go back to the paper ads, this time with want ads of her own that read: "Wanted, a nurse for a little boy. In Calle de Buenos Aires n. 3."[33] On the day in which the ads came out, two women called. One, "a Spaniard by birth," had just lost her baby and was available; according to Grace she had "a most plentiful supply of milk." As it turned out, Dr. Belot knew her and recommended her highly. The baby began to suck her immediately and for a few weeks "lived entirely upon her." Grace and George were satisfied with this new, also nameless, wet nurse, who, according to Grace, devoted herself fully to their child. The only problem that the Backhouses found with the arrangement was that the wet nurse's husband and other relatives gave the Backhouses "more of their company than [they] wished for."[34] The Spanish wet nurse fed Johnny for about a month and then, for some unspecified reason, moved on or was let go. Under her nourishment the baby's condition improved markedly to the point that by late June, as Johnny approached eight months, his mother reported that although "not fat yet" he had "certainly lost the extremely miserable look he had of starvation and wretchedness."[35]

Johnny's next wet nurse was apparently a woman of color; she proved satisfactory until her own baby, Camila, fell ill and the woman who took care of her and "*partly* nursed" her could not do it any longer. The baby's mother then told Grace that she could continue nursing Johnny only if she could nurse her own baby as well. This, Grace was "unwilling to do because the Baby [Camila] is not over clean and *my* Baby wants so very much milk I am afraid she would never have enough for the two."[36]

So off Grace went in search of yet another wet nurse, one that would devote the fullness of her breasts to "master Johnie." She sought a white woman who had placed an ad, but she was already taken. Then she tried a black woman, a slave, but found her "such a savage in appearance & so dirty looking," that she "would not venture upon a trial with her." These failures moved Grace to consider rehiring the previous wet nurse, the one who insisted on bringing little Camila along. Grace felt that Johnny had improved so much with his latest nameless wet nurse that she was willing to allow her to share her milk with her own daughter. For a few weeks the wet nurse's sister also stayed at the Backhouses' to help take care of Camila, who according to Grace did not "feel at home with its mother."[37]

On August 9 the wet nurse's sister left the Backhouse residence and the very next day the wet nurse wanted to be off too. This latest episode sent George and Grace to "some very tumble down street" in search of a new wet nurse; they failed to find one that day. A visit from the wet nurse's sister was enough to keep the wet nurse at the Backhouses. She needed the money and had the milk, Grace had the money and her child needed the milk. In September, Camila's mother wanted to be off again but Dr. Belot gave her a lecture that Grace hoped would "make her patient to the end." In the meantime, ten-month-old Johnny's diet had expanded to include sospiro cakes, tea, coffee, and soup; all of it agreed with him.[38]

When Johnny reached eleven months, Dr. Belot said that the nurse could be relieved of her duties. "[I]t is a very great relief to be rid of her & her little child, who was a great screamer & never clean," Grace wrote her mother-in-law. By the time Johnny was a year old he had been fed by at least five different women, including his own mother, and by two goats. He would grow to be an exceedingly talented man, according to the Yoruba belief. On his first birthday Grace rejoiced in jotting down in her diary, "He is fat, lively, strong, & very merry fellow, but he cannot walk or stand alone yet."[39]

# VIII

## The Return Home

The 1854–55 juncture was marked by increased political tensions with a bearing on George's work at the Mixed Commission. Britain's abolitionist pressures, and the arrival of Captain-General Pezuela, a moderate abolitionist, created a tense environment that sparked the mobilization of pro-slavery interests in both Cuba and the United States. Grace remained hopeful that an international crisis over Cuba would explode and send them home "long before we ever dreamt of coming." This period was also one of personal trials and tribulations for the Backhouses. In 1854, Johnny endured his tormentuous gastrointestinal illness and Grace suffered a miscarriage. It was also the year when the Backhouses lost control over their financial situation and when Grace's closest friends left the island. If the Backhouses' first year in Havana had been difficult and traumatic, many of the problems they faced during their second year heightened their sense of homesickness and brought them to the brink of desperation.

Armed with extraordinary powers and carrying explicit instructions to terminate the slave trade and to liberate those slaves declared emancipados before 1835, Pezuela arrived in Havana on December 2, 1853.[1] Within days of having taken office, Pezuela began an unprecedented crusade against the slave trade that embodied many of

Turnbull's goals of a decade earlier. He declared free all emancipados who had served their terms and established fines and banishment for anyone caught smuggling slaves.[2] Pezuela's January 1, 1854, decree established that all slaves imported since 1835 had been illegally imported and therefore must be declared free. On May 2, 1854, he ordered that plantations suspected of harboring illegally imported slaves be searched, and that from then on all plantations had to keep registers of their slaves. Later that month, Pezuela proceeded with two moves that further convinced his critics that he was seeking to Africanize the island of Cuba, or in other words, to establish a majority population of free blacks. On May 22, Pezuela, in accordance with the bishop of Havana, lifted the ban on interracial marriages. Two days later he issued orders for the reactivation of free black militias. During Pezuela's tenure a record eleven expeditions and 2,699 slaves were captured. Pezuela also forced Francisco Marty to return some of the illegally captured Yucatecan workers that he had brought to Cuba.[3]

Through his controversial decrees against the slave trade, Pezuela managed to alienate virtually all the powerful elements of Cuban society and his actions helped spark a new wave of Cuban annexationism and United States filibusterism, movements that fed on the fear of the island's Africanization.[4] Cuba's white elites viewed Pezuela's measures with great alarm as these seemed to confirm the existence of an Anglo–Spanish conspiracy to liberate Cuba's slaves. Cuba's annexationists responded by pressuring filibusterer leader John A. Quitman into swift action and by starting an annexationist conspiracy under the leadership of the Spaniard Ramón Pintó.[5]

The United States government also responded to Pezuela's measures with much concern. Ten days after the publication of Pezuela's May 3 decree prescribing estate searches, the U.S. consul in Havana reported that the island was "on the eve of a fearful revolution." A special agent deployed to Havana by the U.S. secretary of state echoed the consul's fears and blamed the commotion on British schemes.[6] In part to bridle the growing filibustering expansionist thrust, the Franklin Pierce administration maneuvered to purchase Cuba from Spain, something totally unacceptable for Spain. Frustration over the failure of the Cuba purchase attempt led to a desperate move on the part of U.S. ministers stationed in Europe, who produced the Ostende Manifesto, a document that threatened to take Cuba by force if Spain refused to sell it.[7]

Pezuela's unceremonious recall in September 1854 and the return of Concha to the island's highest post signaled some dramatic changes for Cuba as well as for the triangular geopolitical struggle over it. Concha succeeded in confronting Cuba's pressing political crisis by applying a successful combination of conciliation and force. He first calmed the fears of Cuba's white population by repealing his predecessor's most controversial decrees. Concha reestablished the allotment of emancipados and put in place mechanisms to keep better track of their numbers and their whereabouts.[8] Concha, who during his previous term had dealt harshly with López's filibusterers, uncovered the brewing annexationist conspiracy. "No end of arrests have taken place in Cuba," wrote George to his brother Johnny, "including Priests 2 in number, & several other people of some importance, Creoles, Spaniards, & other nations." Just as on a previous occasion, Concha used strong-arm measures to repress the conspirators, presiding over the executions of his friend Ramón Pintó, Francisco Estrampes, and José Elías Hernández in March 1855. Meanwhile, a month later, the Pierce administration convinced Quitman to abandon the filibuster plans under way. In April 1855 he resigned his command and disbanded his 10,000-troop army. Thus, within a matter of weeks both the internal and external movements that threatened Spain's rule over the island dissipated.[9]

These developments altered the geopolitical equation in profound ways. With the United States no longer hovering menacingly over Cuba, Spain could assert greater independence vis-à-vis the abolitionist pressures of Great Britain. Not once but twice, British pressures for the abolition of the slave trade had backfired, pushing the island's annexationists and North America's expansionists to the brink of liberating Cuba and annexing it to the United States. Following the Africanization scare of 1854 the British government pursued a new Cuba policy of toned-down abolitionism and reduced hostility toward the United States. The limited extent of British abolitionism was made evident by this policy position: Cuba with slaves under Spanish rule was preferable to a slave-based or free-labor Cuba under the United States. George was caught in the middle of this unexpected policy shift.[10]

The Backhouses' financial standing deteriorated in 1854, as evidenced by the frequency with which they addressed economic matters in their diaries and correspondence. They were forced to cut expenses in nonessential areas such as gifts and recreation. Sketches drawn by George and Grace and locks of hair of the Backhouse children replaced shop-purchased gifts for their relatives and friends in England. On the occasion of George's thirty-sixth birthday Grace baked a cake and wished her husband "*many most* happy returns," but regretted that she "could not give him a present because we are so poor." A few days earlier Grace had asked her mother-in-law to purchase a gift for Cattie, her friend in London, "for though we are acting upon *strict, economical principles* just now, yet we cannot give up the pleasure of giving them a wedding present." George and Grace also cut back on horseback riding and other "*luxuries*" in an effort to get rid of their "*nasty debts.*"[11]

Signals of serious economic distress peaked in the spring of 1854. In a letter to her mother-in-law dated May 1, Grace candidly shared the state of their precarious finances: "I am often checked in my wish to get some little toy, so I make a great deal of a pain of new shoes, or a pot of pomatine, or a new bit of soap." At the time, George's bank account at Drummonds, where his salary was deposited by a fellow Foreign Office official, repeatedly ran short of money in the light of mounting pressures from several overdue bills, among them an £120 inn bill incurred during their honeymoon. George's mother made numerous loan deposits to cover his drafts.[12] Personal indebtedness was endemic among middle-class Londoners and even more so among British officials serving abroad.

At this juncture, George and Grace began to explore solutions to their serious money problems and approached their relatives in search of help. On April 2, George wrote what must have been a difficult letter to send home: he asked his mother to inquire with an uncle to see if he would be willing to make him a substantial loan. "I am thinking of asking James Nicholson," he wrote, "if he has any objection to lend me—at not less than 5 per cent per ann: interest—£400. If he could & would do that, I would bind myself to repay it in a year & a half at most." George offered his life insurance policy as security for the proposed loan: "If I should die before the expiration of that time, he must be paid out of my £1200 life insurance." He explained that he did not like the idea of offering such security to any local merchant-lender. Havana, he knew well, was a dangerous place and 1854 was an extraordinarily perilous year.[13]

The object of the loan, Grace explained in another letter, was to consolidate their mounting debts, which at the time were draining one-half of the household income: "If all our debts were paid and we owed to *one person only* a certain sum to be paid off as quickly as we possibly could that we should *right* our affairs much sooner than if we owed money to several people." In the same letter Grace shared with George's mother another option that the couple had discussed in their despair: a "distasteful" plan of temporary separation whereby they would save on servants' wages and other expenses if Grace and the children went to England for a period of time.[14]

Not a month had passed from the time George sent home his letter, requesting a loan, when he sent another one in which he asked his mother to arrange a loan from one of his sisters. The conditions, he proposed, would be the same as those he offered to Nicholson, with interest paid that "would amply compensate to them the loss & bother consequent on the business." "I am very anxious," George concluded, "to have the money before the end of June." He also asked that these requests be kept as private as possible.[15] Doubtless, writing home about these matters was not easy for this young man who had brought his family across the Atlantic to lead Her Britannic Majesty's government's crusade against the slave trade. While corrupt Spanish officials grew wealthy, bribed right and left, George saw himself sink deeper and deeper into debt with the passing of each month. The struggle surrounding the slave trade was, to be sure, an unequal match. It was well known that most captains-general, Pezuela excluded, received two gold-ounce bribes for each imported slave. George's yearly salary (£1,600) was equivalent to the "head money" that a captain-general received for the importation of only 240 slaves, about half of one ship's load. During the first half of the 1850s an average of 7,840 slaves were imported each year, representing around £55,200 in slave-importation bribes for the captain-general alone.[16]

In the spring of 1854 the Backhouses' newfound social network began to collapse, as several of their friends, Grace's in particular, left Cuba. In April, Grace's two closest friends traveled abroad. Mrs. Scharfenberg and her four-year-old son, Carlitos, departed for England early that month. Two weeks later, Mrs. Runge and her four children embarked on a six-month trip to the United States scheduled to coincide with Havana's sickly season. Upon their return to Havana, the Runges began to plan their definite departure from Havana. In March, another family of El Cerro's foreign social circle, the Browns, left

Havana. Cuba, George complained, was a country of transients, where foreigners came to make a quick fortune and then move on.[17]

When the Scharfenbergs closed down their home next door to the Backhouses, Grace purchased a few of the items they put up for sale. She bought their piano for $306, a bed for Alice for $20, and two table cloths for $4. Soon after the Scharfenbergs' departure, the Backhouses moved next door into the house they left vacant.[18] Grace and Mrs. Scharfenberg became very close during the weeks prior to the latter's departure. On April 3 they went together with Alice and Carlitos to have their daguerreotypes taken. This early photographic technology was new in Havana, as it was elsewhere, and most probably neither of them had had theirs taken before. In all, the photographer, whose studio was located at O'Reilly #3, took seven pictures, three of Alice and Grace. Little Alice was "rather fidgetty," as she endured what Grace described as "a long business." Indeed, daguerreotypes required exposures that could take several minutes and could test the patience of the most serene model. The toddler, dressed for the immortalizing event, wore "Aunt Kate's white frock and Aunt Mary's deep blue sash & bows, the sash that came from Rome." Though not entirely pleased with the way they came out, Grace bought two of the daguerreotypes, one with a frame, another frameless at half price. She sent one to her father and one to her mother-in-law.[19]

Mrs. Scharfenberg and her four year-old-son Carlitos embarked for England later that week. As a good-bye present she sent Grace a marble vase with a note. Compelled to reciprocate, Grace answered the note and "did up [her] little gold pencil case as a present from Alice to Carlito [*sic*]." She had hoped to send it early the next day but missed the Scharfenberg carriage, which Grace heard "roll by at 1/2 p. 5." Early that morning the Scharfenberg party boarded a vessel bound for Charleston and New York and eventually sailed across the Atlantic to England.[20]

Later in the month, Grace saw an even closer friend depart, Mrs. Runge, who had been so unselfishly helpful during Johnny's illness earlier in the year. On the eve of her departure, George and Grace stopped by her house to bid her farewell. The next day Mrs. Runge and her children departed bound for New York on board the notorious *Black Warrior,* the U.S. steamship at the heart of a diplomatic controversy between Spain and the United States earlier in the year. She intended to be back in six months, once Cuba's lowlands were safe again.[21]

Thus, in a matter of two weeks Grace saw two of her closest friends leave town. She lost her hike and drive companions and Alice lost her dearest playmates. That spring, El Cerro and El Horcón became bachelors' towns; Mr. Scharfenberg, Mr. Runge, and Mr. Tolmé stayed behind while their wives summered in the North. For Grace, the summer of 1854 promised to be hot, lonely, and long.

That summer, the visit of George's younger brother, Johnny, brought a welcome refreshing torrent to the Backhouse home. On June 22, Johnny Backhouse arrived via England from China, where he continued to hold the vice-consulship at Amoy. The Chinese coolie trade originating precisely at Amoy continued to flourish with the financial backing of Cuban planters and, ironically, under the protection of the British flag. Between the start of the coolie trade in 1853 and July 24, 1854, a total of 7,111 Chinese workers arrived in the port of Havana.[22] It was the day after Johnny's birthday and Grace had baked a cake for the occasion and his arrival. Glasgow ale, Yorkshire ham, and Sunderland cheese completed the welcome banquet for George's brother, whom Grace described as looking "quite fresh and handsome after his sea life." He stayed seven weeks in Havana. Johnny's visit was perhaps the main reason why the Backhouses moved to a larger house earlier that month and why George had been so anxious to receive the loans before the end of June.[23]

Johnny brought with him a piece of England at a time when George and Grace needed it most; as George later put it, his brother helped enliven their new house. Johnny brought a bundle of letters, many gifts, and countless stories to share. He was the first relative or friend that the Backhouses saw since they left London more than a year before. Their precarious finances not withstanding, George and Grace went out of their way to please and entertain George's younger brother. They took him downtown quite often, for dinner, theater, or just for the drive. George still felt that much more could have been done and worried that Johnny may have been bored: "I believe he has read through a number of books while here, consumed several bottles of beer, cigars, & much time in sleep; he eats little, keeps his health & temper both apparently very well. He has had very little of any kind of amusement except the amusement of playing with Alice a great deal."[24]

Johnny's departure on August 9 had a devastating emotional effect on the Backhouse household. "It is a rather melancholy time now Johnny is going," George wrote his mother. "It seems as if, the Family here was breaking up." On the day of his departure, Grace jotted in her diary: "Johnnie left us to day to go by the English steamer via S. Thomas to England. Felt very melancholy at parting, wished heartily we were all going too." Little Alice joined the chorus of broken hearts. According to her mother, she took on "an amusing way of saying with a very grave & sorrowful face & in a very melancholy tone 'Uncle John gone. Uncle John gone.' "[25]

Hilton too suffered from Johnny's departure as she entered into a painful state of homesickness. From the beginning she had disliked Havana and had occasionally exhibited what George described as very insolent behavior. On the very night when Johnny left, Hilton had a row with the wet nurse. She stayed up until two in the morning, trying to write Grace a letter in which she announced her intention to go back to England. Failing to bring out her feelings in written form, Hilton burned the letter and on the next day, in tears, told Grace what she intended to do. "[S]he felt sure," reported Grace, "that the other servants were constantly complaining of her to me. She knew just so much of Spanish as to know when they were talking of her but not enough to justify herself, in fact that she felt so utterly friendless here having no one her equal to talk to." Hilton let Grace know her desire of getting "to England with some family going from here and . . . setting up as dressmaker her young step sister joining her." Despite the seeming urgency of Hilton's plans she assured Grace that she would remain at her service for a few months until a suitable substitute could be found. Grace knew that Hilton was very unhappy and recognized that "there was much here to make her feel dull and lonely."[26]

The return of Mrs. Runge and her four children to Havana in October provided some relief to Grace. Short-lived relief, it turned out to be, because soon after her arrival she announced her definite departure to England. Grace and Mrs. Runge became even closer over the next few months. They got together almost every day, for drives, for walks with their children, and for tea. They also exchanged dinner invitations routinely. "I have been down there, to their house once or twice a day lately," wrote Grace on March 15, 1855.[27]

In one of their many visits, on March 23, 1855, Mrs. Runge proposed that Grace join her on her trip to England. "[I] thought nothing at all about it at first," wrote Grace. "When George came it was mentioned to him—he has often had a wish that way—& said he thought it the best thing I could do." That afternoon, thus, like in other instances in their life, the Backhouses came to an important decision in the swiftest of ways. "You will wonder at the sudden determination," Grace wrote her mother-in-law, "for indeed George and I have settled it at last quite suddenly. Only the day before yesterday did we begin to think of it at all seriously."[28]

George encouraged Grace in her plan although he did not welcome the prospect of staying behind alone. "I am about to be desolate here," George wrote to his brother, adding that he was satisfied that his wife and children were going home. The plan was for Grace, the children, and Hilton to embark on the next British mail steamer; Grace and the children would return in six months with a new English nurse; Hilton would stay in England to pursue her plans. George entrusted his family to his widowed mother, insisting that they stay with her only "under some pecuniary arrangement." Unfortunately, George could not even cover the passage costs at the time. "I must trust to others for getting through the present crisis in my money matters," he wrote his mother shortly after Grace's departure. He requested that she make a deposit at Drummonds to cover the £88 drafted to pay the passage. In the same communication George addressed a "more serious matter." He had failed to make the latest payments of his life insurance premiums and feared a lapse in the policy, "a most serious matter, more especially under the circumstances of my obligation to James Nicholson."[29]

As her diary and correspondence attest, Grace was very excited about the prospect of her voyage home. She was especially glad to be going to England now that she had learned that she was pregnant again. "We think it would be such a good thing," she wrote, "to have my confinement in England where the child might receive Holy Baptism."[30]

Only two weeks after the decision had been reached Grace and her two children embarked on a vessel bound for England. Grace's diary entries stopped temporarily after April 6, 1855, and resumed a month later when she reached London. In her last diary entry in Havana she noted an excursion that she took with George. They took an omnibus to the center of El Cerro and then another one to Marianao, where they combed the river banks in search of shells and fern roots. On the way back their carriage took a side road to avoid interfering with a procession—it was Good Friday. That night they sipped heavy tea and had an "excellent supper." On the next morning George saw his loved ones off.[31]

That very few entries appear in Grace's diary for the duration of the sea journey attests to the difficulties of crossing the Atlantic "in the family way" with two small children. She reported that the passage went smoothly but that she was constantly sick. Though Hilton was there to help, Grace shared her services with Mrs. Runge, who traveled with four small children of her own. The Backhouse party arrived in London safe and well the first week of May 1855. Upon arrival, one of the first things that Grace did was to take communion at St. Paul's Church. A few weeks later she officially inscribed Johnny in the registry of the church as privately baptized in Havana.[32]

Grace enjoyed her stay at 28 Hans Place, George's mother's home. She spent time with her widowed father, John Sandham, who lived a few houses down the street at 49 Hans Place. She also went shopping with her relatives and friends in search of goods for George and herself. She mailed George a cigar case for his thirty-seventh birthday, along with his gold chain, which she had mended in London, and some mustard and tea.[33] Grace wrote and read letters and kept up with her diary as well. In it she kept a faithful register of her correspondence with her beloved George: Friday June 1, "Send off letters to my dearest husband. 1 from me (7 note sheets in close writing)"; Friday June 15, "I had a letter from my dearest husband via N. York, sent from the Havana May 27, very nice dear letter—good accounts." Similar entries followed in Grace's pocket diary. On July 12, Grace gave birth to their third child, a baby girl she named Beatrice Margaret. She was baptized at St. Paul's Church on August 3.[34]

In 1854 and 1855, George faced several problematic situations at work with fellow British official Crawford and with Dalrymple, the Mixed Commission's controversial clerk. Jurisdictional jealousies and Crawford's penchant for self-serving schemes created an uneasy, albeit seemingly polite relation between George and Consul-General Crawford.[35] In the summer of 1854, tensions between Backhouse and Crawford reached a critical point, moving the consul-general to write a letter of complaint to the Foreign Secretary. Crawford accused Backhouse of having written him a letter in a style not suitable for official correspondence. Lord Clarendon looked at the evidence and concluded that there was nothing improper in Backhouse's communication, that there was nothing to be offended by, and that Crawford's complaint had been "unnecessary." There were further instances of friction and lack of cooperation between the two British officials. On one occasion, for example, Crawford refused to surrender letters that Backhouse requested returned so that he could mail them via New York rather than via the delayed English mail. The correspondence surrounding this and other incidents remained civil, but highly impersonal and bureaucratic in tone.[36]

It was Dalrymple, however, who continued to give George his biggest headaches. In November 1854, Backhouse charged Dalrymple with being intoxicated while at work. A few months later, Dalrymple's money problems reached the Mixed Commission again, creating many inconveniences and producing extra work for George. For some time, at Dalrymple's request, George deducted part of the clerk's salary and made payments directly to his creditors, whom according to George were "very numerous and some very urgent." At one point three-fourths of Dalrymple's monthly salary of about £90 went directly to his creditors. George soon grew tired of this inconvenience and of the unending visits of Dalrymple's many creditors to the Mixed Commission and even to the Backhouse residence. In June 1855, George decided to have no further dealings with Dalrymple's creditors and refused to pay them even after a local magistrate ordered him to do so.[37]

A few weeks later in early August 1855, George and Dalrymple had another confrontation. George gave him written instructions on how to proceed with a particular official document. Perhaps under the influence of alcohol, Dalrymple failed to follow George's directions. When George read the document and realized that it had been done wrong he became irate, and, by his own admission, called Dalrymple a "blockhead" and then suspended and ordered him out of the office. Just as on previous occasions, Dalrymple complained directly to the Foreign Office, portraying himself as an innocent victim. In a letter to the Foreign Secretary, Dalrymple reported having received numerous insults and offenses. He stated that "ever since his arrival" George had tried to injure him in any way he could.[38]

Tired of problems at work and looking forward to an early reunion with his children and loving wife, on August 27, George wrote a letter to Lord Clarendon, requesting a month's leave of absence for next November so he could meet and spend some time with his loved ones in New York on their way back from England.[39]

Meanwhile on the other side of the Atlantic, Grace and her children were doing well as good accounts from George continued to arrive in 28 Hans Place. On the morning of September 1, Grace woke up feeling "very sick and headachy" and with an overbearing desire to write to

George, from whom she had not heard for a longer than usual length of time. A week later Hilton called, carrying a short note from George. In it he told Grace not to be alarmed by the lateness of the regular English mail for there had been some rearranging of the mail routes. On September 21, George's usual letter arrived, delayed but with "good accounts."[40]

A page is missing from Grace's diary following her entry for Saturday, September 29; the entries are interrupted for several days after that. The torn page and the ensuing silence suggest that Sunday, September 30, was probably the day on which Mrs. Tolmé, who was in London at the time, paid a visit to the Backhouse residence bearing the terrible news of George's death. Sally Crawford had written two letters, one to Grace, another to George's mother, informing them of the tragic event. She sent these to her mother, Mrs. Tolmé, and commissioned her to deliver the painful news of George's demise.[41]

Over the next few weeks the details of George's death filtered in in a painfully slow way. George was murdered in his own house on the night of August 31—it took about a month for the news to reach London. That night George had dinner with Thomas Callaghan, the clerk substituting the suspended Dalrymple. They were chatting and sipping some after-dinner wine—according to Callaghan they were talking about Grace—when suddenly at about 7:45 two men, one black, the other a mulatto, burst into the house. The black man attacked Callaghan. He overpowered him in no time, tied his hands behind his back, and removed his pocket watch. Meanwhile, the mulatto, reportedly an "exceedingly powerful fellow," attacked George, who fought back with his hands. The assailant drew a knife and pushed it into George's left side. Her Majesty's judge fell to the ground into a puddle of his own blood. The two assailants fled the scene of the crime immediately.[42]

During the attack, Manuel, one of the house servants, jumped over the garden fence and ran for help. A *sereno* and two policemen arrived in no time and managed to arrest a suspicious mulatto they found in the vicinity. Medical help also arrived soon. The first physician to reach the scene was Dr. Valdez, the district surgeon. At about half past eight, some forty-five minutes after the infliction of the wound, Dr. Belot arrived and took over George's care. He ordered the bleeding man leeched.

George's breathing got more and more difficult and the faces of those around him obliterated like tatoos in the chest of an aging sailor; reportedly he remained "quite collected" and aware of what was going on. The local magistrate asked the dying man if he could identify his assailant. George responded that he could not. Later, Crawford asked him if he should take care of his affairs, to which George responded in the affirmative, adding that his property be sold and the proceeds be sent to Grace. The impending presence of death often destroys fixed hierarchies and tames old rivalries. Crawford listened attentively to the agonizing junior official as if his last wishes were commands off the lips of Queen Victoria herself. At eleven o'clock George expired. Only God knows what was going on in George's mind as he faced an imminent death in a strange and inhospitable land, separated from his loving wife and children. He must have held on to his spiritual strength for he died in pain but seemingly with the peace that transcends all understanding. Less than two years before, Dr. Belot had witnessed Johnny Backhouse's first breath; now he stood impotent at the sight of George's last. A postmortem examination the following day revealed that the knife had broken one of George's left ribs and had pierced through his spleen and lung.[43]

On the morning of September 1, at exactly the same time at which George's unsuspecting widow awoke with an unbearable headache and an urgent desire to write him a letter, his lifeless body was taken to Havana's Espada Cemetery and deposited in niche #291. The curate of Nuestra Señora del Pilar entered the death certificate into the parish records. It attested that the fallen man's age, place of birth, and civil status were unknown. The priest presumed that George had been a Roman Catholic and authorized his burial in consecrated ground. Crawford ordered him placed in a mahogany casket lined with zinc or lead, suitable for the transatlantic transfer of the corpse, anticipating that his surviving widow would wish so. The New York press reported that a funeral ceremony took place that was well attended by government functionaries, foreign consuls, and the deceased man's friends.[44]

As established by Spanish colonial law, Crawford had to oversee the wrap-up of his slain compatriot's affairs, especially because he died intestate. On the day following George's murder, Crawford and his wife were busy writing several letters in which they informed George's surviving relatives, friends, and Foreign Office superiors of the horrible crime. Crawford also moved to protect the property George left behind. To prevent looting by the servants and others, he ordered Callaghan to remain in the Backhouse residence and to take custody of all things inside.[45]

Crawford proceeded to have some of George's personal belongings packed and shipped to England: "All the house linens, all his clothes, the plate, all the table ornaments, knick-knacks, and other things familiar to Mrs. Backhouse." He then made an inventory of the furniture and other items not worth shipping to be put up for sale. It included a $1,350 carriage that he never got to ride on, a $272 piano, a revolver, a telescope, dozens of pieces of furniture, a few hundred liquor bottles, and seventeen pounds of tea. The sale of these items produced £590 ($2,877) from which Crawford deducted the customary 2.5 percent fee for his service. Another £21 were added to the Backhouse estate from money owed to George, most of it by Dalrymple. Out of the sale proceeds, $676 were drawn to pay several bills including $163 to Dr. Belot and $25.40 to Dr. Valdez. The estate's balance on February 9, 1856, stood at £477; Crawford remitted £411 to the Backhouse account at Drummonds and kept £66 to cover several matters still pending.[46]

As the person in charge of the late Backhouse's affairs, Crawford faced the disagreeable task of responding to numerous claims against his estate. House servant Manuel claimed that he had not received his salary since May 1853, a significant total of $398. José, the gardener, claimed past wages in the amount of $200. Crawford refused to honor these claims until he heard from Grace "whether it is true what the servants say." Eventually, the claims reached the alcalde who determined that the servants not be paid because they failed to provide evidence to support their case. The grocer, a washerwoman, the milkman, and the baker also presented bills that were paid out of the estate. The Spanish colonial government had a bill of its own in the amount of $100 stemming from the Tribunal de Difuntos' paperwork. Crawford engaged in a prolonged battle to avoid paying this charge. The matter was eventually resolved in Madrid, where Spanish authorities decided to exempt the Backhouse estate from the charge.[47]

Although the enraged New York press anticipated that the murderers would be convicted and garroted within a month of the crime, the case against the suspects did not proceed as officiously and effectively as George's friends and relatives would have desired. On the days following the murder, nine or ten suspects came under police custody for their alleged connection to the crime. The suspects included two white servants of the Backhouse household, and seven or eight men of color. A charge was raised against one of the servants that implicated him with having connived in the robbery but not in the murder. No corroborating evidence ever surfaced, and the case against the accused lacked a single witness, since Callaghan was unable to identify either of the assailants. Moreover, the suspect of the actual murder produced an alibi that could not be challenged in court.[48]

The trial went on for several months. Four months after the crime, Crawford began to signal pessimism about the prospect of anyone being convicted for the crime. "[S]uch is the obscurity which covers their horrible crime," Crawford reported to the Foreign Office, "that I very much fear the authorities, anxious as they are to do so, may not be able to bring them to justice." The suspects, it turned out, enjoyed a very apt defense, "a Gentleman of great legal knowledge and intelligence, as well as of the highest character and integrity." In an effort to help the prosecution, the Foreign Office offered a £100 reward for information on the crime. Crawford made the offer public but wrote to his superiors that he feared that the length of time since the crime—four months—made any conviction virtually impossible. In the end, all suspects were released in the light of insufficient evidence against them.[49] It is very revealing of Britain's new, less antagonistic, and less abolitionist posture that it did not press Spain for further investigations on George's murder.

Who killed George Backhouse, and why, may never be known; the diary he was keeping at the time may have held some clues but it was mysteriously never found. The circumstances surrounding his murder point to a series of possible explanations. The most widely accepted, and the one Crawford subscribed to, presented George as the victim of a common robbery turned violent when George posed resistance. Grace, who never returned to Havana, believed—or wanted to believe—that her beloved husband had been the target of "a slave dealing conspiracy" and claimed that several people subscribed to this theory. Another possibility was that George was the victim of a Ñáñigo initiation rite, whereby inductees to these Afro-Cuban secret societies sometimes had to "test iron" by killing a white person with a sharp knife. Given George's official duties in Havana this would have been a most tragic twist of irony. It is also possible that Dalrymple may have had something to do with the crime.[50]

George's role as activist judge in the Mixed Commission for the Suppression of the Slave Trade certainly placed him in a dangerous position, and the slave-trading interests would have benefited from his death. Although no evidence points to any mastermind beyond the

**Ñáñigo, member of an Afro-Cuban secret society.** (Reprinted from Robert L. Paquette, *Sugar Is Made with Blood*.)

small circle of suspects, all of whom were either servants or people of color, the slave-trading conspiracy remains a plausible explanation. The Ñáñigo theory would be harder to sustain because Backhouse was well known and liked among the city's people of color and thus would have been a most unlikely target of the Ñáñigos's murderous initiation rite. Besides, no evidence ever linked any of the suspects with these secret societies. Dalrymple's involvement remains a possibility; he had proven that he was capable of almost any sin and crime, he was in need of money at the time, and he had just had a bitter confrontation with George, who once again suspended him from his official duties. This would have not been the first time in which Dalrymple appeared to respond to a suspension with a criminal act. This could have been his way of repaying some of the debts that he had contracted with the slave traders with whom he was in debt. Although the least romantic and redeeming, the theory that George was the victim of a common robbery-turned-murder became the official and most accepted interpretation of the tragic event. No concrete fingers pointed to either slave traders, to a disgruntled Dalrymple, or to a Ñáñigo's ritual dagger.

A few weeks after George's murder, letters of condolence began to pour into 28 Hans Place; meanwhile, from across the Atlantic, boxes began to arrive containing painful reminders of the tragic loss. Several items arrived broken and Grace attributed this to the Crawfords' carelessness and disregard. Consul-General Crawford politely responded to these accusations, assuring Grace "that greater care and solicitude could not be used than every body put in practice upon that most melancholy occasion."[51]

Grace endured a prolonged grieving period, marked by deep sadness. She also suffered from paralyzing back pain probably related to her emotional distress. The family physician, Dr. Haden, prescribed rest, pills, and the application of opium plasters. She remained in pain and at home without accepting visits for about five months. On March 11, 1856, Grace stood as godmother for her newborn nephew. They baptized him George Backhouse Sandham, after her late husband.[52]

Grace and George's mother made several applications in search of a pension to help support the family that George left behind. George's mother wrote a personal plea to Foreign Secretary Lord Clarendon. In it she outlined the enormous financial sacrifice at which George accepted the Havana post, draining "his private funds, instead of the appointment being a source of emolument to him." Consequently, she continued, the widow and three surviving children faced "no other prospect than that of becoming dependent upon their relations for their support unless it shall please HM's government to award some provision." Mrs. Backhouse concluded her plea to Lord Clarendon by reminding him of George's father's "long and unremitting services as Under Secretary of State for Foreign Affairs."[53]

Although no such provisions existed for civil officials who died while serving Britain abroad, an exceptional provision was allowed whereby Grace received a £1,200 grant, an amount short of George's salary for one year. Grace thanked Lord Clarendon in writing but requested a larger grant. She explained that the £1,200 plus the small life insurance paid to George's survivors would not generate enough income to maintain George's dependents. She insisted that he had lost his life in Her Majesty's service.[54]

In January 1856, accompanied by her sister Kate, Grace paid a visit to Lord Palmerston, who at the time was Britain's prime minister. On that occasion she requested an additional pension to help her support her children. A month later they returned to Lord Palmerston's private residence to follow up on the request; they were disappointed by his cold reception and by the fact that he had failed to act on the petition. He promised Grace that his own private secretary would take up the matter. Following a few more reminders from Grace, the Queen finally authorized a yearly pension in the amount of £100.[55]

In Havana, meanwhile, Crawford continued to pursue his obligations to wrap up George's affairs. He sent a few remaining items to London, among them Linda, the Backhouses' English Spaniel, at a passage cost of £5. With the £66 balance still in Crawford's hands, he paid a few remaining bills. The last one, £39, for the exhumation of George's corpse for shipment to England. His remains were exhumed on September 8, 1856, and shipped a few days later. The following month, Crawford sent to Drummonds the last 10 shillings that remained in the estate and he informed Grace that he had "now concluded a sad and most distressing duty."[56]

George's mortal remains returned to England three and a half years after he had left with great hopes about the new appointment and the new surroundings. Everything had gone wrong. His coffin arrived in Southampton on November 3, 1856. On the next day, George's remains were transported by rail to London. The funeral ceremonies were carried out shortly before sunset on November 4 in the chapel of Kensall Green Cemetery. George was laid to rest in the same vault in which he had buried his father ten years before. George's brother, Johnny, had arrived from China two months earlier, leaving behind a country ravaged by the Second Opium War. Crippled by disease, Johnny could not enter the cemetery; the cab that transported his aching body had to remain parked outside the cemetery's gates while the rest of the mourning family bid his brother a final farewell. Little over two years earlier, the two Backhouse brothers had spent some great moments together in Havana, enjoying perfect health. Now they were reunited in London, rubble from Britain's foreign service edifice, one dead, the other paralyzed by illness. Despite the sadness of the occasion, George's burial in English soil brought a sense of closure to the tragedy of his death. With the help of her three small children, Grace prepared a funeral wreath with white and pale yellow flowers and myrtle, intertwined with locks of hair from her children and herself. The two older children, Alice then four and Johnny then three, knew where the wreath was going and kissed it. Little Beatrice, only sixteen months old, kissed it too and uttered the word "Papa." Grace later arranged for an obituary light to be lit at St. Paul's Church next to an inscription reading: "To the Glory of God. In Memory of George Canning Backhouse who died August 31, 1855. Aged 37."[57]

Back in Havana, meanwhile, the slave trade continued to flourish and the beheaded Mixed Commission remained a shameful reminder of Britain's impotence as it faced the forces of evil and greed. A few weeks after George's murder Crawford wrote in an official report: "This Island seems to be beset with slavers; they are swarming and what is worse, they appear to succeed in landing their Slaves eluding the vigilance of the Spanish authorities always." Indeed, the five-year period of 1856–60 was the all-time high point of slave importations into Cuba with a total of around 90,000 slaves; another 40,000 Chinese contract laborers arrived during the same quinquennium.[58] Paradoxically, six years after George's death Great Britain openly sided with the pro-slavery Confederacy during the bloody Civil War that tore the United States. During the conflict, the aging Crawford willingly aided the efforts of the Confederate blockade-runners, and it was said that he positioned himself to become Britain's first ambassador to the Confederate States of America. After George's death, Crawford realized another of his goals—he became the Mixed Commission's British judge, while retaining his post as consul-general. He also maneuvered so that his son, John Vincent Crawford, be appointed in place of Dalrymple, whose clerkship became vacant in 1856.[59]

On October 13, 1855, less than a month and a half after George's murder and while the investigation was still proceeding, Dalrymple intended to board the *Cahawba* bound for the port of New York but was intercepted at the pier by several of his creditors. He had requested and received a six-months' leave of absence to go to New York. He managed to escape in June 1856 never to return to his post, or his family, or his creditors. Dalrymple claimed that he could not return for health reasons and he sought—or fabricated—a doctor's certificate, which stated that he suffered from "*a chronic Obstruction of the liver.*" If this was a true diagnosis it most probably stemmed from the heavy drink-

ing with which he was credited. Crawford welcomed Dalrymple's definite departure even though the latter owed him some money. He had
earlier expressed his hopes: "It would be desirable, not only for the
Credit and respectability of the Public Service, but for the well being
and advantage of [Dalrymple], were it convenient to transfer his service to some other place, where his habits might be changed and improved by his being separated from his associates here."[60] While in
New York Dalrymple applied for a clerkship in the Anglo–Portuguese
Mixed Commission in Luanda, in present-day Angola. Perhaps because no other Englishman in his right mind considered serving at such
a deadly post, Dalrymple received the appointment he sought in spite
of his long record of ineptness, corruption, and evil deeds. He held that
post until January 1858 and disappeared from the Foreign Office records after that.[61]

Also leaving Cuba at around the same time was John Baptiste
Dasalu, the Christian emancipado from Lagos who had written to his
relatives informing them of his enslavement and his transatlantic ordeal
to Cuba's shores. Less than a year after Dasalu dictated his hopeful
long-shot letter that eventually reached the Foreign Office, Crawford reported that he had found Dasalu. "Truly it may be said," Crawford wrote,
"we *found* 'the needle in the bundle of straw.'" Crawford promptly secured permission from the local authorities for Dasalu's liberation and
arranged for his departure to Africa via England on July 10, 1856.[62] The
Dahomeans who had enslaved Dasalu continued to harass Lagos and
Abeokuta well into the mid-1860s. By 1867, relations between the British and the Egbas of Abeokuta had deteriorated to the point that all
British traders and missionaries were expelled.

In 1857 Marty sold his Teatro Tacón for three-quarters of a million
pesos. He and his fellow slave traders remained active in the slave
trade during the years following George's murder. In the mid-1860s,
however, a new captain-general, Domingo Dulce, targeted slave traders and had Marty arrested for the importation of several hundred
slaves. Bondage proved unbearable for the Catalan fishmonger, and he
died shortly after his arrest.[63] George's younger brother, Johnny, retired from his post at Amoy in May 1857, never recuperated from his
crippling illness, and died in 1862. War in China did not put an end to
the Chinese coolie trade; thousands of Chinese nationals continued to
arrive into Cuba until their importation came to a halt in 1874.

Grace continued to mourn her murdered husband over the next few years. On the second anniversary of his death she wrote: "Two years ago my beloved husband died. O GOD Thou knowest how unabated is my sorrow." A year later on the same date she jotted in her diary: "My loss—my inseparable loss—seems greater as time goes on." The following year, Grace wrote: "I did not forget the 31st of August—a day so full of sadness. 4 years ago my *beloved* husband was taken from us—4 years only it seems like 14!"[64]

At some unspecified point Grace returned to her diary, to her final entry about her last day with George in Cuba. Next to it she wrote in the elegantly clear handwriting that George had so much admired: "My own dear Husband! What a *delicious* walk that was. How happy we were by the side of that stream, the walk my husband loved best in that foreign land reminding us in some degree of dear old England. . . . When I look back on my happiness this day how I *long* that such hours would come again. How I feel as if I never prized the happiness of being with my dearest husband sufficiently. GOD's will be done GOD grant me grace to bear all He wills becomingly in His sight."[65]

Grace's prayers were answered, and she found consolation in her heart and spirit. She found comfort and reaped many blessings during her remaining days. In 1861 she married the Reverend William Jeudwine, the vicar of Chicheley; the following year she gave birth to Hugh Sandham Jeudwine, who grew up to become a lieutenant general and a knighted sir. He fought in the South African War (1899–1902) and later in World War I. The oldest of the Backhouse children, Alice, married another career officer, the Major Charles Lee Sheppard. She most certainly forgot the Spanish she picked up from the Cuban servants who tended her, and her memories of El Cerro must have sunk into the subconscious corners of her mind. Had she ever returned to Cuba, though, she would have felt uncannily at home. Alice had the good sense to preserve her parents' diaries and correspondence, which she passed on to her only child, Frederick Lee Sheppard, who became a man of the cloth and died a bachelor without direct heirs. He too kept the Backhouse family documents, and doubtless, like his mother before him, returned to their yellowed pages in search of answers. Alice's younger brother, John Sandham Backhouse, lived many years in South Africa, a tense, multiracial, colonial society much like the one in which he was born and his father was killed. He too, perhaps, went back to his parents' journals trying to make sense of those ill-fated years in Havana that forever changed the course of their lives.[66]

# Notes

## Introduction

1. George and Grace Backhouse's documents are part of the John Backhouse Papers of the William B. Hamilton Collection housed at the Special Collections Library, Duke University, Durham, NC (hereafter cited as Backhouse Papers). The collection has an index and includes a mimeographed description of the Backhouse Papers.

2. There is an ample and rich body of nineteenth-century travel accounts by European and United States visitors to Cuba. For a partial listing, see Louis A. Pérez, Jr., *Cuba: An Annotated Bibliography*, 19–28. Also see Harold F. Smith, "A Bibliography of American Travellers' Books about Cuba Published before 1900," 404–12. In a recent compilation, *Slaves, Sugar, and Colonial Society: Travel Accounts of Cuba, 1801–1899*, Pérez reproduces excerpts from several of these travelogues.

3. Several important works describe and analyze Cuba's economy and society during the nineteenth century. Particularly useful are: Manuel Moreno Fraginals, *El ingenio*; Pedro Deschamps Chapeaux, *El negro en la economia habanera del siglo XIX*; Franklin W. Knight, *Slave Society in Cuba during the Nineteenth Century*; Robert Louis Paquette, *Sugar Is Made with Blood*; Robert M. Levine, *Cuba in the 1850s through the Lens of Charles DeForrest Fredricks*; Rebecca J. Scott, *Slave Emancipation in Cuba*; Verena Martínez-Alier, *Marriage, Class and Colour in Nineteenth-Century Cuba*; Laird W. Bergad, *Cuban Rural Society in the Nineteenth Century*; and Louis A. Pérez, Jr., *Cuba: Between Reform and Revolution*, 2nd ed.

4. See Luis Martínez-Fernández, *Torn between Empires*.

5. David Murray, *Odious Commerce*, 245; in Arthur F. Corwin, *Spain and the Abolition of Slavery in Cuba, 1817–1886*, Backhouse is not mentioned once.

6. The 1860 census for Havana included 2,688 non-Spanish white foreigners.

In 1855, 2,693 non-Spanish white foreigners passed through the city's port. Félix Erenchún, *Anales de la Isla de Cuba (1855)*, 1901–11.

## I. Havana Bound

1. The London *Times*, December 17, 18, 1852.

2. George Backhouse to Catherine Backhouse, his mother, December 18, 1852; George Backhouse's Diary (hereafter cited as His Diary), December 17, 1852, both in Backhouse Papers; H.U. Addington to George Backhouse, December 24, 1852, Public Record Office, Kew, England (hereafter cited as PRO), Foreign Office (hereafter cited as FO) 84/870. For earlier salary information, see PRO, FO 366/382–3.

3. For slave importation numbers, see David Eltis, "The Nineteenth-Century Transatlantic Slave Trade," 120–30.

4. His Diary, December 17, 1852; George Backhouse to Catherine Backhouse, December 18, 1852; Grace Backhouse to her aunt, December 22, 1852; Grace Backhouse's Diary (hereafter cited as Her Diary), October 24, 1854, all in Backhouse Papers; Daniel Pool, *What Jane Austen Ate and Charles Dickens Knew*, 51, 268.

5. Mimeographed description of the John Backhouse Papers in Backhouse Papers; J.M. Collinge, compiler, *Office-Holders in Modern Britain*, vol. 8, p. 59; Great Britain, Foreign Office, *The Foreign Office List* (1852), 7–10; appointment letter signed by Lord Palmerston, May 24, 1838, PRO, FO 366/673, p. 363; Charles Ronald Middleton, *The Administration of British Foreign Policy, 1782–1846*, 147, 263; "John Backhouse (obituary)," 95–97.

6. Great Britain, *Foreign Office List* (1852), 7–10.

7. The Great Exhibition was visited by an estimated six million people. At the exhibition the Backhouses probably saw the Cuban collection consisting of fine cigars, sugar samples, chemical products, and various works of art. Great Britain, Royal Commission, *Official Catalogue of the Great Exhibition of the Works of Industry of All Nations, 1851*; His Diary, October 10, 1851, December 11–14, 1852; Her Diary, November 7, 1852; George Backhouse to Catherine Backhouse, December 18, 1852, all in Backhouse Papers.

8. [Charles John] Canning to Catherine Backhouse, October 24, 1852, Backhouse Papers.

9. For some time, Johnny Backhouse served in the Royal Navy. In December 1843, he was appointed senior assistant to the British consul at Canton. In 1847 he became vice-consul at Amoy, where he served until his retirement in 1857. Great Britain, *Foreign Office List* (1857); mimeographed description of the Backhouse Papers, 5.

10. There had been an earlier experiment of Chinese labor importation in 1847 and 1848, which brought some 571 workers to Cuba's shores. The trade began in earnest after 1853. The Backhouses apparently knew Mr. Tait, with whom Grace Backhouse agreed that the Chinese made good servants. George also believed that the Chinese made good servants but questioned the humanity of their servitude. See Juan Pérez de la Riva, "Demografía de los culíes," 55–87, and "Aspectos económicos del tráfico de culíes," 89–110; also see *The Cuba Commission Report*; Grace Backhouse to Catherine Backhouse, April 6, 1854, Backhouse

Papers; George Backhouse to Lord Clarendon, July 10, 1854, PRO, FO 313/26.

11. Her Diary, November 7, 1852 (emphasis in the original); Grace Backhouse to her aunt, December 22, 1852 (emphasis in the original), both in Backhouse Papers.

12. London *Gazette,* December 21, 1852, cited in an unspecified newspaper dated December 22, 1852 (clipping); George Backhouse to Catherine Backhouse, December 18, 21, 1852; His Diary, December 17, 1852, all in Backhouse Papers; Pool, *What Jane Austen Ate,* 312.

13. George Backhouse to Addington, January 1, 1853; Addington to George Backhouse, January 4, 1853, both in PRO, FO 84/898.

14. His Diary, January 20, February 9, 1853; George Backhouse to his sister, Mary Backhouse, May 1, 1853; Grace Backhouse to her aunt, December 22, 1852, all in Backhouse Papers.

15. Her Diary, January 22, 1853; His Diary, January 22, 24, February 3, 1853, all in Backhouse Papers. The artist's name appears in the documents with different spellings: Blakeley, Blakely, and Blaikley.

16. Addington to Kennedy, December 24, 1852, PRO, FO 84/870; Paquette, *Sugar,* 145; Spanish minister in London to the captain-general of Cuba, February 4, 1853, Archivo Nacional de Cuba (hereafter cited as ANC), Gobierno General, leg. 337, exp. 16240; Great Britain, Parliament, House of Commons, *British Parliamentary Papers [Slave Trade]* (hereafter cited as *BPP*), vol. 7, p. 198; George Backhouse to Catherine Backhouse, December 18, 1852, Backhouse Papers.

17. At mid-century there were approximately 1,500 sugar estates in operation. Cuba was the world's biggest sugar producer, with outputs of 322,000 tons (1853), 374,000 tons (1854), and 392,000 tons (1855). Pérez de la Riva, "Demografía," 87; Knight, *Slave Society,* 31, 39, 48; Paquette, *Sugar,* 131; Eltis, "Nineteenth-Century Transatlantic Slave Trade," 122–23; Pérez, *Cuba: Between Reform and Revolution,* 2nd ed., 60.

18. Crawford to Lord Clarendon, August 23, 1853, PRO, FO 84/906.

19. Addington to Kennedy, December 24, 1852, PRO, FO 84/870; George Backhouse to his aunt, March 27, 1853, Backhouse Papers.

20. Addington to Joseph T. Crawford, January 4, 1853, PRO, FO 313/37; His Diary, February 1, 1853, Backhouse Papers.

21. George Backhouse to Catherine Backhouse, December 18, 1852; Grace Backhouse to her aunt, December 22, 1852, both in Backhouse Papers.

22. George Backhouse to Catherine Backhouse, December 18, 1852; George Backhouse to Mary Backhouse, May 1, 1853; His Diary, January 20, February 1, 9, 1853, all in Backhouse Papers; Gustave D'Hespel D'Harponville, *La reine des Antilles.* George refers to a *Historia de España* by Aseangota.

23. Robert Francis Jameson, *Letters from the Havana, during the year 1820*; David Turnbull, *Travels in the West*; Richard Robert Madden, *The Island of Cuba.*

24. His Diary, December 23, 27, 1852, February 9, 1853, Backhouse Papers.

25. His Diary, February 9, 1853, Backhouse Papers; George Backhouse to Lord Wodehouse, February 11, 1853, PRO, FO 84/898.

26. His Diary, December 31, 1852, Backhouse Papers.

27. His Diary, February 17, 1853, Backhouse Papers; log of the *Medea,* PRO, Admiralty (hereafter cited as ADM) 53/5077; muster of the *Medea,* PRO, ADM

38/4099; George Backhouse to Lord Russell, February 17, 1853, PRO, FO 84/898.

28. His Diary, February 18, 1853, Backhouse Papers; log of the *Medea,* PRO, ADM 53/5077.

29. Her Diary, February 21, March 2, 1853; His Diary, March 2, 1853, both in Backhouse Papers.

30. His Diary, February 24, March 8–9, 1853, Backhouse Papers; log of the *Medea,* March 9, 1853, PRO, ADM 53/5077; [Mercedes de Santa Cruz] Condesa de Merlín, *Viaje a la Habana,* 78; Eugene Ney, *Cuba en 1830,* 12–13.

31. Her Diary, March 17–21, 1853; His Diary, March 18–21, 1853, both in Backhouse Papers; log of the *Medea,* March 17–21, 1853, PRO, ADM 53/5077; Maturin Murray Ballou, *Due South,* 117; Ney, *Cuba en 1830,* 14; George Augustus Sala, *Under the Sun,* 48.

32. [Santa Cruz], *Viaje,* 85; Richard Henry Dana, Jr., *To Cuba and Back,* 26; José García de Arboleya, *Manual de la Isla de Cuba,* 2nd ed., 224; *Directorio de artes, comercio e industrias de La Habana,* 47.

33. Turnbull, *Travels,* 199; Robert W. Gibbes, *Cuba for Invalids,* 5; José María de la Torre, "Cuba," 80; [Santa Cruz], *Viaje,* 115; Joaquín Weiss y Sánchez, *La arquitectura colonial cubana,* 1:29–42, 2:126–28. Further from the bay's entrance were located three other forts that were part of the city's defenses: La Chorrera, El Príncipe, and Atarés.

34. Pérez, *Cuba: Between Reform and Revolution,* 2nd ed., 34–39.

35. *Colección de los partes y otros documentos publicados en la Gaceta Oficial de La Habana referentes a la invasión de la gavilla de piratas capitaneada por el traidor Narciso López*; Crawford to Lord Palmerston, PRO, FO 72/793; Robert E. May, *The Southern Dream of a Caribbean Empire, 1854–1861,* 29. Burial certificates of the Bahía Honda expeditionaries are found among the parish records of Nuestra Señora del Pilar, El Cerro.

36. Ramiro Guerra y Sánchez, *Manual de historia de Cuba desde su descubrimiento hasta 1868,* 2:522–27.

37. Alexander von Humboldt, *The Island of Cuba,* 104; Lewis Leonidas Allen, *The Island of Cuba,* 10; James Rawson, *Cuba,* 14; Rachel Wilson Moore, *Journal of Rachel Wilson Moore,* 60; James William Steele, *Cuban Sketches,* 15; George W. Williams, *Sketches of Travel in the Old and New World,* 3; [John George F. Wurdemann], *Notes on Cuba,* 17–18; Ballou, *Due South,* 127; Eliza McHatton Ripley, *Flag to Flag,* 125; George Backhouse to his aunt, August 3, 1853, Backhouse Papers.

38. Data for 1852 from Franklin W. Knight, "Origins of Wealth and the Sugar Revolution in Cuba, 1750–1850," 245; Erenchún, *Anales,* 1877–78.

39. Approximately 39 percent of Cuba's exports went to the United States, and 20 percent headed to British ports. Only 11 percent of Cuba's exports reached Spain. Erenchún, *Anales,* 1885; Martínez-Fernández, *Torn between Empires,* 70.

40. De la Torre, "Cuba," 80; Roberto Marte, *Cuba y la República Dominicana,* 49, 191; [Santa Cruz], *Viaje,* 82; Dana, *To Cuba,* 7; [Wurdemann], *Notes,* 18; Henry Ashworth, *A Tour in the United States, Cuba, and Canada,* 48; Cirilo Villaverde, *Cecilia Valdés,* 157; Ballou, *Due South,* 125–26.

41. *La Gaceta de La Habana,* April 1, 1853.

42. His Diary, March 21, 1853; Her Diary, March 21, 1853, both in Back-

house Papers; log of the *Medea,* March 21, 1853, PRO, ADM 53/5077.

43. An order of December 2, 1826, established fines for captains who allowed passengers to disembark without the approval of the health official and jail terms for boatmen transporting them ashore. ANC, Asuntos Políticos, leg. 298, exp. 46.

44. William Cullen Bryant, *Letters of William Cullen Bryant,* 3:25–26; [Santa Cruz], *Viaje,* 90–91; Henry Tudor, *Narrative of a Tour in North America,* 2:104; Abiel Abbot, *Letters Written in the Interior of Cuba,* 2; John Stevens Cabot Abbott, *South and North,* 42; [Wurdemann], *Notes,* 18; Sala, *Under the Sun,* 63; Dana, *To Cuba,* 8, 13; Her Diary, March 21, 1853, Backhouse Papers.

45. Log of the *Medea,* PRO, ADM 53/5077; Moore, *Journal,* 3; Reau Campbell, *Around the Corner to Cuba,* 6; Fredrika Bremer, *The Homes of the New World,* 2:257; [Wurdemann], *Notes,* 4, 24; [Julia Louisa Matilda Woodruff] pseud., W.M.L. Jay, *My Winter in Cuba,* 19–20; Amelia Matilda Murray, *Letters from the United States, Cuba and Canada,* 2:52–53; Dana, *To Cuba,* 8.

46. Levine provides the following population figures for 1850: 605,560 whites, 118,200 free mulattoes, 87,370 free blacks, 11,100 slave mulattoes, and 425,000 black slaves for a total of 1,247,230. Levine, *Cuba,* 7.

47. See Knight, *Slave Society,* esp. ch. 5; also see Martínez-Alier, *Marriage,* 98, 71–81. Martínez-Alier identifies nine different categories among the free of color: (1) free-born pardo, white on one side; (2) ex-slave pardo, white on one side; (3) free-born pardo on both sides; (4) ex-slave, pardo on both sides; (5) free, free-born chino; (6) ex-slave chino; (7) free-born Creole moreno; (8) ex-slave Creole moreno; (9) ex-slave African-born. These categories point to the preeminence of color shade in establishing hierarchy among the free of color. At the top are included the pardos (mulatto offspring of black and white or of two mulattoes), followed by the chinos (offspring of black and mulatto), and finally the morenos (offspring of blacks). Below the free of color were the slaves in the following hierarchy: pardo slave, moreno Creole slave, African-born slave.

48. The census of 1841 provides detailed neighborhood-by-neighborhood demographic information about Havana. For all of Havana's urban districts the information is as follows: 61,614 whites (35,076 male, 26,538 female); 35,713 free of color (17,208 male, 18,505 female); 40,171 slaves (22,717 male, 17,454 female), for a total of 137,498 (75,001 male, 62,497 female). Census figures for 1860 reflect a total population of 158,587 broken down as follows: 95,963 whites, 319 Yucatecans, 2,008 Asians, 28,990 free of color, and 31,307 slaves. For the entire island, including Havana, the information for 1841 is as follows: 418,291 whites (227,144 male, 191,147 female); 152,838 free of color (75,703 male, 77,135 female); 436,495 slaves (281,250 male, 155,245 female), for a total of 1,007,624 (584,097 male, 423,527 female). Census of 1841 reproduced in Cuba, Instituto de Investigaciones Estadísticas, *Los censos de población y viviendas en Cuba,* 89–98; Erenchún, *Anales,* 1902–1903; Paquette, *Sugar,* 39–40.

49. Erenchún, *Anales,* 1911; *Directorio de artes,* 61; Levine, *Cuba,* 12. At mid-century, one Spanish peso was equivalent to one U.S. dollar. A gold Spanish doubloon (onza de oro) was equivalent to 17 pesos/dollars. A British pound was equivalent to 5.1 pesos/dollars. Five pesetas were equivalent to one peso, and ten reales de plata constituted one peso.

50. Julia Ward Howe, *A Trip to Cuba,* 35; Alexander Jones, *Cuba in 1851,* 18; Levine, *Cuba,* 12.

51. Steele, *Cuban Sketches,* 19.

52. Walter Goodman, *The Pearl of the Antilles,* 1–2; Gibbes, *Cuba for Invalids,* 8; Dana, *To Cuba,* 9; Bremer, *Homes,* 2:258; Samuel Hazard, *Cuba with Pen and Pencil,* 35; [Wurdemann], *Notes,* 19; Howe, *Trip,* 30.

53. Grace Backhouse to Mary Backhouse, June 30, 1853, Backhouse Papers.

54. *La Gaceta de La Habana* of March 22, 1854, reported that in the city, the sun set at 6:04.

55. His Diary, March 21, 1853, Backhouse Papers; George Backhouse to Lord Russell, March 21, 1853, PRO, FO 313/24.

56. Sala, *Under the Sun,* 71–73; [Woodruff], *My Winter,* 72; Ballou, *Due South,* 130; Howe, *Trip,* 37, 110; [William Henry Hurlbert], *Gan-Eden,* 96; Ashworth, *Tour,* 49; Murray, *Letters,* 2:54; Abbott, *South and North,* 44; Antonio Carlo Napoleone Gallenga, *The Pearl of the Antilles,* 25; Edwin F. Atkins, *Sixty Years in Cuba,* 2.

57. Her Diary, March 21, 1853; George Backhouse to his aunt, March 27, 1853, both in Backhouse Papers.

58. Alexander Gilmore Cattell, *To Cuba and Back in Twenty-Two Days,* 16; Hazard, *Cuba,* 166; Dana, *To Cuba,* 109; [Santa Cruz], *Viaje,* 207; [Wurdemann], *Notes,* 25; Steele, *Cuban Sketches,* 20, 106; Ripley, *Flag to Flag,* 139; Gallenga, *Pearl,* 35; George Backhouse to Catherine Backhouse, May 11, 1855, Backhouse Papers.

59. Jameson, *Letters,* 60 (emphasis in the original); [Woodruff], *My Winter,* 73; Gallenga, *Pearl,* 92; Ballou, *Due South,* 141–2; Carlton H. Rogers, *Incidents of Travel in the Southern States and Cuba,* 66; Steele, *Cuban Sketches,* 20; for a literary description of Havana's smells, Alejo Carpentier, *Explosion in a Cathedral,* 13–14.

60. Demoticus Philalethes, *Yankee Travels through the Island of Cuba,* 9–10; Antonio de las Barras y Prado, *Memorias, La Habana a mediados del siglo XIX,* 69; Hazard, *Cuba,* 59; Gibbes, *Cuba for Invalids,* 9; Abbott, *South and North,* 44; His Diary, March 21, 1853, Backhouse Papers.

61. His Diary, March 21, 1853; Her Diary, March 21–22, 1853, both in Backhouse Papers; Williams, *Sketches,* 7; Ballou, *Due South,* 121–2, 179; Philalethes, *Yankee Travels,* 2–3; Sala, *Under the Sun,* 66, 123–4; Dana, *To Cuba,* 12–13; Hazard, *Cuba,* 23, 40; [Woodruff], *My Winter,* 31–32; Howe, *Trip,* 41, 136–7; [Hurlbert], *Gan-Eden,* 30–31; Nicolás Tanco Armero, "La Isla de Cuba," 109; George W. Carleton, *Our Artist in Cuba.*

62. Her Diary, March 23, 1853, Backhouse Papers.

63. His Diary, March 21, 1853, Backhouse Papers.

## II. Settling in the Tropics

1. Leví Marrero, *Cuba: Economía y sociedad,* 14:161; [Woodruff], *My Winter,* 31–32; Dana, *To Cuba,* 106; Ballou, *Due South,* 134; Villaverde, *Cecilia Valdés,* 167.

2. Great Britain, Foreign Office, *Foreign Office List,* 1864.

3. Paquette, *Sugar,* 145; José Luciano Franco, *Comercio clandestino de esclavos,* 227, 366.

4. George Backhouse to his aunt, March 27, 1853; His Diary, March 22, 1853, both in Backhouse Papers; Crawford to Lord Russell, February 26, 1853, PRO, FO 84/905.

5. [Wurdemann], *Notes,* 4; His Diary, March 23, 1853, Backhouse Papers.

6. Her Diary, March 22, 1853, Backhouse Papers; George Backhouse to Lord Clarendon, November 6, 1854, PRO, FO 313/27; Great Britain, Foreign Office, *Foreign Office List* (1878), 83.

7. His Diary, August 3, 12, 1851, March 29, 30, 1853; George Backhouse to his aunt, March 27, 1853, all in Backhouse Papers.

8. Allen, *Island of Cuba,* 16; Cuba, Comisión de Estadística, *Cuadro estadístico de la siempre fiel Isla de Cuba* (1846); Emilio Roig de Leuchsenring, *La Habana* (1939 ed.), 38; Francisco González del Valle, *La Habana en 1841,* 93; Moore, *Journal,* 24–25; Weiss y Sánchez, *Arquitectura colonial,* 1:148; Felicia Chateloin, *La Habana de Tacón,* 109.

9. Hazard, *Cuba,* 69, 142; Ballou, *Due South,* 180–81; Moore, *Journal,* 54.

10. [Hurlbert], *Gan-Eden,* 61; Ballou, *Due South,* 180–81.

11. Weiss y Sánchez, *La arquitectura cubana del siglo XIX,* 2nd ed., xii–xvii; D'Hespel D'Harponville, *Reine,* 116–17; de la Torre, *Lo que fuimos y lo que somos,* 98; Joseph John Gurney, *A Winter in the West Indies,* 205; Dana, *To Cuba,* 92; Cuba, Comisión de Estadística, *Cuadro estadístico* (1846), 46; Hazard, *Cuba,* 142–43; Rogers, *Incidents,* 97; Levine, *Cuba,* 56; *Directorio de artes,* 32, 245; *Anuario y directorio de La Habana,* 179, 272–80; [Hurlbert], *Gan-Eden,* 60. Among the *quintas* of El Cerro were those of Santovenia, Doña Leonor de Herrera, the Count of Lombillo, Peñalver, and the Marquis of Las Delicias. Emilio Roig de Leuchsenring, *La Habana: Apuntes históricos* (1963 ed.), 2:19; Roberto Gómez Reyes, "Informe histórico sobre la casa #256 de la Calle Tulipán," Archivo del Museo del Cerro, Havana, file 4.1.10.

12. Bremer, *Homes,* 2:271 (emphasis added); Williams, *Sketches,* 10; Rogers, *Incidents,* 97; Ballou, *Due South,* 268–69; [Hurlbert], *Gan-Eden,* 61; Howe, *Trip,* 239.

13. Dana, *To Cuba,* 46; Ashworth, *Tour,* 54–55; George Backhouse to Mary Backhouse, May 1, 1853, Backhouse Papers; [Woodruff], *My Winter,* 38.

14. [Hurlbert], *Gan-Eden,* 61; Howe, *Trip,* 67; [Wurdemann], *Notes,* 301–9; Ballou, *Due South,* 213–15; James Mursell Phillippo, *The United States and Cuba,* 455; Jameson, *Letters,* 127; George Backhouse to Mary Backhouse, May 1, 1853; His Diary, May 9, 1853; Grace Backhouse to Mary Backhouse, June 30, 1853, all in Backhouse Papers.

15. His Diary, May 15, 1853; Her Diary, May 15, 1853, both in Backhouse Papers.

16. La Calle Buenos Aires was within the *barrio* (ward) of El Cerro; El Cerro belonged to the jurisdiction of the district of El Horcón, one of Havana's rural districts. Erenchún, *Anales,* 1875; His Diary, April 2, 13, 1853, Backhouse Papers.

17. His Diary, April 2, 1853, Backhouse Papers.

18. George Backhouse to Catherine Backhouse, May 11, 1855; Her Diary April 1, 1853; His Diary, October 12, 1853; Grace Backhouse to Mary Backhouse, June 30, 1853, all in Backhouse Papers.

19. George Backhouse to Mary Backhouse, May 1, 1853; Grace Backhouse to Mary Backhouse, January 6, 1854, both in Backhouse Papers.

20. Grace Backhouse to Mary Backhouse, January 6, 1854; Her Diary, April, 3, June 12–14, 1854; inventory dated January 29, 1856, all in Backhouse Papers; Pool, *What Jane Austen Ate,* 197.

21. Grace Backhouse to Catherine Backhouse, January 4, 1854; Grace Backhouse to Mary Backhouse, June 30, 1853; Her Diary, July 4–5, September 1, 1854, all in Backhouse Papers; Pool, *What Jane Austen Ate,* 218.

22. His Diary, September 22, 1853, Grace Backhouse to her aunt, October 7, 1853, both in Backhouse Papers.

23. Her Diary, April 12, September 29, 1853, September 5, 1854; Grace Backhouse to Catherine Backhouse, January 4, 1854, all in Backhouse Papers.

24. Grace Backhouse to Catherine Backhouse, May 1, 1854; Her Diary, January 27, May 17, 1854: George Backhouse to Mary Backhouse, July 29, 1853, all in Backhouse Papers; [Woodruff], *My Winter,* 202.

25. Howe, *Trip,* 120; Her Diary, March 18, August 10, 1854; Grace Backhouse to Catherine Backhouse, September 4, 1854, all in Backhouse Papers.

26. Her Diary, July 15, August 10, 1854; Grace Backhouse to Catherine Backhouse, January 4, March 19, 1854, all in Backhouse Papers. The reference to "very tumble down streets" is probably about one of Havana's predominantly working-class districts: Belén, Chavez, or Jesús María. Paquette, *Sugar,* 39–40.

27. Crawford to Lord Palmerston, June 14, 1851, PRO, FO 72/793; Anthony Trollope, *The West Indies and the Spanish Main,* 140–47; Phillippo, *United States,* 428; Marrero, *Cuba,* 9:102; Her Diary, May 3, 18, 1853, August 19, 1854; Crawford to Thomas Staveley, September 8, 1855 (copy); Grace Backhouse to Catherine Backhouse, April 6, 1854, all in Backhouse Papers. Crawford also spent £300 on domestic service annually; Crawford to Lord Palmerston, June 14, 1851, PRO, FO 72/793.

28. Phillippo, *United States,* 428; [Wurdemann], *Notes,* 44; statement by Crawford for U.S. Consul Charles Helm, November 27, 1858; Helm to the U.S. secretary of state, November 29, 1858, both in National Archives, College Park, MD (hereafter cited as NA), Record Group 59, General Records of the Department of State, Diplomatic Despatches of the Havana Consulate (hereafter cited as Havana Despatches), vol. 39; Crawford to Lord Clarendon, May 29, 1854, PRO, FO 72/852; Crawford to John Bidwell, July 27, 1850, PRO, FO, 72/771; Crawford to Lord Palmerston, June 14, 1851, PRO, FO 72/793; Gallenga, *Pearl,* 25; Captain-General José de la Concha's 1851 report in España, Ministerio de Ultramar, *Cuba desde 1850 a 1873,* compiled by Carlos de Sedano, 37; D'Hespel D'Harponville, *Reine,* 256; [Hurlbert], *Gan-Eden,* 31.

29. George Backhouse to Mary Backhouse, February 13, 1851, George Backhouse to Jane Backhouse, May 4, 1851: George Backhouse to Mary Backhouse, May 1, 1853, all in Backhouse Papers; George Backhouse to Lord Clarendon, November 6, 1854, PRO, FO 313/27.

30. His Diary, March 21, 1853, Backhouse Papers; Murray, *Letters,* 2:55; Sala, *Under the Sun,* 73.

31. George Backhouse to Mary Backhouse, May 1, 1853; His Diary, April 30, 1853, both in Backhouse Papers.

32. González del Valle, *La Habana en 1841,* 169–70; D'Hespel D'Harponville, *Reine,* 442; Philalethes, *Yankee Travels,* 46–49; Moore, *Journal,* 33, Gibbes, *Cuba for Invalids,* 66; Paquette, *Sugar,* 46; Murray, *Letters,* 2:57, 78; Ashworth,

*Tour,* 63; Tudor, *Narrative,* 2:106–8; [Santa Cruz], *Viaje,* 102; Phillippo, *United States,* 408; Turnbull, *Travels,* 94.

33. George Backhouse to Mary Backhouse, May 1, 1853; George Backhouse to his aunt, August 3, 1853; Grace Backhouse to Mary Backhouse, June 30, 1853, all in Backhouse Papers.

## III. The Mixed Commission and Cuba's *Emancipados*

1. Sworn statement dated March 26, 1853, ANC, Gobierno General, leg. 337, exp. 16240.
2. His Diary, March 26, 1853, Backhouse Papers; Crawford's yearly report as acting commissary judge, January 1, 1853, PRO, FO 313/24; Reyneiro G. Lebroc, *Cuba: Iglesia y sociedad,* 181.
3. Spanish minister in London to the captain-general of Cuba, February 4, 1853, ANC, Gobierno General, leg. 337, exp. 16240.
4. Robert W. Shufeldt, "Secret History of the Slave Trade to Cuba," 218–35.
5. Great Britain, *British and Foreign State Papers,* 1816–17, pp. 33–74; Marrero, *Cuba,* 9:47; Leslie Bethell, "The Mixed Commissions for the Suppression of the Transatlantic Slave Trade in the Nineteenth Century," 80–81. The indemnification amount was £400,000.
6. Spanish minister in London to Lord Clarendon, June 11, 1856, Archivo Histórico Nacional, Madrid (hereafter cited as AHN), Estado, leg. 8047; Great Britain, *British and Foreign,* 1834–35, pp. 343–74.
7. Eltis, "Nineteenth-Century Transatlantic Slave Trade," 122–23.
8. Great Britain, *British and Foreign,* 1834–35, pp. 343–74.
9. Spanish first secretary of state to the captain-general of Cuba, January 1, 1850, ANC, Reales Órdenes y Cédulas, leg. 151, exp. 123.
10. Inés Roldán de Montaud, "Origen, evolución y supresión del grupo de negros 'emancipados' en Cuba," 569–70, 610; Rodolfo Sarracino, *Los que volvieron a África,* 70–71.
11. George Backhouse and Crawford to Lord Clarendon, October 10, 1854, PRO, FO 313/27.
12. See report in PRO, FO 313/24, p. 87. George Backhouse to Lord Clarendon, January 2, 1854, PRO, FO 84/929; Crawford to Lord Palmerston, December 31, 1851, PRO, FO 313/24.
13. Paquette, *Sugar,* 153.
14. Murray, *Odious Commerce,* 141–55; Paquette, *Sugar,* 138–39, 150–54.
15. Murray, *Odious Commerce,* 141–56, 178; Philip S. Foner, *A History of Cuba and Its Relations with the United States,* 1:210–11; Paquette, *Sugar,* 138–39, 150–54; Martínez-Fernández, *Torn between Empires,* 17.
16. George Backhouse to Lord Clarendon, August 7, 1854, PRO, FO 313/26; Corwin, *Spain and the Abolition,* 62; Great Britain, *BPP,* vol. 7, p. 96.
17. John G. Taylor, *The United States and Cuba,* 289; Gurney, *Winter,* 206; Murray, *Letters,* 2:61, 86.
18. Marrero, *Cuba,* 9:102; Roncali ruled Cuba between 1848 and 1850.
19. See William B. Taylor, *Drinking, Homicide, and Rebellion in Colonial Mexican Villages,* 101–6.

20. Bethell, "Mixed Commissions," 80–87; Mariano Díaz to the president of the Spanish Council of Ministers, August 7, 1854, AHN, Estado, 8047; Lord Clarendon to Crawford, May 19, 1853, PRO, FO 84/905; George Backhouse to Lord Clarendon, August 30, 1853, PRO, FO 313/25; Turnbull, *Travels,* 40–42; George Backhouse to Lord Clarendon, May 10, 1853, PRO, FO 313/24 and November 6, 1854, PRO, FO 313/27.

21. Moreno Fraginals, *El ingenio,* 1:279, 284; Bethell, "Mixed Commissions," 92; Gurney, *Winter,* 206, 213–19.

22. Shufeldt, "Secret History," 218–35.

23. Testimony by Kennedy in Great Britain, *BPP,* vol. 7, p. 96; Her Diary, December 16, 1854, Backhouse Papers; Taylor, *United States,* 282; George Backhouse to Lord Clarendon, May 8, 1854, PRO, FO 313/26; Chateloin, *La Habana,* 68; Paquette, *Sugar,* 44.

24. George Backhouse to Lord Clarendon, November 6, 1854, PRO, FO 313/27; testimony by Francis Ross Cocking quoted in Paquette, *Sugar,* 144; Kennedy to Lord Stanley, October 26, 1852, PRO, FO 84/870; Great Britain, *BPP,* vol. 7, p. 89; Edward Sullivan, *Rambles and Scrambles in North and South America,* 250.

25. Murray, *Odious Commerce,* 141; Paquette, *Sugar,* 144–45; Marrero, *Cuba,* 9:77.

26. Records of the case, and George Backhouse to Lord Clarendon, August 8, 1853, both in PRO, FO 313/25; Mariano Díaz to the president of the Spanish Council of Ministers, August 7, 1854, AHN, Estado, 8047.

27. Document signed by Crawford dated March 21, 1853, PRO, FO 313/24, p. 145; Judge Esteva to the president of the Spanish Council of Ministers, May 10, 1854, AHN, Estado, leg. 8047.

28. Documents signed by the Spanish secretary of state, April 7, 1855, and January 13, 1857; George Backhouse to Judge Esteva, March 23, 1854, and April 24, 1854 (copies), all in AHN, Estado, leg. 8047.

29. His Diary, April 20, 27, May 31, 1853; Her Diary, April 17, 1853, both in Backhouse Papers; George Backhouse to Lord Clarendon, May 10, 1853, and other case documents in PRO, FO 313/24; Crawford to Lord Clarendon, April 21, 1853, PRO, FO 84/905.

30. Captain Hancock to Crawford, June 29, 1854; George Backhouse to Lord Clarendon, July 10, 1854, both in PRO, FO 313/26; Crawford to Lord Clarendon, July 6, 1854, PRO, FO 84/937.

31. Documents pertaining to the case in PRO, FO 313/28, p. 46; George Backhouse to Lord Clarendon, June 18, 1855, PRO, FO 313/27; Lord Clarendon to Backhouse, September 29, 1855, and Crawford to Lord Clarendon, October 25, 1855, both in Great Britain, *BPP,* vol. 42, Class A, pp. 75–76.

32. According to the law, there were two categories of emancipados: the *aprendices* (those serving their first five-year term) and the *ladinos* (those serving beyond their first five-year term). The consignment fees for aprendices were higher than those of ladinos because the trustees of ladinos had to pay, in addition, a nominal salary to their emancipados; aprendices, on the other hand, only received food, clothing, and shelter. Consignment fees established in 1854 were as follows: those younger than eight years, free of charge; aprendices 8 to 15

years old, 5 pesos per month if male, 3 pesos per month if female; aprendices 15 years old or older, 6 pesos per month if male, 4 pesos per month if female; ladinos, 2.6 pesos per month if male, and 2 pesos per month if female. Ladinos were supposed to receive from their trustees wages of 6 pesos per month if male, and 4.5 pesos per month if female; in either case this was a very low wage, between one-third and one-half of what they could earn as free laborers. In the case of those emancipados with special skills such as cigar-making, these salaries represented close to only one-fifth of what they could earn as free laborers. Emancipado legislation also established that the Cuban-born children of emancipadas be consigned along with their mothers. Annex C to 1835 treaty, Great Britain, *British and Foreign,* 1834–35; Francisco Dionisio Vives, *Condiciones con que se reparten los negros que se emancipan por el Gobierno* (document signed by the captain-general of Cuba in 1829; copy in the Cuban Collection of the Biblioteca Nacional José Martí, Havana); José de la Concha, *Memoria sobre el ramo de emancipados de la Isla de Cuba;* Budget of the Junta de Emancipados of 1856, ANC, Gobierno General, leg. 337, exp. 16254, and leg. 940, exp. 33151; Roldán de Montaud, "Origen," 597; case of the thirteen-year-old daughter of Olalla, tin ticket 120, of the Isle of Pines expedition, ANC, Gobierno General, leg. 258, exp. 13376. Also see Luis Martínez-Fernández, "The Havana Anglo-Spanish Mixed Commission for the Suppression of the Slave Trade and Cuba's *Emancipados.*"

33. File on labor of emancipados in Matanzas (1832–33), ANC, Gobierno Superior Civil, leg. 105, exp. 5363; de la Concha, *Memoria,* 4–5; Spanish first secretary of state to the captain-general of Cuba, June 20, 1836, ANC, Reales Órdenes y Cédulas, leg. 100, exp. 14.

34. Decree of December 28, 1854, in *La Gaceta de La Habana,* December 29, 1854.

35. Concha, *Memoria,* 5–6; Lord Palmerston to the Spanish government, March 27, 1851, AHN, Estado, leg. 8044.

36. George Backhouse to Lord Clarendon, January 1, 1854, PRO, FO 313/27.

37. Grace Backhouse to Catherine Backhouse, January 6, 1854; Grace Backhouse to Mary Backhouse, June 30, 1853; Her Diary, July 14–15, September 1, 1854, all in Backhouse Papers.

38. Decree of December 28, 1854, in *La Gaceta de La Habana,* December 29, 1854; de la Concha, *Memoria,* 9; ANC, Gobierno General, leg. 258, exp. 13376.

39. Roldán de Montaud, "Origen," 599.

40. George Backhouse to Lord Clarendon, December 9, 1853, PRO, FO 313/25 and FO 84/900.

41. George Backhouse to Lord Clarendon, November 10, 1853, PRO, FO 84/900 and FO 313/25; George Backhouse to Lord Clarendon, October 10, 1853, PRO, FO 313/25.

42. Crawford to Lord Clarendon, February 1, 1855, PRO, FO 84/965.

43. Miguel Estorch cited in Roldán de Montaud, "Origen," 581; Crawford to Lord Clarendon, June 1, 1855, AHN, Estado, leg. 8048; Paquette, *Sugar,* 135; Crawford to Lord Clarendon, January 3, 1855, in Great Britain, *BPP,* vol. 41, Class B, p. 563; D'Hespel D'Harponville, *Reine,* 279–80.

44. Vives, *Condiciones.*

45. Case file in ANC, Asuntos Políticos, leg. 41, exp. 58.
46. Jacobo de la Pezuela cited in Roldán de Montaud, "Origen," 559.
47. Roldán de Montaud, "Origen," 580. There are, however, some indications of cordial interaction between emancipados and both free blacks and slaves including marriages. Sarracino, *Los que volvieron,* 200–8.
48. His Diary, May 10, 1853, Backhouse Papers.
49. Cañedo to George Backhouse, November 17, 1853, PRO, FO 313/25 and 84/900; Cañedo to Crawford, March 4, 1853, PRO, FO 84/905.
50. Foner, *History,* 2:76–77; copy of January 1 decree in PRO, FO 313/25, pp. 162–67; *La Gaceta de La Habana,* May 3–4, 1854; Murray, *Odious Commerce,* 233–55; de la Concha, *Memoria,* 8.
51. Un Hacendado [Cristóbal F. Madan], *Llamamiento de la Isla de Cuba a la nación española,* 97–98. An anonymous leaflet entitled "Gratitud de los Cubanos al General Pezuela" circulated in Havana following his departure. It was, however, more of an anti-Concha leaflet than anything praising Pezuela. Copy of leaflet in ANC, Asuntos Políticos, leg. 220, exp. 7; Crawford to Concha, March 31, 1855, in Great Britain, *BPP,* vol. 42, Class B, p. 379.
52. Crawford to Lord Clarendon, September 27, 1854, in Great Britain, *BPP,* vol. 41, Class B, p. 533; George Backhouse to Lord Clarendon, September 30, 1854, PRO, FO 313/27; de las Barras y Prado, *Memorias,* 26–27; Grace Backhouse to Catherine Backhouse, October, 5, 1854, Backhouse Papers.
53. George Backhouse to Lord Clarendon, December 9, 1853, and January 30, 1854, PRO, FO 313/25.
54. George Backhouse to Lord Clarendon, February 7, 1855, PRO, FO 84/959 and 313/27; general director of the Spanish Secretariat of State to the captain-general of Cuba, April 13, 1855, ANC, Reales Órdenes y Cédulas, leg. 183, exp. 223.
55. Crawford to the Earl of Malmesbury, January 24, 1853, and Cañedo to Crawford, March 4, 1853, PRO, FO 84/905.
56. George Backhouse to Lord Clarendon, September 9, 1853, PRO, FO 84/899; George Backhouse to Lord Clarendon, October 10, 1853, PRO, FO 313/25; George Backhouse to Cañedo, October 21, 1853, PRO, FO 313/25 and 84/900.
57. George Backhouse to Lord Clarendon, December 9, 1853; George Backhouse to Lord Clarendon, January 30, 1854, PRO, FO 313/25.
58. José Esteva to Crawford, December 24, 1853, PRO, FO 313/37; George Backhouse to Lord Clarendon, November 10, 1853, and January 30, 1854, both in PRO, FO 313/25.
59. The correspondence on the Dasalu case is in PRO, FO 313/38.
60. Fernando Ortiz Fernández, *Travesía y trata negrera,* 58.
61. Her Diary, March 22, 1853; His Diary, March 30, 1853, both in Backhouse Papers; George Backhouse to Lord Clarendon, November 6, 1854, PRO, FO 313/27; other documents on Dalrymple in PRO, FO 313/25, pp. 174–78.
62. His Diary, May 20, 1853; Her Diary May 22, 1853, both in Backhouse Papers.
63. Crawford to Lord Clarendon, June 7, 1853, PRO, FO 72/830.
64. Crawford to Lord Clarendon, June 8, 1853, PRO, FO 313/24; Crawford to Lord Clarendon, June 7, and August 24, 1853, PRO, FO 72/830; Kennedy

to Lord Palmerston, August 24, 1850, Lord Palmerston to Kennedy, September 26, 1850, and Kennedy to Lord Palmerston, July 26, 1850, all three in PRO, FO, 72/771.

65. Crawford to Lord Clarendon, September 8, 1853, and draft of Lord Palmerston to Crawford, July 28, 1853, both in PRO, FO 72/830.

66. Chateloin, *La Habana,* 159–62; [Wurdemann], *Notes,* 59; Dana, *To Cuba,* 93–94.

67. Madden, *Island of Cuba,* 79; draft of Lord Palmerston to Crawford, July 28, 1853, and Crawford to Lord Clarendon, September 8, 1853, both in PRO, FO 72/830; Marrero, *Cuba,* 14:35–6; Dana, *To Cuba,* 93–94; Gurney, *Winter,* 212; Dalrymple to Lord Clarendon, December 9, 1853, PRO, FO 84/898.

68. His Diary, May 26, June, 6, 7, 8, 14, 20, 24, 1853, Backhouse Papers; Lord Wodehouse to Dalrymple, July 27, 1853, PRO, FO 313/37.

69. His Diary, July 13, 1853, Backhouse Papers; Lord Wodehouse to Dalrymple, July 27, 1853, PRO, FO 313/37; Crawford to Lord Clarendon, September 8, 1853, PRO, FO 72/830.

70. Crawford to Lord Clarendon, June 7, and September 8, 1853, PRO, FO 72/830; note signed by Crawford, PRO, FO 72/852.

71. Crawford to Lord Clarendon, June 7, September 8, 1853, PRO, FO 72/830; Dalrymple to Lord Clarendon, July 20, 1854, PRO, FO 313/38.

72. Ballou, *Due South,* 188–96; His Diary, July 13, August 2, 1853, Backhouse Papers; George Backhouse to Lord Clarendon, August 9, and September 9, 1853, PRO, FO 313/25; Dalrymple to Lord Clarendon, December 9, 1853, PRO, FO 84/898.

73. Francisco Marty to the captain-general of Cuba, July 19, 1842, ANC, Gobierno Superior Civil, leg. 994, exp. 34299; Paquette, *Sugar,* 218; Franco, *Comercio clandestino,* 226–28.

74. George Backhouse to Lord Clarendon, September 9, 1853, PRO, FO 313/25; His Diary, September 9, 1853, Backhouse Papers; George Backhouse to Dalrymple, September 9, 1853, PRO, FO 84/898.

75. Spanish captain-general to Crawford, December 2, 1853, and Crawford to Lord Clarendon, April 6, 1854, both in PRO, FO 72/852; George Backhouse to Lord Clarendon, January 11, 1854, PRO, FO 313/25; George Backhouse to Lord Clarendon, February 27, 1854, PRO, FO 313/26; Lord Clarendon to Dalrymple, January 27, 1854, PRO, FO 313/38.

76. First Spanish secretary of state to the captain-general of Cuba, September 18, 1844, ANC, Reales Órdenes y Cédulas, leg. 165, exp. 40; Kennedy to the captain-general of Cuba, January 10, 1849, ANC, Gobierno Superior Civil, leg. 1119, exp. 41188; Kennedy to the captain-general of Cuba, April 9, 1850, ANC, Gobierno Superior Civil, leg. 1113, exp. 41234; Crawford to Lord Clarendon, September 8, 1853, PRO, FO, 72/830.

77. Dalrymple to Lord Clarendon, July 20, 1854, and other related documents in PRO, FO 313/38; George Backhouse to Lord Clarendon, November 6, 1854, PRO, FO 313/27 and FO 84/930; PRO, FO 313/24, p. 82.

78. George Backhouse to Lord Clarendon, November 6, 1854, PRO, FO 84/930; Lord Wodehouse to Dalrymple, December 7, 1854, PRO, FO 313/38; Dalrymple to Lord Clarendon, December 9, 1853, PRO, FO 84/898.

## IV. Life in a "Male City"

1. See, for example, [Hurlbert], *Gan-Eden*, 2; Phillippo, *United States*, 465; Steele, *Cuban Sketches*, 22, 210–19; Williams, *Sketches*, 5; John A. Perry, *Thrilling Adventures of a New Englander*, 12; Abbott, *South and North*, 52; Howe, *Trip*, 94; Rogers, *Incidents*, 172–73; Henry Anthony Murray, *Lands of the Slave and the Free*, 1:297; Tudor, *Narrative*, 2:104; also see Luis Martínez-Fernández, "Life in a 'Male City': Native and Foreign Elite Women in Nineteenth-Century Havana," 27–49.

2. Howe, *Trip*, 30.

3. Steele, *Cuban Sketches*, 214.

4. Gallenga, *Pearl*, 29, 36; Tanco Armero, "Isla," 112; [Wurdemann], *Notes*, 40.

5. Census of 1861, reproduced in Cuba, Instituto de Investigaciones Estadísticas, *Censos*, 1:111–13.

6. At mid-century the sex imbalance among rural slaves aged 12–60 was 136,600 males to 69,256 females; there were instances of plantations having all-male work forces. Among urban slaves of the same age group, however, the imbalance was inverted and much lighter: 22,891 men to 25,232 women. John S. Thrasher, "Preliminary Essay," in Humboldt, *Island of Cuba*, 75; García de Arboleya, *Manual*, 116; in 1853, Crawford reported resumption of male-only importations in the last five years and many plantations with no females, Crawford to Lord Clarendon, April 28, 1853, PRO, FO 84/905. Also see Madden, *Island of Cuba*, 4; Martínez-Alier, *Marriage*, 57. Census of 1861 in Cuba, Instituto de Investigaciones Estadísticas, *Censos*, 1:111–13; most of these demographic shifts were nineteenth-century developments related to the dramatic social and economic transformations brought about by the sugar revolution. As late as 1810 the population of Havana was sexually balanced; in fact, it was closer to the typical Latin American metropolitan area with a slight female majority (48,470 women to 47,644 men). For demographic information on Mexico City see Silvia Arróm, *The Women of Mexico City*, 106.

7. Even in the capital of neighboring Puerto Rico, women could walk the streets. In San Juan in 1846 the number of males per 100 women was 60.4 among whites and 48.3 among the free of color. De las Barras y Prado, *Memorias*, 178; Jay Kinsbruner, *Not of Pure Blood*, 83. It is true that other societies in the hemisphere had similar social structures. Several factors, however, explain why restrictions on female behavior were not as severe in other parts of Latin America. For one, the prolonged wars of independence and the republican legislation that followed their success disturbed traditional morality codes and allowed for greater freedom for the women of post-independence Latin America. In the case of Brazil, with a slave-based social structure similar to that of Cuba, the arrival of the Portuguese court in 1808 also allowed for a greater degree of freedom for the women of Rio de Janeiro and other coastal cities. See Johanna S.P. Mendelson, "The Feminine Press," and June E. Hahner, "The Nineteenth-Century Feminist Press and Women's Rights in Brazil"; Martínez-Alier, *Marriage*, 109, xiii.

8. Martínez-Alier, *Marriage*, 109, xiii.

9. Editors of *La Verdad, Cuestión negrera de la Isla de Cuba,* 8.

10. Philalethes, *Yankee Travels,* 11 (italics in the original); Thrasher, "Preliminary Essay," in Humboldt, *Island of Cuba,* 69–71; political governor of Havana to the captain-general of Cuba, March 3, 1855, ANC, Gobierno Superior Civil, leg. 1373, exp. 53615.

11. Philalethes, *Yankee Travels,* 11; Ballou, *Due South,* 130; Williams, *Sketches,* 12; García de Arboleya, *Manual,* 262; Benjamin Moore Norman, *Rambles by Land and Water,* 28–29; Gibbes, *Cuba for Invalids,* 11; Howe, *Trip,* 43; Dana, *To Cuba,* 10; [Santa Cruz], *Viaje,* 107.

12. [Hurlbert], *Gan-Eden,* 12; Dana, *To Cuba,* 10. Interestingly, these restrictions were also extended to those practicing the so-called world's oldest profession. According to one traveler, street walking was not permitted in Havana and "these women are allowed to 'ply their vocation' from the windows of their houses." Hazard, *Cuba,* 199.

13. [Santa Cruz], *Viaje,* 107; John Mark, *Diary of My Trip to America and Havana,* 66; Tudor, *Narrative,* 2:120; Gallenga, *Pearl,* 28; de las Barras y Prado, *Memorias,* 116–17; Bremer, *Homes,* 2:376; José María Gómez Colón, *Memoria sobre la utilidad del trabajo de la muger pobre en la Isla de Cuba y medios para conseguirlo,* 49–50.

14. Gallenga, *Pearl,* 29; Williams, *Sketches,* 13; [Woodruff], *My Winter,* 125; Phillippo, *United States,* 421; Bryant, *Letters,* 3:28; Norman, *Rambles,* 29; Hazard, *Cuba,* 404; Ballou, *Due South,* 135; Philalethes, *Yankee Travels,* 201. Julia Ward Howe was born in New York City but lived many years in Boston. Howe, *Trip,* 43.

15. Ballou, *Due South,* 175; García de Arboleya, *Manual,* 262; Phillippo, *United States,* 421; Williams, *Sketches,* 13; Norman, *Rambles,* 28–29; Ashworth, *Tour,* 49–50; Dana, *To Cuba,* 17; Hazard, *Cuba,* 161; Tanco Armero, "Isla," 135; Philalethes, *Yankee Travels,* 16–19; [Hurlbert], *Gan-Eden,* 42.

16. Howe, *Trip,* 44–45; Richard J. Levis, *Diary of a Spring Holiday in Cuba,* 25. Throughout the text I use the term *volanta* because contemporary visitors applied it generically to both volantas and quitrines. The main difference between volantas and quitrines was that the quitrines had a top that could be folded back whereas the volantas' top was fixed. Quitrines were more highly esteemed than volantas. The term *quitrín* is a corruption of the Catherine-type suspension coils used in both quitrines and volantas. Ney, *Cuba en 1830,* 29, n. 30 (note by Jorge J. Beato Núñez); Ballou, *Due South,* 129–30; [Santa Cruz], *Viaje,* 210; Hazard, *Cuba,* 176–77; [Woodruff], *My Winter,* 29–30, 48; Trollope, *West Indies,* 144; [Wurdemann], *Notes,* 25.

17. Rogers, *Incidents,* 81; [Santa Cruz], *Viaje,* 101–7; Trollope, *West Indies,* 144; Sala, *Under the Sun,* 149; Tanco Armero, "Isla," 131.

18. Levis, *Diary,* 25; Hazard, *Cuba,* 160–77; [Santa Cruz], *Viaje,* 210; Gibbes, *Cuba for Invalids,* 11; Trollope, *West Indies,* 144–50; Ballou, *Due South,* 159; Steele, *Cuban Sketches,* 113; [Woodruff], *My Winter,* 26–29; Tanco Armero, "Isla," 131; Ashworth, *Tour,* 50; Tudor, *Narrative,* 2:116–17.

19. Rogers, *Incidents,* 92; Ripley, *Flag to Flag,* 137; Frances Calderón de la Barca, *Life in Mexico during a Residence of Two Years in that Country,* 16; Philalethes, *Yankee Travels,* 189–90; Bryant, *Letters,* 3:27–28; [Wurdemann], *Notes,* 41–42; Campbell, *Around the Corner,* 28; Ballou, *Due South,* 168; Murray,

*Letters,* 2:55; Norman, *Rambles,* 16; Howe, *Trip,* 45; [Woodruff], *My Winter,* 30, 69–70; Hazard, *Cuba,* 157.

20. Arróm, *Women,* 66; Erenchún, *Anales,* 223; Captain-General Valentín Cañedo to the president of the Council of Ministers, July 5, 1853, AHN, Ultramar, leg. 1683, exp. 28.

21. [Santa Cruz], *Viaje,* 145.

22. Bryant, *Letters,* 3:31; Dana, *To Cuba,* 21; [Wurdemann], *Notes,* 22; James Edward C.B. Alexander, *Transatlantic Sketches,* 1:338–41; Taylor, *United States,* 294–97; Cattell, *To Cuba,* 33–35; Steele, *Cuban Sketches,* 175; Williams, *Sketches,* 13; [Woodruff], *My Winter,* 167; Ballou, *Due South,* 139.

23. Dana, *To Cuba,* 28–29; Hazard, *Cuba,* 184; Steele, *Cuban Sketches,* 147; de las Barras y Prado, *Memorias,* 48; Villaverde, *Cecilia Valdés,* 192.

24. James O'Kelly, *The Mambi Land,* 26; [Wurdemann], *Notes,* 42; Gallenga, *Pearl,* 36; Hazard, *Cuba,* 158; [Woodruff], *My Winter,* 204, 294; Bremer, *Homes,* 2:281.

25. Steele, *Cuban Sketches,* 214; Howe, *Trip,* 43–44, 85.

26. Moore, *Journal,* 37; [Woodruff], *My Winter,* 70–71.

27. Marrero, *Cuba,* 14:53, 73–74; Emilio Roig de Leuchsenring, *Médicos y medicina en Cuba,* 39–49.

28. Philalethes, *Yankee Travels,* 193.

29. Howe, *Trip,* 38, 106; Moore, *Journal,* 56; Allen, *Island,* 22; Williams, *Sketches,* 13; Ballou, *Due South,* 152, 203–4; [Woodruff], *My Winter,* 27; Tudor, *Narrative,* 2:116; Campbell, *Around the Corner,* 28; Bryant, *Letters,* 3:26; Murray, *Letters,* 2:61.

30. Grace Backhouse to Mary Backhouse, February 7, 1854, Backhouse Papers.

31. W.J. Reader, *Life in Victorian England,* 8.

32. Her Diary, May 3, October 24, 1854; George Backhouse to Catherine Backhouse, January 8, 1854, all in Backhouse Papers; copies of official letters in Grace's handwriting in PRO, FO 72/830 and FO 313/26.

33. Howe, *Trip,* 116; Bremer, *Homes,* 2:283–84; His Diary, April 27, 1853; George Backhouse to Catherine Backhouse, April 2, 1854; Her Diary, April 9, 1853, Backhouse Papers.

34. Her Diary, April 30, 1853, May 11, June 6, 21, 1854, Backhouse Papers.

35. Her Diary, October and November 1854; January 12, 19, 25, and February 9, 1854, all in Backhouse Papers.

36. Her Diary, November 14, 21, 22, 1854, Backhouse Papers.

37. Bryant, *Letters,* 3:34; Hazard, *Cuba,* 143; Bremer, *Homes,* 2:274; Howe, *Trip,* 55; Murray, *Letters,* 2:58; His Diary, May 27, 1853; Her Diary, November 21, 1854, all in Backhouse Papers.

38. Gibbes, *Cuba for Invalids,* 131–32; Tudor, *Narrative,* 2:140–41; Hazard, *Cuba,* 53–54; His Diary, September 5, 1853; Her Diary, July, 26, 1854, all in Backhouse Papers.

39. George Backhouse to Catherine Backhouse, April 2, 1854; His Diary, April 22, 1851, and October 18, 1853; Grace Backhouse to Mary Backhouse, February 7, 1854, all in Backhouse Papers; Moore, *Journal,* 55.

40. In anticipation of the British mail steamer, Grace would sometimes try to spot the vessel from the roof of her house. Her Diary, May 23, June 22, August 23, 1853, February 25, April 24, July 22, October 23, 1854; Grace Backhouse to

Catherine Backhouse, March 25, 1855; Grace Backhouse to Catherine Backhouse, January 4, May 1, 1854; Her Diary, June 22, 1853, and May 11, 1854; Her Diary, June 22, July 22, August 23, 1853, February 25, December 23, 1854; Grace Backhouse to Catherine Backhouse, April 6, 1854, all in Backhouse Papers.

41. Her Diary, May 10, June 9, July 9, October 10, November 10, 1853, May 10, July 10, September 9, October 10, 1854. See, for example, Grace Backhouse to Catherine Backhouse, May 1, and July 4, 1854; Grace Backhouse to Catherine Backhouse and to her sisters-in-law, March 25, 1855; George Backhouse to Catherine Backhouse, April 2, 1854, all in Backhouse Papers.

42. Grace Backhouse to Catherine Backhouse, January 22, 1854 (emphasis in the original); George Backhouse to his aunt, August 3, 1853; George Backhouse to Mary Backhouse, July 29, 1854; Grace Backhouse to Mary Backhouse, June 30, 1853; Grace Backhouse to Catherine Backhouse, April 6, 1854, June 5, 1854, all in Backhouse Papers.

43. Grace Backhouse to Catherine Backhouse, January 22, June 5, and September 4, 1854; George Backhouse to his aunt, August 3, 1854, George Backhouse to Mary Backhouse, July 29, 1854, all in Backhouse Papers.

44. Grace Backhouse to Catherine Backhouse, March 19, June 5, 1854; Grace Backhouse to Catherine Backhouse and to her sisters-in-law, June 21, 1854, all in Backhouse Papers.

45. Her Diary, June 5, 1853; Grace Backhouse to Mary Backhouse, February 7, 1854; Grace Backhouse to Catherine Backhouse, May 1, 1854, all in Backhouse Papers.

## V. Leisure and Pleasure

1. Murray, *Letters*, 2:56; *El Siglo*, February 14, 1867; Ripley, *Flag to Flag*, 130.

2. Her Diary, November 20, 1854, Backhouse Papers; Herminio Portell Vilá, *Historia de Cuba en sus relaciones con los Estados Unidos y España*, 2:13; Steele, *Cuban Sketches*, 217. Britons and Cubans applied the pejorative term "Yankee" indistinctively to citizens from all regions of the United States. Howe, *Trip*, 36.

3. George Backhouse to Catherine Backhouse, March 10, 1854, Backhouse Papers.

4. George Backhouse to Catherine Backhouse, April 2, 1854; mimeographed guide to the Backhouse Papers, both in Backhouse Papers.

5. Grace Backhouse to Catherine Backhouse, January 22, 1854, Backhouse Papers.

6. Her Diary, March 31, and September 12, 1853, Backhouse Papers; Steele, *Cuban Sketches*, 210.

7. His Diary, August 20, 1853, Backhouse Papers.

8. His Diary, April 27, and July 22, 1853; George Backhouse to Mary Backhouse, July 29, 1853, all in Backhouse Papers; Bremer, *Homes*, 2:268–9.

9. George Backhouse to Catherine Backhouse, April 2, 1854; Her Diary, July 21, 1853, and March 28, 1854, all in Backhouse Papers.

10. Her Diary, October 31, 1854 (emphasis in the original); inventory dated January 29, 1856, both in Backhouse Papers.

11. Pool, *What Jane Austen Ate,* 205–10.

12. Her Diary, March 24, 1854, Backhouse Papers (emphasis in the original).

13. Her Diary, May 18, 1853, November 7, 1854; Grace Backhouse to Mary Backhouse, December 3, 1853; Grace Backhouse to Catherine Backhouse, July 4, 1854, all in Backhouse Papers.

14. Her Diary, May 19, 1853, and March 25, 1854, Backhouse Papers.

15. George Backhouse to Catherine Backhouse, March 10, and May 11, 1855, both in Backhouse Papers.

16. His Diary, August 20, 1853; invitation to a ball at Buckingham Palace for May 5, 1852; Her Diary, June 2, 1854, all in Backhouse Papers.

17. Crawford to Lord Clarendon, June 7, 1853, PRO, FO 72/830; Kennedy to Lord Palmerston, November 15, 1850, PRO FO 72/771; Her Diary, November 14, 1854; His Diary August 17, 1853, Backhouse Papers.

18. His Diary, May 14, 1853, Backhouse Papers; Philalethes, *Yankee Travels,* 227; Hazard, *Cuba,* 156; Gibbes, *Cuba for Invalids,* 9. *La Gaceta de La Habana* of March 29, 1855, advertised a "somewhat used but very decent volanta" for 8 gold ounces (136 pesos). An inventory dated January 29, 1856, reflects that the Backhouses owned a carriage with harnesses valued at $1,350; it listed no horses, however.

19. García de Arboleya, *Manual,* 368; de la Torre, *Lo que fuimos,* 120; de las Barras y Prado, *Memorias,* 69; Levine, *Cuba,* 56; Marrero, *Cuba,* 14:295; Her Diary, April 6, 1855, Backhouse Papers.

20. Her Diary, January 31, 1854, April 6, 1855; Grace Backhouse to Mary Backhouse, February 7, 1854 (emphasis in the original), Backhouse Papers. The earlier meaning of the term snob was someone of low social standing; Pool, *What Jane Austen Ate,* 374.

21. His Diary, April 26 and 30, 1853; Grace Backhouse to Catherine Backhouse, January 22, 1854, all in Backhouse Papers.

22. Turnbull, *Travels,* 7; Ashworth, *Tour,* 51; Ballou, *Due South,* 219–21; [Hurlbert], *Gan-Eden,* 10–11; Calderón de la Barca, *Life,* 10; Murray, *Lands,* 1:281; Steele, *Cuban Sketches,* 17; Villaverde, *Cecilia Valdés,* 118; Dana, *To Cuba,* 9.

23. [Hurlbert], *Gan-Eden,* 10–11; Bremer, *Homes,* 2:266; Calderón de la Barca, *Life,* 10; Ballou, *Due South,* 219–20; [Wurdemann], *Notes,* 22; Murray, *Lands,* 1:283; Compadre [pseud.], "El Calesero," 425–29.

24. Sala, *Under the Sun,* 147; Abbott, *South and North,* 44; [Woodruff], *My Winter,* 20, 28 ; Norman, *Rambles,* 12; Phillippo, *United States,* 433; [Hurlbert], *Gan-Eden,* 11; Turnbull, *Travels,* 6.

25. Murray, *Letters,* 2:75; Ballou, *Due South,* 39, 228–29; Tudor, *Narrative,* 2:112–13; Murray, *Lands,* 1:281; [Woodruff], *My Winter,* 28–29; Villaverde, *Cecilia Valdés,* 141.

26. Mariano Torrente, *Bosquejo económico político de la Isla de Cuba,* 1:171; Tudor, *Narrative,* 2:112–13.

27. [Wurdemann], *Notes,* 99; Bremer, *Homes,* 2:266.

28. According to the official census there were 467 quitrines and 2,184 volantas in Havana in 1827, and 2,649 carriages of various types in Havana in 1846. Another source claims that there were 8,500 volantas in 1841. See Chateloin, *La Habana,* 26, 95; and González del Valle, *La Habana,* 217.

29. [Wurdemann], *Notes,* 4; Erenchún, *Anales,* 1802; Gibbes, *Cuba for Invalids,* 9; Abbott, *South and North,* 44; Hazard, *Cuba,* 59; de las Barras y Prado,

*Memorias,* 69; Grace Backhouse to Catherine Backhouse, January 22, 1854, Backhouse Papers.

30. Dana, *To Cuba,* 35; *La Gaceta de La Habana,* April 9, 1853.

31. Philalethes, *Yankee Travels,* 9–10; Hazard, *Cuba,* 58–59; Abbott, *South and North,* 44; [Wurdemann], *Notes,* 179.

32. Howe, *Trip,* 45; Philalethes, *Yankee Travels,* 8; Compadre, "Calesero," 425–29.

33. Her Diary, June 5, 1853, and June 2, 1854, Backhouse Papers.

34. Among Havana's commercial establishments were: 12 drugstores, 22 bakeries, 18 jewelry stores, 19 hotels, 57 furniture stores, 20 perfume shops, 138 eateries, 7 bookstores, 969 dry goods stores, 145 tailor shops, 113 barber shops, 8 guest houses, 139 shoe stores, and 164 doctors' offices. Erenchún, *Anales,* 1905–1907; His Diary, April 30, and May 14, 1853; Her Diary, April 12, May 5 and 12, June 2 and 5, 1853, March 18, 1854; Grace Backhouse to Catherine Backhouse, May 1, 1854, all in Backhouse Papers.

35. Chateloin, *La Habana,* 95. For a street-by-street description of Havana, see Manuel Fernández Santalices, *Las calles de La Habana Intramuros.*

36. Hazard, *Cuba,* 63; [Hurlbert], *Gan-Eden,* 13; [Wurdemann], *Notes,* 40; Gibbes, *Cuba for Invalids,* 206–7; González del Valle, *La Habana,* 219–27, 279; Ballou, *Due South,* 167; Philalethes, *Yankee Travels,* 11; *The Cuban Messenger,* March 24, 1861; also see various advertisements in *Directorio de artes,* passim, and *Anuario y directorio,* passim.

37. Calderón de la Barca, *Life,* 16; [Wurdemann], *Notes,* 41; Hazard, *Cuba,* 36, 162; Steele, *Cuban Sketches,* 105–6; Dana, *To Cuba,* 10; Ballou, *Due South,* 167; [Hurlbert], *Gan-Eden,* 13; Rogers, *Incidents,* 91–92; [Woodruff], *My Winter,* 76; Sala, *Under the Sun,* 74.

38. Ballou, *Due South,* 167; Paquette, *Sugar,* 41; Tanco Armero, "Isla," 110–11.

39. [Wurdemann], *Notes,* 41; Ballou, *Due South,* 168; Murray, *Letters,* 2:55.

40. Chateloin, *La Habana,* 122; Cattell, *To Cuba,* 16; Abbott, *South and North,* 46–47; Diary of Susan Hathorn, February 8, 1855, at the Special Collections Library, Duke University.

41. Murray, *Lands,* 1:290–91; Tanco Armero, "Isla," 138–39; Campbell, *Around the Corner,* 8; Gibbes, *Cuba for Invalids,* 49; [Woodruff], *My Winter,* 98; [Wurdemann], *Notes,* 74; Rogers, *Incidents,* 93; Ballou, *Due South,* 174–75; Erenchún, *Anales,* 1797.

42. Chateloin, *La Habana,* 125–26; *Directorio de artes,* 33; Erenchún, *Anales,* 1733; Franco, *Comercio clandestino,* 236; Ballou, *Due South,* 185–86; [Wurdemann], *Notes,* 35–36; Williams, *Sketches,* 44; Ashworth, *Tour,* 54; Bremer, *Homes,* 2:289; Rogers, *Incidents,* 98–99; Norman, *Rambles,* 36.

43. Advertisement section of *Anuario y directorio,* passim; Gallenga, *Pearl,* 38; Dana, *To Cuba,* 12–13; González del Valle, *La Habana,* 220; Chateloin, *La Habana,* 32.

44. His Diary, March 22 and 29, 1853; Her Diary, April 1, May 5, 1853; June 6, 14, August 10, 1854, all in Backhouse Papers.

45. Cattell, *To Cuba,* 31; [Woodruff], *My Winter,* 30; Howe, *Trip,* 35, 99, 106; Norman, *Rambles,* 16; Williams, *Sketches,* 8–9.

46. Chateloin, *La Habana,* 32; Dana, *To Cuba,* 10, 102; Abbott, *South and North,* 45; Gibbes, *Cuba for Invalids,* 128; Roland T. Ely, *Cuando reinaba su*

*majestad el azúcar,* 751; Jameson, *Letters,* 74–75; Hazard, *Cuba,* 155, 234; Ballou, *Due South,* 260; Campbell, *Around the Corner,* 16; Williams, *Sketches,* 11–12; D'Hespel D'Harponville, *Reine,* 254; Cattell, *To Cuba,* 22–31; Rogers, *Incidents,* 66; Bremer, *Homes,* 2:267; Howe, *Trip,* 110.

47. X. Marmier, "Cuba en 1850," 121; Howe, *Trip,* 107–9; Dana, *To Cuba,* 108; Norman, *Rambles,* 16; [Woodruff], *My Winter,* 30; Her Diary, May 5, 1853, June 10, 14, 19, 1854, Backhouse Papers.

48. García de Arboleya, *Manual,* 373; [Hurlbert], *Gan-Eden,* 4; Roig de Leuchsenring, *La Habana,* (1939 ed.), 87; Bremer, *Homes,* 2:272; Julio Le Riverend, *La Habana,* 138.

49. [Woodruff], *My Winter,* 45; Bremer, *Homes,* 2:261–64; Tanco Armero, "Isla," 131; Villaverde, *Cecilia Valdés,* 182–83; Trollope, *West Indies,* 148.

50. Moore, *Journal,* 54; Levine, *Cuba,* 56; [Woodruff], *My Winter,* 45–6; Hazard, *Cuba,* 69, 142; [Hurlbert], *Gan-Eden,* 61; Rogers, *Incidents,* 97; Gibbes, *Cuba for Invalids,* 131.

51. *Directorio de artes,* 35.

52. His Diary, April 6, 26, 30, June 6, 1853; Her Diary, June 5, 1853, all in Backhouse Papers.

53. Ashworth, *Tour,* 50–51; Steele, *Cuban Sketches,* 113; Villaverde, *Cecilia Valdés,* 184; González del Valle, *La Habana,* 413; Richard Burleigh Kimball, *Cuba and the Cubans,* 153.

54. Villaverde, *Cecila Valdés,* 183.

55. [Woodruff], *My Winter,* 26–27; Gibbes, *Cuba for Invalids,* 11, 30; Ashworth, *Tour,* 50; Bryant, *Letters,* 3:26; Dana, *To Cuba,* 16–17; Norman, *Rambles,* 45; Rogers, *Incidents,* 95–96; Levine, *Cuba,* 44.

56. Construction file of El Teatro Tacón in ANC, Gobierno Superior Civil, leg. 994, exp. 34299; Chateloin, *La Habana,* 196–99; Hazard, *Cuba,* 186; Campbell, *Around the Corner,* 11; Calderón de la Barca, *Life,* 11; [Hurlbert], *Gan-Eden,* 51; Rogers, *Incidents,* 165; Steele, *Cuban Sketches,* 146; Roig de Leuchsenring, *La Habana,* (1939 ed.), 64–65; Dana, *To Cuba,* 28; [Santa Cruz], *Viaje,* 112; Norman, *Rambles,* 35; [Wurdemann], *Notes,* 37; Ballou, *Due South,* 152–54; Paquette, *Sugar,* 218; Weiss y Sánchez, *Arquitectura cubana,* xx.

57. Francisco Marty to the captain-general of Cuba, March 3, 1852, ANC, Gobierno Superior Civil, leg. 1000, exp. 34748; also see leg. 1258, exp. 49706; de las Barras y Prado, *Memorias,* 72–73; García de Arboleya, *Manual,* 250; Calderón de la Barca, *Life,* 11; Ely, *Cuando reinaba,* 677–79; Levine, *Cuba,* 44.

58. Her Diary, July 28, August, 3, 16, November 25, 1854, Backhouse Papers; *La Gaceta de La Habana,* April 9, 1853.

59. Tanco Armero, "Isla," 125; Ballou, *Due South,* 152–53; Bryant, *Letters,* 3:33; Norman, *Rambles,* 35.

60. Grace Backhouse to Catherine Backhouse, April 6, 1854, Backhouse Papers.

## VI. Protestants in Roman Catholic Cuba

1. His Diary, August 3, June 15, December 5, 1851; Her Diary November 2, 1851, and December 15, 1856, and mimeographed description of the Backhouse Papers, all in Backhouse Papers.

2. Phillippo, *United States,* 404; Andrew Blythe to William Cass, July 20, 1857, NA, Havana Despatches, roll 36.

3. Marcos Antonio Ramos, *Panorama del protestantismo en Cuba,* 63; Paquette, *Sugar,* 155; Marrero, *Cuba,* 9:73; Corwin, *Spain and the Abolition,* 73; Murray, *Odious Commerce,* 157.

4. British minister in London to Lord Palmerston, September 22, 1851, PRO, FO 83/159; Jerónimo Bécker, *Historia de las relaciones exteriores de España durante el siglo XIX,* 2:213–14.

5. George Backhouse to his aunt, August 3, 1853, Backhouse Papers; Spanish consul at Kingston to the captain-general of Cuba, October 17, 1853, ANC, Asuntos Políticos, leg. 48, exp. 33.

6. Kennedy to the captain-general of Cuba, May 7, 1850, PRO, FO 72/886; Earl of Malmesbury to the British minister in Madrid, April 23, 1852, AHN, Estado, 8565; Minister [Pidal] to the British minister in Madrid, August 19, 1850, PRO, FO 72/886; George Backhouse to Lord Clarendon, June 20, 1855, in Great Britain, *BPP,* vol. 42, Class A, p. 67; Ramos, *Panorama,* 65.

7. "Real Cédula de 21 de octubre de 1817, sobre aumentar la población blanca de la Isla de Cuba," in ANC, Gobierno Superior Civil, leg. 1657, exp. 82745.

8. Vice-Consul of Ponce Peter Mineville to the San Juan consul, March 22, 1872, NA, Record Group 84, Records of Foreign Service Posts, San Juan Consulate, vol. 7117; Grace Backhouse to Mary Backhouse, January 6, 1854, Backhouse Papers; Williams, *Sketches,* 21.

9. Various sources in the ANC point to the fact that not much evidence was required. In 1818 the British subject George Booth arrived in Havana to establish himself as a carpenter; he had no documents to prove it, but insisted that he was a Roman Catholic. On December 23, he was granted domicile by the Spanish authorities. ANC, Gobierno Superior Civil, leg. 1656, exp. 82742. David Clark had no supporting documents either, but the testimonies of people who knew him sufficed. ANC, Gobierno Superior Civil, leg. 727, exp. 26754. Also see the domiciliation and oath papers of Mary Callaghan, ANC, Gobierno Superior Civil, leg. 791, exp. 26855. Also see George Backhouse to his aunt, August 3, 1853, Backhouse Papers; Crawford to Lord Palmerston, January 22, 1852, PRO, FO 72/886; [Wurdemann], *Notes,* 166; Taylor, *United States,* 297; Turnbull, *Travels,* 67; Kennedy to Lord Palmerston, June 21, 1850, PRO, FO 72/886; British minister in Madrid to Claudio Antón de Luzuriaga, April 4, 1855, PRO, FO 72/885.

10. Dana, *To Cuba,* 20; Abbot, *Letters,* 76; Allen, *Island,* 10.

11. His Diary, March 24, 1853; Her Diary, March 24, and April 3, 1853, both in Backhouse Papers.

12. Weiss y Sánchez, *Arquitectura colonial,* 2:73–74.

13. Allen, *Island,* 10, 23; Ashworth, *Tour,* 51; Levis, *Diary,* 103; Williams, *Sketches,* 41; Diary of the Reverend William Norwood (1844), Virginia Historical Society, Richmond; Trollope, *West Indies,* 147–48.

14. Allen, *Island,* 10; Tudor, *Narrative,* 2:115–16; [Wurdemann], *Notes,* 50; Steele, *Cuban Sketches,* 176–77.

15. Abbot, *Letters,* 76; Her Diary, April 13, 1854, Backhouse Papers; Dana, *To Cuba,* 38; Steele, *Cuban Sketches,* 176–77; Ballou, *Due South,* 37; Norwood Diary (1844); [Wurdemann], *Notes,* 181; [Woodruff], *My Winter,* 56–58.

16. Williams, *Sketches*, 6; Hazard, *Cuba*, 127, 431; Steele, *Cuban Sketches*, 175–81; Dana, *To Cuba*, 86–87; Allen, *Island*, 10; Tudor, *Narrative*, 2:115–16; Rogers, *Incidents*, 88–89; Norwood Diary (1844); [Wurdemann], *Notes*, 22, 49; Calderón de la Barca, *Life*, 13; [Woodruff], *My Winter*, 58.

17. Norman, *Rambles*, 38; Hazard, *Cuba*, 130; Rogers, *Incidents*, 89; Bremer, *Homes*, 2:375.

18. Steele, *Cuban Sketches*, 175; Kimball, *Cuba*, 153; Williams, *Sketches*, 6.

19. Steele, *Cuban Sketches*, 175; [Woodruff], *My Winter*, 58; Kimball, *Cuba*, 153; Rogers, *Incidents*, 88. Curate of Monserrate to the captain-general of Cuba, September 1, 1868, and superior civilian governor of Cuba to the chief of police of Havana, September 3, 1868, both in ANC, Gobierno Superior Civil, leg. 743, exp. 75436.

20. Norwood Diary (1844); Bremer, *Homes*, 2:269, 302; [Woodruff], *My Winter*, 55, 156, 172; Steele, *Cuban Sketches*, 183; Philalethes, *Yankee Travels*, 224; Ballou, *Due South*, 145; Abbot, *Letters*, 62, 68, 74–75; Williams, *Sketches*, 39, 43–44.

21. Her Diary, March 25, 27, 1853, Backhouse Papers.

22. Bremer, *Homes*, 2:375; [Woodruff], *My Winter*, 190; Erenchún, *Anales*, 1791.

23. Norman, *Rambles*, 101; Bryant, *Letters*, 3:29; de las Barras y Prado, *Memorias*, 68; [Woodruff], *My Winter*, 191.

24. His Diary, March 25, 1853, Backhouse Papers; Steele, *Cuban Sketches*, 180–82; Bryant, *Letters*, 3:27; [Hurlbert], *Gan-Eden*, 35; Bremer, *Homes*, 2:376; Rogers, *Incidents*, 161–62.

25. Bremer, *Homes*, 2:376.

26. His Diary, October 23, 1853, and Her Diary, April 6, 1855, Backhouse Papers. Twelfth cakes were richly decorated cakes baked for the celebration of the twelfth night after Christmas, the eve of the day of the Epiphany. Pantomime was a festive and comical theatrical production with drama, music, and dance; Pool, *What Jane Austen Ate*, 349, 386.

27. [Wurdemann], *Notes*, 194; Abbot, *Letters*, 103; Tanco Armero, "Isla," 134.

28. David Lockmiller, "The Settlement of the Church Property Question in Cuba," 488–89.

29. Trollope, *West Indies*, 135; Bremer, *Homes*, 2:376; Gallenga, *Pearl*, 155.

30. Philalethes, *Yankee Travels*, 52, 222; Steele, *Cuban Sketches*, 200; Ashworth, *Tour*, 52; [Wurdemann], *Notes*, 209; Marrero, *Cuba*, 14:168; [Hurlbert], *Gan-Eden*, 168; Rawson, *Cuba*, 28; Phillippo, *United States*, 404–5.

31. Hazard, *Cuba*, 191; Williams, *Sketches*, 5; Dana, *To Cuba*, 119.

32. Cock fights, in fact, could only be held on Sundays and other holidays. Cuba's laws prohibited them during work days and owners of cock pits could be fined 200 pesos for holding cock fights on work days. ANC, Gobierno Superior Civil, leg. 996, exp. 34407.

33. Steele, *Cuban Sketches*, 179–80; Rogers, *Incidents*, 159; Hazard, *Cuba*, 191; Phillippo, *United States*, 405; Williams, *Sketches*, 6; Moore, *Journal*, 40; Ballou, *Due South*, 59; Her Diary, November 19, 1854, Backhouse Papers.

34. His Diary, March 27, 1853, George Backhouse to his aunt, March 27, 1853, both in Backhouse Papers.

35. George Backhouse to his aunt, August 3, 1853; Grace Backhouse to Mary Backhouse, July 29, 1853; Grace Backhouse to her aunt, September 6, 1853, all in Backhouse Papers.

36. Gurney, *Winter*, 211; [Woodruff], *My Winter*, 157.

37. George Backhouse to his aunt, August 3, 1853; His Diary, March 25, 1853; Her Diary, April 24, and November 20, 1853, and June 12, November 19, 1854, all in Backhouse Papers.

38. Her Diary, February 4, and March 18, 1855, Backhouse Papers; Murray, *Letters*, 2:64, 77; [Wurdemann], *Notes*, 348; Rogers, *Incidents*, 173–74.

39. Rogers, *Incidents*, 173–75; Norwood Diary (1844); Ramos, *Panorama*, 78.

40. Grace Backhouse to Mary Backhouse, June 30, 1853, Backhouse Papers.

41. Grace Backhouse to Mary Backhouse, June 30, 1853, and January 6, 1854; George Backhouse to his aunt, August 3, 1853; His Diary, June 18–19, 1853, all in Backhouse Papers.

42. Steele, *Cuban Sketches*, 184, 173.

43. Her Diary, October 30, 1853, and October 30, 1855; certified copy of baptismal certificate of John Sandham Backhouse, both in Backhouse Papers.

44. Howe, *Trip*, 178; Steele, *Cuban Sketches*, 185.

45. Steele, *Cuban Sketches*, 174; Ramos, *Panorama*, 140.

46. Philalethes, *Yankee Travels*, 251, 222; Ramos, *Panorama*, 77.

47. Allen, *Island*, 17; [Hurlbert], *Gan-Eden*, 136–37; Norwood Diary (1844); Bryant, *Letters*, 3:27–31; Turnbull to the captain-general of Cuba, September 16, 1841, ANC, Gobierno Superior Civil, leg. 744, exp. 25346; also see exp. 25546.

48. ANC, Gobierno Superior Civil, leg. 1530, exps. 70685, 70885; Abbot, *Letters*, 17; Charles Helm to Cass, April 21, 1860, NA, Havana Despatches, roll 40.

49. Perry, *Thrilling Adventures*, 12.

## VII. A Land Flowing with Milk and Pestilence

1. Grace Backhouse to her aunt, December 22, 1852, Backhouse Papers; Crawford to the Earl of Malmesbury, September 9, 1852, PRO, FO 72/793; Jorge Le-Roy y Cassá, *Estudios sobre la mortalidad de La Habana durante el siglo XIX y comienzos del actual*, 19; Crawford to Lord Russell, February 3, 1853, PRO, FO 72/830.

2. D. Ramón Hernández Poggio, *Aclimatación é higiene de los europeos en Cuba*, 67–70; Marte, *Cuba*, 191, 123; Le-Roy y Cassá, *Estudios*, 6; Ángel José Cowley, *Ensayo estadístico-médico de la mortalidad de la diócesis de La Habana durante el año de 1843*, 1–41.

3. William H. Robertson to William Marcy, July 27, 1854, NA, Havana Despatches, vol. 28; Ballou, *Due South*, 141; Jameson, *Letters*, 59, 119 (emphasis in the original).

4. Le-Roy y Cassá, *Estudios*, 28; Hernández Poggio, *Aclimatación*, 123; de las Barras y Prado, *Memorias*, 67–68; Marrero, *Cuba*, 14:66; Philalethes, *Yankee Travels*, 3.

5. Cowley, *Ensayo*, 3–6; Hernández Poggio, *Aclimatación*, 45; Marrero, *Cuba*, 9:176; "1857 Sick to Hospitals of Havana from American Vessels," NA, Havana Despatches, roll 39.

6. Thomas Savage to William Marcy, August 3, 1856, NA, Havana Despatches, roll 33; Alexander M. Clayton, "The Relations of the United States and Cuba in 1853 & 54, by A.M. Clayton," manuscript in file 151, Claiborne Papers, Southern Historical Collection, Chapel Hill, NC; see also "Alex M. Clayton to Hon. J.F.H. Claiborne," 364–68.

7. [Wurdemann], *Notes,* 3; D'Hespel D'Harponville, *Reine,* 73; Marrero, *Cuba,* 14:66; Hernández Poggio, *Aclimatación,* 74; Hazard, *Cuba,* 24; Cattell, *To Cuba,* 47; George Backhouse to Mary Backhouse, July 29, 1853; and Grace Backhouse to Catherine Backhouse, October 5, 1854, both in Backhouse Papers.

8. His Diary, March 24, 1853; George Backhouse to his aunt, March 27, 1853; Her Diary, April 11, 19, 21, 1854, all in Backhouse Papers.

9. Her Diary, March 24, 1853, Backhouse Papers; John V. Crawford to the Earl of Malmesbury, July 1, 1858, in Great Britain, Foreign Office, *Confidential Series, Collection 541, The Slave Trade,* vol. 1, p. 36; certificate signed by Dr. Belot, June 18, 1856, with Robertson to Marcy, June 20, 1856, NA, Havana Despatches, vol. 33; *The Cuban Messenger,* March 24, 1861; González del Valle, *La Habana,* 176; Archivo del Arzobispado de La Habana, Expedientes Ultramarinos, April 1853, no. 17; Erenchún, *Anales,* 1790.

10. U.S. consul to the captain-general of Cuba, December 30, 1843, ANC, Gobierno Superior Civil, leg. 1530, exp. 70691.

11. Undated note signed by Consul Blythe [1858?], NA, Havana Despatches, vol. 39; Consul Helm to Cass, April 28, 1860, NA, Havana Despatches, vol. 40; Belot to Helm, April 27, 1860, in id.; Marrero, *Cuba,* 14:79.

12. His Diary, September 18, 19, 20, 1853, Backhouse Papers.

13. His Diary, September 22, 1853; Grace to her aunt, October 7, 1853; Her Diary, October 2, 1853, all in Backhouse Papers; George Backhouse to Lord Clarendon, October 10, 1853, PRO, FO 313/25.

14. Her Diary, May 13, 16, 25, 26, 28, 1854; Grace Backhouse to Catherine Backhouse, May 1, 1854, all in Backhouse Papers.

15. Howe, *Trip,* 200; Pool, *What Jane Austen Ate,* 279; Her Diary, September 7, 1853.

16. Grace Backhouse to her aunt, October 7, 1853, Backhouse Papers; Her Diary, May 4, 1854; Grace to her mother-in-law, June 5, 1854, all in Backhouse Papers.

17. His Diary, October 26, 1853, Backhouse Papers.

18. Grace Backhouse to Mary Backhouse, January 6, 1854; Grace Backhouse to Catherine Backhouse, January 4, 22, 1854, all in Backhouse Papers.

19. Her Diary, February 20–28, 1854; Grace Backhouse to Catherine Backhouse, March 3, 1854, all in Backhouse Papers.

20. Her Diary, March 10–11, 1854, Backhouse Papers.

21. Letter signed F.R[unge], dated March 11, 1854, Backhouse Papers.

22. Her Diary, February 14, and March 11–13, 1854; Grace Backhouse to Catherine Backhouse, March 19, 1854, all in Backhouse Papers.

23. Her Diary, March 18, 1854; George Backhouse to Catherine Backhouse, April 2, 1854, both in Backhouse Papers.

24. Her Diary, March 13–15, 1854; Grace Backhouse to Catherine Backhouse, March 19, 1854, both in Backhouse Papers.

25. Her Diary, March 13, 14, 1854; Grace Backhouse to Catherine Backhouse, March 19, 1854, all in Backhouse Papers; Ballou, *Due South,* 175.

26. George Backhouse to Catherine Backhouse, April 2, 1854; Her Diary, April 2, 4, 9, 1854, all in Backhouse Papers.

27. Her Diary, April 16, 1854, Backhouse Papers.

28. Londa Schiebinger, "Why Mammals Are Called Mammals: Gender Politics in Eighteenth-Century Natural History," 383; Grace Backhouse to Catherine Backhouse, March 19, 1854 (emphasis in the original); Her Diary, March 15, 1854; Grace Backhouse to Catherine Backhouse, January 4, 1854; Grace Backhouse to Mary Backhouse, December 3, 1853 (emphasis in the original), all in Backhouse Papers.

29. Grace Backhouse to Catherine Backhouse, June 5, 1854, Backhouse Papers.

30. Kenneth F. Kipple, *The Caribbean Slave,* 128; Fernando Ortiz Fernández, *Hampa afro-cubana,* 100; Villaverde, *Cecilia Valdés,* 280, 522.

31. *La Gaceta de La Habana,* May 27, 1854, and March 29, 1853.

32. Her Diary, May 27, 28, 1854, and Grace Backhouse to Catherine Backhouse, July 4, 1854, all in Backhouse Papers.

33. *La Gaceta de La Habana,* May 30, 1854.

34. Her Diary, May 30, June 4, 9, 1854; and Grace Backhouse to Catherine Backhouse, June 4, 1854, all in Backhouse Papers.

35. Her Diary, June 9, 1854; Grace Backhouse to Catherine Backhouse and to her sisters-in-law, June 21, 1854, both in Backhouse Papers.

36. Grace Backhouse to Catherine Backhouse, July 4, 1854, Backhouse Papers.

37. Her Diary, July 5, 16, 17, 1854; Grace Backhouse to Catherine Backhouse, July 4, 1854, all in Backhouse Papers.

38. Her Diary, August 10, 13, 1854; Grace Backhouse to Catherine Backhouse, January 22, 1854, and September 4, 1854, all in Backhouse Papers.

39. Grace Backhouse to Catherine Backhouse, September 4, and October 5, 1854; Her Diary, September 30, and October 26, 1854, all in Backhouse Papers.

## VIII. The Return Home

1. Bécker, *Historia,* 2:330; Murray, *Odious Commerce,* 233; George Backhouse to Lord Clarendon, December 5, 1853, PRO, FO 313/25; Grace Backhouse to Catherine Backhouse, June 5, 1854, Backhouse Papers; Foner, *History,* 2:76; de la Concha, *Memoria,* 8.

2. De la Concha, *Memoria,* 6–8; Foner, *History,* 2:77.

3. Copy of January 1 decree in PRO, FO 313/25; *La Gaceta de La Habana,* May 3–4, 1854; John S. Thrasher, *A Preliminary Essay on the Purchase of Cuba,* 71; Guerra y Sánchez, *Manual de historia de Cuba,* 540–46; George Backhouse to Lord Clarendon, August 19, 1854, PRO, FO 313/27; Murray, *Odious Commerce,* 253; Marrero, *Cuba,* 9:110; Franco, *Comercio clandestino,* 230.

4. [Madan], *Llamamiento,* 97–98.

5. Foner, *History,* 2:94; May, *Southern Dream,* 48.

6. William H. Robertson to Marcy, April 21, and May 10 and 14, 1854; report of Davis to Marcy, May 22, 1854, NA, Havana Despatches, vol. 27; Marcy to Charles W. Davis, NA, Special Missions, reel 154.

7. Basil Rauch, *American Interest in Cuba,* 279; Foner, *History,* 2:97; Robert F. Smith, ed., *What Happened in Cuba?* 64–67.

8. Murray, *Odious Commerce,* 255; Crawford to de la Concha, March 31, 1855, in Great Britain, *BPP,* vol. 42, Class B, p. 379; Roldán de Montaud, "Origen," 629; C. Stanley Urban, "The Africanization of Cuba Scare, 1853–1855," 29–45; Proclamation of February 12, 1855, in PRO, FO 72/878; Foner, *History,* 2:108; Martínez-Fernández, *Torn between Empires,* 40–50. George Backhouse to Johnny Backhouse, April 7, 1855, Backhouse Papers. "Resignation of General Quitman," New York *Tribune,* April 30, 1855; *La Gaceta de La Habana,* May 24, 1855.

9. Cristóbal F. Madan to Consul Allen Owen, June 6, 1851, NA, Havana Despatches, vol. 24; files on repression against conspirators in AHN, Ultramar, leg. 4645, exps. 4, 11; George Backhouse to Johnny Backhouse, April 7, 1855, Backhouse Documents; "Resignation of General Quitman," New York *Tribune,* April 30, 1855.

10. Lord Napier to Lord Clarendon, May 26, 1857, quoted in Gavin B. Henderson, ed., "Southern Designs on Cuba, 1854–1857, and Some European Opinions," 384; Christopher J. Bartlett, "British Reaction to the Cuban Insurrection of 1868–1878," 297.

11. Her Diary, November 10, 1853, May 11, 1854; Grace Backhouse to Catherine Backhouse, May 1, and August 6, 1854 (emphasis in the original), all in Backhouse Papers.

12. Grace Backhouse to Catherine Backhouse, May 1, 1854; George Backhouse to Catherine Backhouse, April 2, 1854, both in Backhouse Papers.

13. George Backhouse to Catherine Backhouse, April 2, 1854, Backhouse Papers.

14. Grace Backhouse to Catherine Backhouse, April 6, 1854, Backhouse Papers.

15. George Backhouse to Catherine Backhouse, April 2, 21, 1854, all in Backhouse Papers.

16. Eltis, "Nineteenth-Century Transatlantic Slave Trade," 121–22.

17. Grace Backhouse to Catherine Backhouse, March 19, 1854; George Backhouse to Catherine Backhouse, March 28, April 2, 27, 1854, all in Backhouse Papers.

18. Her Diary, March 28, April 3, 1854, Backhouse Papers.

19. Her Diary, April 3, 1854; Grace Backhouse to Catherine Backhouse, April 6, 1854, both in Backhouse Papers; Levine, *Cuba,* 26.

20. Her Diary, April 7–8, 1854; Grace Backhouse to Catherine Backhouse, April 6, 1854, all in Backhouse Papers.

21. Her Diary, April, 27, 28, 1854, Backhouse Papers.

22. Crawford to Lord Clarendon, August 7, 1855, in Great Britain, *BPP,* vol. 42, Class B, pp. 397–98; George Backhouse to Lord Clarendon, July 10, 1854, PRO, FO 313/26; Great Britain, *Foreign Office List* (1857); mimeographed description of the Backhouse Papers, 5.

23. Her Diary, June 21, 22, 1854; Grace Backhouse to Catherine Backhouse and to her sisters-in-law, June 21, 1854; Grace Backhouse to Catherine Backhouse, July 4, 1854, all in Backhouse Papers.

24. Her Diary, June 21, 22, July 28, August, 3, 1854; George Backhouse to Catherine Backhouse, August 6, 1854, all in Backhouse Papers.

25. George Backhouse to Catherine Backhouse, August 6, 1854; Grace Backhouse to Catherine Backhouse, September 4, 1854; Her Diary, August 9, 1854, all in Backhouse Papers.

26. His Diary, August 20, 28, 1853; Her Diary, August 10, 1854; Grace Backhouse to Catherine Backhouse, September 4, 1854, all in Backhouse Papers.

27. Grace Backhouse to Catherine Backhouse, October 5, 1854; Her Diary, October 24–29, November 1–7, 1854, March 15, 1855, all in Backhouse Papers.

28. Her Diary, March 23, 1855; Grace Backhouse to Catherine Backhouse, March 25, 1855, both in Backhouse Papers.

29. George Backhouse to Johnny Backhouse, April 7, 1855; Grace Backhouse to Catherine Backhouse, March 25, 1855; George Backhouse to Catherine Backhouse, April 9 and 12 and May 11, 1855, all in Backhouse Papers.

30. Grace Backhouse to Catherine Backhouse, March 25, 1855, Backhouse Papers.

31. Grace Backhouse to Catherine Backhouse, March 25, 1855; Her Diary, April 6, 1855, both in Backhouse Papers.

32. Her Diary, April 19, 1855, May, 6, 25, 1855, Backhouse Papers.

33. *Post Office London Directory* (1852); Her Diary, June 1, 21, 30, 1855, Backhouse Papers.

34. Her Diary, June 1, May 19, June 15, July 2, August 3, 1855; letter dated July 30, no name given, all in Backhouse Papers.

35. In 1854 the two officials produced conflicting estimates of the slave trade; George's was about 1,000 higher and the Foreign Office preferred Crawford's lower estimate. Murray, *Odious Commerce,* 245.

36. Crawford to Lord Clarendon, July 14, 1854, PRO, FO 84/937; Lord Clarendon to Crawford, August 17, 1854, PRO, FO 313/38; George Backhouse to Lord Clarendon, August 21, 1855, PRO, FO 84/959.

37. George Backhouse to Lord Clarendon, August 3, 1855, PRO, FO 313/28; George Backhouse to Lord Clarendon, June 21, 1855, PRO, FO 313/28 and FO 84/959; George Backhouse to Lord Clarendon, July 24, 1855, PRO, FO 313/38; Lord Clarendon to George Backhouse, August 31, 1855, PRO, FO 84/959.

38. George Backhouse to Lord Clarendon, August 3, 1855, PRO, FO 313/28; Lord Clarendon to Crawford, October 26, 1855, PRO, FO 84/959; George Backhouse to Dalrymple, August 6, 1855, PRO, FO 313/38; Dalrymple to Lord Clarendon, August 6, 1855, PRO, FO 84/959 and FO 313/38.

39. George Backhouse to Lord Clarendon, August 27, 1855, PRO, FO 313/28.

40. Her Diary, September 1, 9, 21, 1855, Backhouse Papers.

41. Crawford to Thomas Staveley, September 8, 1855 (copy); Sally Crawford to Catherine Backhouse, September 8, 1855, both in Backhouse Papers.

42. Crawford to Lord Clarendon, September 1, 1855 (copy); Crawford to Staveley, September 8, 1855 (copy); Callaghan to Staveley, September 8, 1855 (copy); Jane Callaghan to Grace Backhouse, May 4, 1856; several undated clippings of the London press, all in Backhouse Papers. Captain-General de la Concha to the Spanish minister of state, September 10, 1855, AHN, Ultramar, leg. 4646, exp. 32.

43. Crawford to Lord Clarendon, September 1, 1855, PRO, FO 72/878.

44. Crawford to Staveley, September 8, 1855 (copy); undated newspaper clippings, Backhouse Papers. Death certificate in Archivo Parroquial de Nuestra Señora del Pilar.

45. Crawford to Grace Backhouse, September 22, 1856, Backhouse Papers.

46. Callaghan to Staveley, September 8, 1855 (copy); Crawford to Staveley,

September 8, 1855 (copy); Crawford to Grace Backhouse, February 9, 1856; inventory dated January 29, 1856, all in Backhouse Papers.

47. Crawford to Staveley, September 8, 1855 (copy); Crawford to Grace Backhouse, February 9, and October 14, 1856, Backhouse Papers. Spanish secretary of state to the mister of Fomento y Ultramar, August 15, 1856, AHN, Ultramar, leg. 4646, exp. 32.

48. Undated newspaper clippings, Backhouse Papers; Crawford to Lord Clarendon, November 23, 1855, in Great Britain, *BPP,* vol. 42, Class A, pp. 76–77; Crawford to Lord Clarendon, October 9, 1855, PRO, FO 72/878.

49. Crawford to Lord Clarendon, November 23, 1855, in Great Britain, *BPP,* vol. 42, Class A, pp. 76–77; Foreign Office to Crawford, November 27, 1855, PRO, FO 72/878; Crawford to Lord Clarendon, February 28, 1856, PRO, FO 72/902.

50. Grace Backhouse to Lord Clarendon (undated copy), Backhouse Papers; de las Barras y Prado, *Memorias,* 123–24; Marrero, *Cuba,* 14:287.

51. Her Diary, November 8, 1855; Crawford to Grace Backhouse, September 22, October 14, 1856, Backhouse Papers.

52. Her Diary, November 3, 13, 19, December 1–18, 1855, March 11, 1856, all in Backhouse Papers.

53. Catherine Backhouse to Lord Clarendon (undated copy); Lord Wodehouse to Grace Backhouse, January 10, 1856, Backhouse Papers.

54. Grace Backhouse to Lord Clarendon (undated copy), Backhouse Papers.

55. Her Diary, January 17, February 18, March 4, and November 5, 1856, Backhouse Papers.

56. Crawford to Grace Backhouse, September 22, October 14, 1856, Backhouse Papers.

57. Her Diary, November 13, 1856, and December 15, 1856, Backhouse Papers.

58. Crawford to Lord Clarendon, Oct. 6, 1855, PRO, 84/965; Pérez, *Cuba: Between Reform and Revolution,* 2nd ed., 111; Pérez de la Riva, "Demografía," 87.

59. Savage to Seward, October 4, 1861, NA, Havana Despatches, vol. 42; Shufeldt to Seward, November 27, 1861, id., vol. 41; Thomas E. Taylor, *Running the Blockade,* 146. Clarendon to Lord Crawford, December 22, 1855, PRO, FO 313/38; *Foreign Office List* (1878), 81.

60. Crawford to Lord Clarendon, October 8 and 13, and November 24, 1855, PRO, FO 313, vol. 28; Crawford to George Backhouse, August 15, 1855, PRO, FO 313/38; certificate apparently signed by Dr. José Andrés de Piedra, dated May 10, 1856, in PRO, FO 84/984; memo by Thomas Ward on letter of Dalrymple dated July 2, 1856, PRO, FO 84/984.

61. Lord Clarendon to Crawford, July 31, 1856, PRO, FO 313/38; Bethell, "Mixed Commissions," 81; Great Britain, *Foreign Office List* (1878), 83.

62. Crawford to Lord Clarendon, June 28, 1856, and July 10, 1856, PRO, FO 84/988.

63. Ely, *Cuando reinaba,* 679; Franco, *Comercio clandestino,* 235–36, 389.

64. Her Diary, August 31, 1857, 1858, and 1859, Backhouse Papers.

65. Her Diary, note following the entry of April 6, 1855, Backhouse Papers (emphasis and capitals in the original).

66. Mimeographed description of the Backhouse Papers, 5.

# Bibliography

## Archival Materials

Archivo del Arzobispado de La Habana.
Expedientes Ultramarinos.

Archivo del Museo del Cerro, Havana. Files 2.3.2, 4.1.10, 4.12, 4.17, 4.19, 6.1.1.

Archivo Histórico Nacional, Madrid.
Sección Estado, legs. 8047, 8565.
Sección Ultramar, leg. 4646.

Archivo Nacional de Cuba, Havana.
Asuntos Políticos, legs. 48, 220, 298.
Gobierno General, leg. 337.
Gobierno Superior Civil, legs. 743, 744, 791, 994, 996, 1113, 1119, 1530, 1656, 1657.
Reales Órdenes y Cédulas, legs. 165, 183.

Archivo Parroquial de la iglesia Salvador del Mundo, El Cerro, Havana. Libros de Bautismos, Matrimonios, y Defunciones.

Archivo Parroquial de la iglesia Nuestra Señora del Pilar, El Cerro, Havana. Libros de Bautismos, Matrimonios, y Defunciones.

Duke University, Special Collections Library, Durham, NC.
Diary of Susan Hathorn.
John Backhouse Papers.

National Archives, College Park, MD.
Record Group 59, General Records of the Department of State, Despatches from
    U.S. Consuls in Havana, T-20, rolls 33–40; Records of Special Missions, reel
    154.
Record Group 84, Records of Foreign Service Posts, San Juan Consulate, vol.
    7117.

Public Record Office, Kew, England.
ADM (Admiralty) 38, 53.
FO (Foreign Office) 72, 83, 84, 313, 366.

Southern Historical Collection, Chapel Hill, NC.
Claiborne Papers.

Virginia Historical Society, Richmond, VA.
Diary of the Reverend William Norwood.

## Contemporary Sources

Abbot, Abiel. *Letters Written in the Interior of Cuba.* Boston: Bowles and Dear-
    born, 1829.
Abbott, John Stevens Cabot. *South and North; or Impressions Received during a
    Trip to Cuba and the South.* New York: Abbey & Abbot, 1860. Reprint New
    York: Negro Universities Press, 1969.
Alexander, James Edward C.B. *Transatlantic Sketches.* 2 vols. London: Richard
    Bentley, 1833.
Allen, Lewis Leonidas. *The Island of Cuba; or, Queen of the Antilles.* Cleveland:
    Harris, Fairbanks, 1852.
*Anuario y directorio de La Habana.* Havana: 1859.
Ashworth, Henry. *A Tour in the United States, Cuba, and Canada.* London: A.W.
    Bennett, [1861].
Atkins, Edwin F. *Sixty Years in Cuba.* Cambridge, MA: Privately printed at the
    Riverside Press, 1926. Reprint New York: Arno Press, 1980.
Ballou, Maturin Murray. *Due South or Cuba, Past and Present.* Boston:
    Houghton, Mifflin, 1885.
Bremer, Fredrika. *The Homes of the New World.* 2 vols. New York: Harper &
    Brothers, 1854.
Bryant, William Cullen. *Letters of William Cullen Bryant.* Edited by William
    Cullen Bryant II and Thomas G. Voss. 4 vols. New York: Fordham University
    Press, 1975–84.
Calderón de la Barca, Frances. *Life in Mexico during a Residence of Two Years in
    that Country.* London: J.M. Dent, N.D.
Campbell, Reau. *Around the Corner to Cuba.* New York: C.G. Crawford, 1889.
Carleton, George W. *Our Artist in Cuba: Fifty Drawings on Wood.* New York:
    privately printed, 1865.
Cattell, Alexander Gilmore. *To Cuba and Back in Twenty-Two Days.* Philadel-
    phia: The Times Printing House, 1874.

Clayton, Alex M. "Alex M. Clayton to J.F.H. Claiborne." *Hispanic American Historical Review* 9:3 (1929): 364–68.

*Colección de los partes y otros documentos publicados en la Gaceta Oficial de La Habana referentes a la invasión de la gavilla de piratas capitaneada por el traidor Narciso López.* Havana: Imprenta del Gobierno, 1851.

Compadre [pseud.], "El Calesero." *Noticioso y Lucero,* January 1, 1842. Reproduced in González del Valle, *La Habana,* 425–29.

Cowley, José Ángel. *Ensayo estadístico-médico de la mortalidad de la diócesis de La Habana durante el año de 1843.* Havana: Imprenta del Gobierno, 1845.

Cuba, Comisión de Estadística. *Cuadro estadístico de la siempre fiel Isla de Cuba* (1846). Havana: Imprenta del Gobierno y la Capitanía General, 1847.

*The Cuba Commission Report: A Hidden History of the Chinese in Cuba.* Introduction by Denise Helly. Baltimore: Johns Hopkins University Press, 1993.

Dana, Richard Henry, Jr. *To Cuba and Back: A Vacation Voyage.* Boston: Ticknor and Fields, 1859. Reprint C. Harvey Gardiner, ed. Carbondale: Southern Illinois University Press, 1966.

de la Concha, José. *Memoria sobre el ramo de emancipados de la Isla de Cuba.* Madrid: Imprenta de la América, 1861.

de la Torre, José María. "Cuba." In Richard S. Fisher, ed. *The Spanish West Indies: Cuba and Porto Rico.* New York: J.H. Colton, 1861.

———. *Lo que fuimos y lo que somos o La Habana antigua y moderna.* Havana: Spencer, 1857.

de las Barras y Prado, Antonio. *Memorias, La Habana a mediados del siglo XIX.* Madrid: Ciudad Lineal, 1925.

D'Hespel D'Harponville, Gustave. *La reine des Antilles.* Paris: Gide et Baudry, 1850.

*Directorio de artes, comercio e industrias de La Havana.* Havana: Tiburcio V. Cuesta, 1860.

Editors of *La Verdad. Cuestión negrera de la Isla de Cuba.* New York: La Verdad, 1851.

Erenchún, Félix. *Anales de la Isla de Cuba (1855).* Havana: Imprenta del Tiempo-Imprenta La Antilla, 1856–59.

España, Ministerio de Ultramar. *Cuba desde 1850 a 1873.* Carlos de Sedano, compiler. Madrid: Imprenta Nacional, 1873.

Gallenga, Antonio Carlo Napoleone. *The Pearl of the Antilles.* London: Chapman and Hall, 1873. Reprint New York: Negro Universities Press, 1970.

García de Arboleya, José. *Manual de la Isla de Cuba.* 2nd ed. Imprenta del Tiempo, 1859.

Gibbes, Robert W. *Cuba for Invalids.* New York: W.A. Townsend, 1860.

Gómez Colón, José María. *Memoria sobre la utilidad del trabajo de la muger pobre en la Isla de Cuba y medios para conseguirlo.* Havana: Imprenta de Manuel Soler, 1857.

Goodman, Walter. *The Pearl of the Antilles or an Artist in Cuba.* London: Henry S. King, 1873.

Great Britain. *British and Foreign State Papers.* 1816–17, 1834–35. London: Ridgway and Sons, 1838, 1852.

Great Britain, Foreign Office. *Confidential Series, Collection 541, the Slave Trade.*

————. *The Foreign Office List*. London: Harrison & Son, 1852–78.

Great Britain, Parliament, House of Commons. *British Parliamentary Papers [Slave Trade]*. 95 vols. Shannon, Ireland: Irish University Press, 1968–71.

Great Britain, Royal Commission. *Official Catalogue of the Great Exhibition of the Works of Industry of All Nations, 1851*. London: Spicer Brothers, 1851.

Gurney, Joseph John. *A Winter in the West Indies*. London: John Murray, 1840.

Hazard, Samuel. *Cuba with Pen and Pencil*. Hartford: Hartford Publishing, 1871.

Hernández Poggio, D. Ramón. *Aclimatación é higiene de los europeos en Cuba*. Cádiz, Spain: Imprenta de la Revista Médica, 1874.

Howe, Julia Ward. *A Trip to Cuba*. Boston: Ticknor and Fields, 1860. Reprint New York: Fredrick A. Praeger, 1969.

[Hurlbert, William Henry]. *Gan-Eden: Or, Pictures of Cuba*. Boston: Jewett, 1854.

Jameson, Robert Francis. *Letters from the Havana, during the Year 1820*. London: John Miller, 1821.

"John Backhouse (obituary)." *The Gentleman's Magazine* (new series) 25 (January–June 1846): 95–97.

Jones, Alexander. *Cuba in 1851*. New York: Stringer and Townsend, 1851.

Kimball, Richard Burleigh. *Cuba and the Cubans*. New York: S. Hueston and G. Putnam, 1850.

Le-Roy y Cassá, Jorge. *Estudio sobre la mortalidad de La Habana durante el siglo XIX y comienzos del actual*. Havana: Lloredo y Cía, 1913.

Levis, Richard J. *Diary of a Spring Holiday in Cuba*. Philadelphia: Porter and Coates, 1872.

[Madan, Cristóbal F.] Un Hacendado. *Llamamiento de la Isla de Cuba a la nación española*. New York: Estevan Hallet, 1854.

Madden, Richard Robert. *The Island of Cuba: Its Resources, Progress, and Prospects*. London: Partridge and Oakey, 1853.

Mark, John. *Diary of My Trip to America and Havana, in October and November 1884*. Manchester: A. Ireland and Company, 1885.

May, B. *Álbum pintoresco de la Isla de Cuba*. Havana: B. May, 1853.

Moore, Rachel Wilson. *Journal of Rachel Wilson Moore, Kept During a Tour to the West Indies and South America in 1863–64*. Philadelphia: T.E. Ellwood, 1867.

Murray, Amelia Matilda. *Letters from the United States, Cuba and Canada*. 2 vols. London: John W. Parker, 1856.

Murray, Henry Anthony. *Lands of the Slave and the Free*. 2 vols. London: J.W. Parker and Son, 1855.

[Neely, F. Tennyson]. *Greater America: Heroes, Battles, Camps, Dewey Islands, Cuba, Porto Rico*. New York: F. Tennyson Neely, 1898.

Ney, Eugene. *Cuba en 1830: Diario de viaje de un hijo del Mariscal Ney*. Introduction and Notes by Jorge J. Beato Núñez. Miami: Ediciones Universal, 1973.

Norman, Benjamin Moore. *Rambles by Land and Water, or Notes to Travel in Cuba and Mexico*. New York: Paine and Burguess, 1845.

O'Kelly, James. *The Mambi Land*. Philadelphia: J.B. Lippincott, 1874.

Perry, John A. *Thrilling Adventures of a New Englander*. Boston: Redding, 1853.

Philalethes, Demoticus. *Yankee Travels Through the Island of Cuba; or the Men and Government, the Laws and Customs of Cuba, as Seen by American Eyes.* New York: D.A. Appleton, 1856.

Phillippo, James Mursell. *The United States and Cuba.* London: Pewtress, 1857.

*Post Office London Directory.* London: 1852.

Rawson, James. *Cuba.* New York: Lane & Tippet, 1847.

Ripley, Eliza McHatton. *From Flag to Flag: A Woman's Adventures and Experiences in the South during the War, in Mexico, and in Cuba.* New York: Appleton, 1889.

Rogers, Carlton H. *Incidents of Travel in the Southern United States and Cuba.* New York: R. Craighead, 1862.

Sala, George Augustus. *Under the Sun: Essays Mainly Written in Hot Countries.* London: Tinsley Brothers, 1872.

[Santa Cruz, Mercedes de] Condesa de Merlín. *Viaje a La Habana.* Havana: Editorial de Artes y Literatura, 1974.

Shufeldt, Robert W. "Secret History of the Slave Trade to Cuba." Edited by Frederick C. Drake. *Journal of Negro History* 53:3 (July 1970): 218–35.

Steele, James William. *Cuban Sketches.* New York: Putnam's Sons, 1881.

Sullivan, Edward. *Rambles and Scrambles in North and South America.* London: Richard Bentley, 1852.

Tanco Armero, Nicolás. "La Isla de Cuba," in Juan Pérez de la Riva, ed., *La Isla de Cuba en el siglo XIX vista por extranjeros.* Havana: Editorial de Ciencias Sociales, 1981.

Taylor, John G. *The United States and Cuba: Eight Years of Change and Travel.* London: Richard Bentley, 1851.

Taylor, Thomas E. *Running the Blockade: A Personal Narrative of Adventure, Risks, and Escapes during the American Civil War.* 4th ed. London: John Murray, 1912.

Thrasher, John S. *A Preliminary Essay on the Purchase of Cuba.* New York: Derby and Jackson, 1859.

Torrente, Mariano. *Bosquejo económico político de la Isla de Cuba.* 2 vols. Madrid: M. Pita-Barcina, 1852–53.

Trollope, Anthony. *The West Indies and the Spanish Main.* New York: Harper and Brothers, 1860. Reprint London: Frank Cass, 1968.

Tudor, Henry. *Narrative of a Tour in North America.* 2 vols. London: James Duncan, 1834.

Turnbull, David. *Travels in the West: Cuba with Notices of Porto Rico and the Slave Trade.* London: Longman, 1840. Reprint New York: Negro Universities Press, 1969.

Villaverde, Cirilo. *Cecilia Valdés.* Havana: Consejo Nacional de Cultura, 1964.

Vives, Francisco Dionisio. *Condiciones con que se reparten los negros que se emancipan por el gobierno.* Document dated 1829 in Cuban collection of the Biblioteca Nacional José Martí.

von Humboldt, Alexander. *The Island of Cuba.* Translation, notes, and preliminary essay by John S. Thrasher. New York: Derby and Jackson, 1856.

Williams, George W. *Sketches of Travel in the Old and New World.* Charleston, SC: Walker, Evans & Cogswell, 1871.

[Woodruff, Julia Louisa Matilda] Jay, J.L.M., pseud. *My Winter in Cuba.* New York: E.P. Dutton, 1871.

[Wurdemann, John George F.]. *Notes on Cuba*. Boston: James Munroe, 1844. Reprint New York: Arno Press, 1971.

## Newspapers

*The Cuban Messenger*
La Gaceta de La Habana
The London *Gazette*
The London *Times*
*El Siglo*

## Secondary Sources

Arróm, Silvia. *The Women of Mexico City*. Stanford: Stanford University Press, 1985.

Barret-Ducrocq, Françoise. *Love in the Time of Victoria*. London: Verso, 1991.

Bartlett, Christopher J. "British Reaction to the Cuban Insurrection of 1868–1878." *Hispanic American Historical Review* 37:3 (August 1957): 296–312.

Bécker, Jerónimo. *Historia de las relaciones exteriores de España durante el siglo XIX.* 3 vols. Madrid: Jaime Ratés-Voluntad, 1924–26.

Bergad, Laird W. *Cuban Rural Society in the Nineteenth Century: The Social and Economic History of Monoculture in Matanzas*. Princeton: Princeton University Press, 1990.

Bethell, Leslie. "The Mixed Commissions for the Suppression of the Transatlantic Slave Trade in the Nineteenth Century." *Journal of Negro History* 7:1 (1966): 79–93.

Carpentier, Alejo. *Explosion in a Cathedral*. London: Gollancz, 1963.

Chateloin, Felicia. *La Habana de Tacón*. Havana: Editorial de Letras Cubanas, 1989.

*Cien planos de La Habana en los archivos españoles*. Ministerio de Obras Públicas y Urbanismo: Madrid, 1985.

Collinge, J.M., compiler. *Office-Holders in Modern Britain*. Vol. 8, Foreign Office Officials, 1782–1870. London: University of London, 1979.

Corwin, Arthur F. *Spain and the Abolition of Slavery in Cuba, 1817–1886*. Austin: University of Texas Press, 1967.

Cuba, Instituto de Investigaciones Estadísticas. *Los Censos de población y viviendas en Cuba*. One vol. to date. Havana: Instituto de Investigaciones Estadísticas, 1988.

Deschamps Chapeaux, Pedro. *El negro en la economia habanera del siglo XIX*. Havana: Unión de Escritores y Artistas Cubanos, 1971.

Eltis, David. "The Nineteenth-Century Transatlantic Slave Trade: An Annual Time Series of Imports into the Americas Broken Down by Region." *HAHR* 67:1 (February 1987): 109–38.

Ely, Roland T. *Cuando reinaba su majestad el azúcar: Estudio histórico-sociólogico de una tragedia latinoamericana*. Buenos Aires: Editorial Sudamericana, 1963.

Fernández Santalices, Manuel. *Las calles de La Habana Intramuros*. Miami: Saeta Ediciones, 1989.

Foner, Philip S. *A History of Cuba and its Relations with the United States*. 2 vols. New York: International Publishers, 1962–63.

Franco, José Luciano. *Comercio clandestino de esclavos.* Havana: Editorial de Ciencias Sociales, 1985.

González del Valle, Francisco. *La Habana en 1841.* Havana: Oficina del Historiador de La Habana, 1952.

Guerra y Sánchez, Ramiro. *Manual de historia de Cuba.* Madrid: Editorial R., 1972.

————. *Manual de historia de Cuba desde su descubrimiento hasta 1868.* 2 vols. Havana: Editorial Pueblo y Educación, 1987.

Hahner, June E. "The Nineteenth-Century Feminist Press and Women's Rights in Brazil." In *Latin American Women.* Asunción Lavrin, ed., 254–85.

Henderson, Gavin B. "Southern Designs on Cuba, 1854–1857, and Some European Opinions." *Journal of Southern History* 5 (August 1939): 371–85.

Kinsbruner, Jay. *Not of Pure Blood: The Free People of Color and Racial Prejudice in Nineteenth-Century Puerto Rico.* Durham, NC: Duke University Press, 1996.

Kipple, Keneth F. *The Caribbean Slave: A Biological History.* Cambridge: Cambridge University Press, 1984.

Knight, Franklin W. "Origins of Wealth and the Sugar Revolution in Cuba, 1750–1850." *HAHR* 57:2 (May 1977): 231–53.

————. *Slave Society in Cuba during the Nineteenth Century.* Madison: University of Wisconsin Press, 1970.

Lavrin, Asunción, ed. *Latin American Women: Historical Prespectives.* Westport: Greenwood Press, 1978.

Lebroc, Reyneiro G. *Cuba: Iglesia y sociedad (1830–1860).* Madrid: no publisher, 1976.

Le Riverend, Julio. *La Habana.* Madrid: Editorial Mapfre, 1992.

Lockmiller, David. "The Settlement of the Church Property Question in Cuba." *HAHR* 17:4 (November 1937): 488–98.

Levine, Robert M. *Cuba in the 1850s Through the Lens of Charles DeForrest Fredricks.* Tampa: University of South Florida Press, 1990.

Marmier, X. "Cuba en 1850." *Revista Bimestre Cubana* LIV:2 (1944): 105–33.

Marrero, Leví. *Cuba: Economía y sociedad.* 15 vols. Madrid: Editorial Playor, 1971–92.

Marte, Roberto. *Cuba y la República Dominicana: Transición económica en el Caribe del siglo XIX.* Santo Domingo: Universidad APEC, no date [1988?].

Martínez-Alier, Verena. *Marriage, Class and Colour in Nineteenth-Century Cuba.* Ann Arbor: University of Michigan Press, 1989.

Martínez-Fernández, Luis. "The Havana Anglo-Spanish Mixed Commission for the Suppression of the Slave Trade and Cuba's *Emancipados.*" *Slavery and Abolition* 16:2 (August 1995): 205–25.

————. "Life in a 'Male City': Native and Foreign Elite Women in Nineteenth-Century Havana." *Cuban Studies* 25 (1995): 27–50.

————. *Torn between Empires: Economy, Society, and Patterns of Political Thought in the Hispanic Caribbean, 1840–1878.* Athens: University of Georgia Press, 1994.

May, Robert E. *The Southern Dream of a Caribbean Empire, 1854–1861.* Baton Rouge: Louisiana State University Press, 1973. Reprint Athens: University of Georgia Press, 1989.

Mendelson, Johanna S.P. "The Feminine Press: The View of Women in the Colonial Journals of Spanish America, 1790–1810." In *Latin American Women*. Asunción Lavrin, ed., 198–218.

Middleton, Charles Ronald. *The Administration of British Foreign Policy, 1782–1846*. Durham, NC: Duke University Press, 1977.

Moreno Fraginals, Manuel. *El ingenio: El complejo económico social del azúcar.* 3 vols. Havana: Editorial de Ciencias Sociales, 1978.

Murray, David. *Odious Commerce: Britain, Spain, and the Abolition of the Cuban Slave Trade.* Cambridge: Cambridge University Press, 1980.

Ortiz Fernández, Fernando. *Hampa afro-cubana. Los negros brujos (apuntes para un estudio de etnología criminal).* Miami: Ediciones Universal, 1973.

———. *Travesía y trata negrera.* Havana: Publicigraf, 1993.

Paquette, Robert Louis. *Sugar Is Made with Blood.* Middletown, CT: Wesleyan University Press, 1988.

Pérez, Louis A., Jr. *Cuba: An Annotated Bibliography.* New York: Greenwood Press, 1988.

———. *Cuba: Between Reform and Revolution.* 2nd ed. New York: Oxford University Press, 1995.

———. *Slaves, Sugar, and Colonial Society: Travel Accounts of Cuba, 1801–1899.* Wilmington, DE: Scholarly Resources, 1992.

Pérez de la Riva, Juan. "Aspectos económicos del tráfico de culíes. Chinos a Cuba (1853–1874)." In Pérez de la Riva, ed. *El Barracón,* 89–110.

———. "Demografía de los culíes. Chinos en Cuba (1853–1874)." In Pérez de la Riva, ed. *El Barracón,* 55–87.

———. *El Barracón: Esclavitud y capitalismo en Cuba.* Barcelona: Editorial Crítica, 1978.

Pool, Daniel. *What Jane Austen Ate and Charles Dickens Knew.* New York: Touchstone Books, 1993.

Portell Vilá, Herminio. *Historia de Cuba en sus relaciones con Estados Unidos y España.* 4 vols. Havana: Montero, 1938–41.

Ramos, Marcos Antonio. *Panorama del protestantismo en Cuba.* San José, Costa Rica: Editorial Caribe, 1986.

Rauch, Basil. *American Interest in Cuba: 1848–1855.* New York: Columbia University Press, 1948.

Reader, W.J. *Life in Victorian England.* New York: Capricorn Books, 1967.

Roig de Leuchsenring, Emilio. *La Habana: Apuntes históricos.* Havana: Municipio de La Habana, 1939.

———. *La Habana: Apuntes históricos.* 3 vols. Havana: Consejo Nacional de Cultura. 1963.

———. *Médicos y medicina en Cuba: Historia, biografía, costumbrismo.* Havana: Academia de Ciencias de Cuba, 1965.

Roldán de Montaud, Inés. "Origen, evolución y supresión del grupo de negros 'emancipados' en Cuba (1817–1870)." *Revista de Indias* 42 (July–December 1982): 559–641.

Sarracino, Rodolfo. *Los que volvieron a África.* Havana: Editorial de Ciencias Sociales, 1988.

Schiebinger, Londa. "Why Mammals Are Called Mammals: Gender Politics in Eighteenth-Century Natural History." *American Historical Review* 98:2 (April 1993): 382–411.

Scott, Rebecca J. *Slave Emancipation in Cuba: The Transition to Free Labor, 1860–1899.* Princeton: Princeton University Press, 1985.

Smith, Harold F. "A Bibliography of North American Travellers' Books about Cuba Published before 1900." *The Americas* 22:4 (April 1966): 404–12.

Smith, Robert F. Editor. *What Happened in Cuba? A Documentary History.* New York: Twayne, 1963.

Taylor, William B. *Drinking, Homicide, and Rebellion in a Colonial Mexican Village.* Stanford: Stanford University Press, 1979.

Urban, C. Stanley. "The Africanization of Cuba Scare, 1853–1855." *HAHR* 37:1 (February 1937): 29–45.

Weiss y Sánchez, Joaquín. *La arquitectura colonial cubana.* 2 vols. Havana: Editorial de Letras Cubanas, 1979–85.

———. *La arquitectura cubana del siglo XIX.* 2nd ed. Havana: Editorial Pueblo y Educación, 1989.

# Index

References to illustrations are italicized; references to notes are in brackets.

**Luis Martínez-Fernández** was born in Havana, the city that serves as this book's setting. He received his B.A. and M.A. in history from the University of Puerto Rico and his history Ph.D. from Duke University, where he discovered the previously unused Backhouse Family documents. Martínez-Fernández has published extensively on diverse topics of Cuban, Puerto Rican, and Dominican history. His most recent book is entitled *Torn between Empires: Economy, Society, and Patterns of Political Thought in the Hispanic Caribbean, 1840–1878* (1994). Martínez-Fernández teaches Latin American and Caribbean history at Rutgers University, where he currently acts as Chair of the Department of Puerto Rican and Hispanic Caribbean Studies.